Using Film to Unlock Textual Literacy

NCTE Editorial Board

Steven Bickmore
Catherine Compton-Lilly
Deborah Dean
Antero Garcia
Bruce McComiskey
Jennifer Ochoa
Staci M. Perryman-Clark
Anne Elrod Whitney
Vivian Yenika-Agbaw
Kurt Austin, Chair, ex officio
Emily Kirkpatrick, ex officio

Using Film to Unlock Textual Literacy

A Teacher's Guide

Robert B. Crisp
Myers Park High School, Charlotte, North Carolina

NATIONAL COUNCIL OF TEACHERS OF ENGLISH
340 N. NEIL ST., SUITE #104, CHAMPAIGN, ILLINOIS 61820
WWW.NCTE.ORG

Staff Editor: Bonny Graham
Manuscript Editor: Michael Ryan
Interior Design: Jenny Jensen Greenleaf
Cover Design: Pat Mayer and Robert Bryant Crisp

NCTE Stock Number: 54465; eStock Number: 54472
ISBN 978-0-8141-5446-5; eISBN 978-0-8141-5447-2

© 2021 by the National Council of Teachers of English.

All rights reserved. No part of this publication may be reproduced or transmitted in any form or by any means, electronic or mechanical, including photocopy, or any information storage and retrieval system, without permission from the copyright holder. Printed in the United States of America.

It is the policy of NCTE in its journals and other publications to provide a forum for the open discussion of ideas concerning the content and the teaching of English and the language arts. Publicity accorded to any particular point of view does not imply endorsement by the Executive Committee, the Board of Directors, or the membership at large, except in announcements of policy, where such endorsement is clearly specified.

NCTE provides equal employment opportunity (EEO) to all staff members and applicants for employment without regard to race, color, religion, sex, national origin, age, physical, mental or perceived handicap/disability, sexual orientation including gender identity or expression, ancestry, genetic information, marital status, military status, unfavorable discharge from military service, pregnancy, citizenship status, personal appearance, matriculation or political affiliation, or any other protected status under applicable federal, state, and local laws.

Every effort has been made to provide current URLs and email addresses, but because of the rapidly changing nature of the web, some sites and addresses may no longer be accessible.

Library of Congress Cataloging-in-Publication Data

Names: Crisp, Robert B., 1974- author.
Title: Using film to unlock textual literacy : a teacher's guide / by Robert B. Crisp.
Description: Champaign, Illinois : National Council of Teachers of English, 2021. | Includes bibliographical references and index. | Summary: "Shows high school ELA teachers how to teach film with the same degree of forethought and intent that goes into teaching print texts"—Provided by publisher.
Identifiers: LCCN 2021034867 (print) | LCCN 2021034868 (ebook) | ISBN 9780814154465 (trade paperback) | ISBN 9780814154472 (adobe pdf)
Subjects: LCSH: Motion pictures—Study and teaching—United States. | English language—Study and teaching—Foreign speakers.
Classification: LCC PN1993.8.U5 C75 2021 (print) | LCC PN1993.8.U5 (ebook) | DDC 808.2/0309353—dc23
LC record available at https://lccn.loc.gov/2021034867
LC ebook record available at https://lccn.loc.gov/2021034868

*To Bud, for teaching me to appreciate a good story,
and to Bill, for showing me how to teach it*

Film analysis enables us to recognize how the filmmakers have their magic on us, how all the constituent elements of the film have combined to create that magic. Rather than rob us of the pleasures of watching films, this approach affords us the even greater pleasure of deep engagement.
—Jon Lewis, *Essential Cinema: An Introduction to Film Analysis*

Imagination is more important than knowledge. For knowledge is limited, whereas imagination embraces the entire world, stimulating progress, giving birth to evolution.
—Albert Einstein, *What Life Means to Einstein*

Contents

ACKNOWLEDGMENTS xi

INTRODUCTION TO THE COURSE 1

SAMPLE LESSONS 17

LESSON 1 The Kuleshov Effect: Making Meaning through Juxtaposition 19

LESSON 2 Intro to Film Study: Group Dynamics 28

LESSON 3 Spec Scripts: Transforming a Classic for the Silver Screen 40

LESSON 4 The Filmmaker's Toolkit: From Building Blocks to Works of Art 50

LESSON 5 *Edward Scissorhands*: Snow Globes, Visual Rhyming, and the Fine Art of Mise-en-Scène 72

LESSON 6 Looking like You Know What You're Doing: Avoiding Bathroom Selfie Cinematography 87

LESSON 7 Casey for the Win: Exploring Director's Prerogative 94

LESSON 8 *Othello*: Getting More from the Moor of Venice 121

LESSON 9 From the Stars to the Silver Screen: A Technical Analysis of the Opening Scene of Spielberg's *E.T. The Extra-Terrestrial* 136

LESSON 10	That Night on the Marge of Lake Lebarge: The Art of the Smooth Transition	152
LESSON 11	Documenting the Action: Not Your Everyday Short Story Analysis	163
LESSON 12	*Unbroken*: Guiding Audience Response	171
APPENDIX A	FILM VOCABULARY	179
APPENDIX B	Charts and Rubrics	183
APPENDIX C	Sample Film Technique Assessments	191
APPENDIX D	Storyboard Templates	221
APPENDIX E	Common Core State Standards	224

WORKS CITED	231
INDEX	233
AUTHOR	241

Acknowledgments

"Notice how the images here reflect what is happening in the story. See those background elements? What do you think Tim Burton is trying to say here?" Cheryl Harris, our presenter for this part of the workshop, scanned the room, gauging the reactions on her participants' faces.

I was hooked.

It was the first time I had ever seen anyone use film as more than a reward for staying awake in class. I was learning about a text, analyzing it deeply, and seriously enjoying the process. And to top it off, the text in question was the film *Edward Scissorhands*.

Since that summer, roughly two and a half decades ago now, I have been fascinated with fleshing out this approach to use with my own students, more than a few of whom have since gone on to study film in college and work in the film industry.

Having said that, one of the most important lessons the journey has taught me is that no man is an island. I could not have written this book alone. I owe more than a few people a tremendous debt of gratitude for helping to make this book a reality.

Thank you to my family—whether by birth, love, choice, or marriage—for supporting me all of these years. Whether helping grade papers and assessments, lending a hand with personal film projects, being willing to pose for photographs or video clips to be used in class lessons or quizzes, giving me time to explore ideas, or encouraging me to keep going, you are incredible. There is no way I could do any of this without you. Penni Beth, Garrett, and Caroline, you are and will always be my *Why*.

To my grandfather Bud, you were the greatest storyteller I ever knew. You taught me that good storytelling is about so much more than the words. I am humbled to stand in your shoes and will forever be trying to fill them.

To my great uncle Bryan, your photography inspired a passion in me for visual storytelling that continues to this day. The day you saw something good in my own photography was a moment I will always cherish.

To Bill McBride, who has been so much more than a mentor to me for so many years now, I can never say thank you enough. We have shared steak, coffee, and midnight snacks. We have written together and presented together, and once, you snuck me into a national convention. You taught me what it means to be an educator. You are also one of the most faithful and supportive friends I have ever had.

Thank you to my colleagues and administrators at Myers Park High School for supporting me. In particular, thank you to Allyson Davis, a truly incredible assistant principal, for being such a staunch supporter of the program, for helping submit the proposal that allowed my students to earn honors credit, and for encouraging me to write a second level for the course.

Thank you as well to Kristen Angerer for being an incredible department chair and for allowing me to indulge my passion project. Not many department chairs would have been so willing to fill my schedule with an elective course in which we "just watch movies." Having you in my corner means the world.

Moreover, to my cadre of film teacher colleagues, Katherine Cates, Mark Jenkins, Melissa Hefner, and Kristen Angerer, I am blown away by your subject knowledge, your passion for educating your students, your work ethic, and your sheer intelligence. You are a daily reminder that the students at MPHS are in very capable hands. You make me better, and I don't do a good enough job of telling you that.

And thank you to our incredible counseling staff, who took the time to understand the course we have worked so hard to build and for encouraging students to add Literature and Film to their schedules.

To that end, thank you to my students. I wish I could list every one of you here, but as there are nearly five thousand of you now, the space is far too limited to do you justice. You are incredible human beings, and you keep me going. Seeing the curiosity stoked as we break down everything from shot details to conspiracy theories surrounding Kubrick's *The Shining* makes getting up early on Monday mornings worth it and celebrating Black Keys Fridays all the more enjoyable. I love you all.

Among those thousands of students, I would like to single out a few who have come back through the years to visit and to offer their expertise to my current students. To Gabriel Kauntiz and Conor Butner, you guys gave up your spring breaks back during your college years to teach my students for a week—and you did it for four years running. Who does that? And you were amazing! You were among the first to show me that what I was doing really mattered, and I will be forever grateful to you for that.

To Graham Keever and David Knuckles, you remain two of the most passionate and talented filmmakers with whom I have ever worked. I am proud of you for chasing your dreams and humbled that you have kept in touch after all these years. I continue to be amazed by your talent and humbled by your passion. I look forward to seeing you receive your Oscars. Thank you for considering me your "Mr. Feeny." That remains one of the greatest compliments I have ever received.

And to Eric Ugland and Jordan Imbrey, the creative masterminds behind Ugly Embryo Productions (one of the more creative monikers ever to grace my classes), you guys still amaze me. Eric, I enjoy following your work as a focus puller, and the rigs you get to play with are incredible. And Jordan, though you were never technically in my class, the fact that you participated in all of our projects impressed me to no end. I have enjoyed following your film career as well. I appreciate you guys for allowing me to help out with your *Airborne* trilogy, and for my resulting IMDB page. It doesn't get much traffic, but it's there!

To Alexandra French, for whom Guillermo del Toro's *El laberinto del fauno* (*Pan's Labyrinth*) was a gateway to a career in LA, thank you for coming back to share your stories with my students. And the makeup your team designed for that performance at the Grammy Awards—that was truly something else. I am so very proud of you! And thank you, by the way, for telling Señor del Toro about us.

To Caroline Donnelly and Grant Eaton, former students who provided some of the illustrations for this book, I will forever be both grateful and in awe of your talents. You are amazing people, and I love that we were able to do this together.

To Peitz Greene, thank you for teaching me never to underestimate students who learn differently. Your incredible technical expertise—like the time you turned all of our school computers into a collective render farm—will never cease to amaze me. And thank you for that behind-the-scenes film set tour you took my students on via Zoom. The fact that we stayed live an hour past when class was supposed to end, yet not a single student left, says everything that needs saying.

I'd also like to thank those who regularly participated in the After Party for keeping me sane during a very strange time in education. COVID, masks, online classes, hybrid schedules, greatly increased expectations and responsibilities, and sometimes even ridicule, suspicion, and indifference toward educators from both certain corners of the public and certain lawmakers have made teaching an incredibly difficult prospect. But you—Lucy Osborn, Spencer Robinson, Anna Carpenter, Lucy Caldwell, Riley Puckett, Sophie Thrasher, Ryan Lynch,

Anna Ten Eyck, and Josh "Two Shacks" Matushak—you helped me keep keep my head on straight.

To Julian Exum, owner-operator of SouthSide Productions, even before you took my film class, the expertise you were willing to share with your classmates was impressive. Believe me, I was taking notes, too. And the fact that you and I were able to put together a feature-length documentary about Myers Park students' experiences with online instruction during COVID still blows me away. Who needs a staff of hundreds?

As for our tech theater students, without your support and expertise, there is no way we would be able to pull off our annual student film festival—going on twenty years now. I hope you know that the excitement you see on students' faces when their films are on screen or when they come down front to accept their awards is due in part to you. And thank you to Hilary Petta, Caitlin Cornwell, and Amanda Roberts for all of your assistance and expertise over the years in that regard.

And Darryl Thompson, thank you for all of those 1 a.m. text messages and long conversations about film and philosophy—and for showing me that Janet Leigh could indeed lie herself across the side of that tub with her face on the floor and avoid blinking for an extended period of time. That will always be one of my favorite teaching moments. And I still have that photograph!

I likewise owe a tremendous debt of gratitude to my copy editor, Michael Ryan, for making me sound intelligent, and for reminding me what students feel like when they get their papers back, all marked up with deletions, corrections, and suggestions. Your enthusiasm for this project truly meant the world. It was an absolute pleasure working with someone so talented, and I hope to do it again soon.

Also, thank you to Kurt Austin, senior editor, and Bonny Graham, staff editor, at NCTE, for taking a complex idea and helping shape it into something accessible. I know I put a lot on your plate, and you delivered admirably.

To Pat Mayer, I very much enjoyed working with you to design the cover. It took a while, but I think it was worth it. I am so impressed by your expertise.

Oh, and John Golden, I very much enjoyed our discussions all those years ago when we were traveling the country working as consultants together. Thank you for laying such incredible groundwork in the field of film study in language arts classrooms. Your work continues to inspire me, and I will always appreciate and respect the example you set.

And thank you to Cheryl Harris and Betsy James for that workshop all those years ago that started me down this road. You lit a fire in me.

Introduction to the Course

This distinction between form and experience is not pedantic, but fundamental: a form can express the Transcendent, an experience cannot. A form can express the common ground in which all things share. An experience can only express one man's reaction to that common ground.

—Paul Schrader, *Transcendental Style in Film: Ozu, Bresson, Dreyer*

When we talk about meeting kids where they are, we have to mean it. Film, after all, is ubiquitous. We are surrounded by screens—television, film, cell phones, ads on the sides of buildings, even fast-food menus. We are inundated with shows, games, and advertisements. As a result, we understand film viscerally, if not intellectually. It is a language we can comprehend and from which we can make meaning, even when we may not understand the technical aspects of how that process happens.

So, if that is the case, we as educators should take advantage of that fact. Reach kids where they are, right? The problem is that most of us learned to teach print texts in college, not films. Only relatively recently have large numbers of English teachers begun to see film as a viable form of nonprint text. The National Council of Teachers of English (NCTE), recognizing the value of such texts, has published quite a few books and articles on the subject.

The simple fact is that telling stories via the medium of film requires every bit of the forethought and intent that constructing print text requires. Technical considerations are inherent in the medium, of course, but at its core, the process is the same. Want the audience to relate? Develop the characters. Want to hook your reader/viewer? Build suspense. Develop a conflict. Insert complicating actions. And given the degree of intent required, it stands to reason that film can therefore be read in much the same way as print text can be read.

The difficulty with reading film texts stems from the lack of specific training many English teachers received in college. The interesting fact about reading film, though, is that the medium allows for a visceral experience that print text cannot. We understand the tension, we feel the suspense, and we understand the characters, all without the advantage of technical expertise. Film is designed to be felt—we just don't always understand the *how* of it all.

The difficulty with reading print texts is of a different type entirely. English teachers become English teachers for a variety of reasons, but the common thread is that we are all good readers. We see the characters in our mind's eye. We hear their voices. The worlds they inhabit become real for us. And when the texts we read are made into film, we often complain that the characters do not *look* right, do not *sound* right, and *that just isn't how that place is supposed to look*. We take for granted that not all of our students come to class with this same skill set, so we spend a tremendous amount of time attempting to overcome this deficit. Film study can be a fantastic way to bridge that gap.

For instance, film study can be a wonderful way to teach our students how to use their imaginations. My seventh grader mentioned to me the other day that she was glad she got to see the film version of a book she had read because, "Now I get to see what they look like!" But for film to be effective as a teaching tool, we should take the opposite approach. For example, give students a text and have them plan it out first, and then compare to a film version. Or compare multiple film versions of a given scene to see how different directors envision the story. The important takeaway is that a film represents one director's vision, which is a very different thing from saying it represents "The Truth." By extension, then, every person—every student—is entitled to their own vision as well.

Once students are able to internalize that their perspective is valid, they learn to trust it. Then they learn to develop it. Finally, when they go back to that print text, they have an entirely different experience. They "see" the world of the story. They can "hear" the characters' voices. And they begin to interact with the text in a whole new way. Why did that happen? Why couldn't this happen? They begin to evaluate, to analyze, and to consider options. And isn't that what we want?

Moreover, one of the major goals of teachers of literature is to lead students through a close reading of the text in order to identify the techniques a writer uses in order to make meaning. Once identified, those techniques are analyzed in terms of their effectiveness. Ultimately, as students begin to identify the *how* and *why* regarding the techniques good writers use, the thinking is those students will be more likely to be able to incorporate those techniques into their own writing, thereby becoming better writers.

With regard to film, the goals of the storyteller are the same. Convey a setting. Craft relatable characters. Weave an engaging conflict. Build toward a resolution. All this while connecting with the reader and guiding that reader's emotions. The difference when studying film is that the filmmaker has many more tools with which to accomplish these goals.

When examining print texts, instructors generally pose similar questions. Why did the author use this word instead of that one? How does the author develop given characters? How does the author's sentence construction build suspense? We study characters, conflicts, mood, tone, connotation, denotation, sentence structure, plot structure, irony, foreshadowing, voice, intent, diction, the effect of audience on style and message, and many other literary elements.

When examining film texts, instructors can pose the same questions. The difference, though, is there are now many more elements to consider. Why, for instance, would the filmmaker begin the scene with shots of a second-floor inner-city classroom? Why would the filmmaker film this character from a high angle? Why would the filmmaker use side lighting for that character? What does the filmmaker's use of a trombone shot on this character convey about what the character is thinking or feeling?

At the end of the day, whether one studies print text or film, the goal is still to break down how storytellers tell their stories. The flip side to that coin is to use that knowledge to the benefit of our own writing. Learn to receive; learn to create.

This book is designed to help you teach film in your classroom to equip your students with the skills they could then apply to the creation of their own films. The underlying philosophy is that by engaging students in a familiar medium, by teaching them the tools storytellers utilize to make their audiences feel, engage, and relate, students can develop a skill set that will help print texts come alive for them in ways it never has before.

And if your students have fun along the way? Even better!

You may have never been trained to teach film, but the important idea to understand is that you can do this even without such specialized training. The lessons in this book are designed to equip you with the skills and knowledge necessary to teach film effectively in your classroom with your existing skill set. To that end, you will find lesson plans (in the Sample Lessons section), a glossary of film terms (Appendix A and in lists specific to each unit lesson); comparison and observation charts and rubrics (Appendix B), assessments (Appendix C), storyboard templates (Appendix D), Common Core State Standards addressed in each unit lesson (see Appendix E for the complete list), and more generally, step-by-step instructions designed to make planning and implementation easier for you. Try a lesson and see how your students respond!

Developing Effective Course Objectives

Success involves failing first. Ask any successful person. Ask any experienced person, really. It's all part of the creative process, so sit back and allow the artist within you to sprout, blossom and flourish. You must accept that your first, second, and third attempt at something might suck. It's a necessary step in improving your skill. Failure is your teacher, not your judge.

—CONNOR FRANTA, *A Work in Progress*

In general, your objectives when teaching film mirror those when you are teaching print text. You want your students to examine how a particular author utilizes a particular technique in a particular text to make meaning. No sense in reinventing the wheel—keep that basic template, but sub in directors for authors, film titles for print titles, etc. For example, the following are a few sample objectives (or objective stems) covered in this course:

- We will examine [a scene/scenes] from [text title] to determine how [director] uses [film technique] in order to impact meaning and influence audience perception.
- We will examine [a scene/scenes] from [text title/titles] to determine basic elements of [director's] voice/style.
- We will examine [a scene/scenes] from [text title/titles] to determine basic elements of [given film movement].
- We will examine how [director] uses [film techniques] to make meaning and use our understanding of this director's approach to craft our own scenes in this director's style.

The important thing to notice in this case is how closely these objectives mirror those one might find adorning the board in a more traditional English classroom. We will examine Robert Service's poem "My Prisoner" in order to determine how he uses dialect and nonstandard spelling in order (just kidding about the "in order" part!) to impact meaning and influence audience perspective. After all, when teaching reading, the English teacher's goal can generally be simplified to helping students learn to see and evaluate the techniques authors use to make meaning or influence an audience.

For instance, take a look at the first objective listed above:

TEMPLATE: We will examine [a scene/scenes] from [text title] to determine how [director] uses [film technique] to impact meaning and influence audience perception.

VERSION 1: We will examine the poem "next to of course god america i" to determine how E. E. Cummings uses capitalization, enjambment, and sarcasm to impact meaning and influence audience perception.

VERSION 2: We will examine the shower scene from *Psycho* to determine how Hitchcock uses montage, point-of-view shots, and pacing to impact meaning and influence audience response.

In short, contrary to what you might expect, this book does not ask you to stray far from how you were taught to teach. We will still teach our students how to break down challenging texts, identify the storytelling techniques we discover, and use those techniques to craft our own new stories. What this book does ask you to do is to use a form of text with which your students are familiar to positively impact their understanding of the craft of storytelling, thereby building student literacy.

For your convenience, more specific objectives are listed at the beginning of each unit.

Different Skills Pay Different Bills: A Note Regarding Differentiation

Science Technology Engineering and Math is still necessary to know if you dream of being a filmmaker. Filmmaking is an art form, but with the use of STEM.

—Kailin Gow

We all look for the best way to reach our kids, and we have heard the old admonition that we should "reach kids where they are" a thousand times. *Differentiate. Check.* We also know that doing so in a class of thirty-five or more kids is challenging, to say the least. How, then, does one differentiate in a film class?

Film is an incredibly rich, fantastically thorough collaboration of a wide variety of people with a wide variety of skills and talents. Each person is important; each role on a film set is invaluable. The overall project would not work if any one of those roles were not filled.

To that end, we begin by exploring those different roles. We write treatments. We write scripts. We scout locations. We storyboard. We do basic filming and editing. And as we fill these different roles, we gain a more thorough understanding of the process and a better understanding of our own strengths and weaknesses. As that process unfolds, we gravitate toward the roles that most interest us. In the end, students gravitate toward cinematography, or editing, or writing, or directing, etc.—each of whom plays a different "instrument," so to speak, in the orchestra that is the filmmaking process.

As the teacher, you then may take advantage of what students have learned about themselves. For example, you may assign students a text as homework, and students may then choose whether they wish to complete storyboards, prepare a treatment, write interior monologues for the characters, or design the set. Each job is important, and the overall project needs them all. Not every poet, for example, must be a master of rhyme.

This understanding is important as well when teaching students to manage collaborative groups. Students should recognize they will need each skill set to be represented in each group. Every film project will need a producer. Every film project will require a director. A cinematographer. A writer. An editor. The skill sets these people bring to the table are very different, and none of those jobs is expendable.

In that sense, a film class is the very model of what a differentiated classroom should look like. Every student is working toward the same goal—a completed film—but each is working in a way that best fits that student's skill set.

For your benefit, each unit is preceded by materials that include ideas for differentiating within each lesson.

It Takes a Village: Film Set Hierarchy

Make films that purify the soul with the flow of rational, vigorous and compassionate thinking.

—Abhijit Naskar, *The Film Testament*

There are hundreds of jobs on a film set, and every one of them adds in some important way to the finished product. There are thousands of personal, logistical, and artistic considerations, and every one of these decisions falls under the jurisdiction of one of those jobs. For the sake of simplicity, though, in a classroom context, these jobs will need to be condensed quite a bit. Additionally, some responsibilities may be reassigned for the sake of balancing the workload.

To that end, I am a firm believer that every person in a group should have a specific set of responsibilities. In this way, students understand how they contribute to the group's overall success. As important, they understand that if they do not fulfill their responsibilities, the project will not be successful. The types of assignments in this class, after all, do not allow for the "You do the odd questions, and I'll do the even ones" approach.

Consequently, students need to know exactly what roles they will be expected to fill. In virtually every collaborative assignment in this book, the following roles should suffice.

Producer

The producer oversees all of the logistics, which include correspondence with the actors and crew as well as supervising the shooting schedule and securing locations for filming. The producer brings aboard the actors for the film (which may include auditions) and makes sure every group member knows when they are needed for filming (call sheets). In a condensed classroom setting, the producer may also need to do location scouting to find an appropriate place for the group to film. In short, the producer is responsible for making sure the director has everything they need in order to complete the project. It should be noted that the responsibilities delineated here actually go beyond the scope of what a Hollywood producer would be required to do. Those additional responsibilities have been rolled into the producer's job description simply as a way to help balance the workload among group members.

Director

The director is the person with the creative vision for the film in general. The director must make sure everyone knows their responsibilities and that they will be able to fulfill those responsibilities. Further, the director will set the due dates for each phase of the process. The director is responsible for working closely with the actors to determine how they should perform their roles. Additionally, the director is responsible for crafting a treatment for the scriptwriter (an added role intended to help balance group responsibilities) and then using the subsequent script to develop the storyboards.

Scriptwriter/Supervisor

Some of the following roles have been expanded beyond what one might expect to see in Hollywood for the sake of balancing group members' workloads. We begin with the scriptwriter. The scriptwriter is responsible for writing the script. Once the director has completed the treatment for the film, the scriptwriter uses the treatment to craft a script. The script is the blueprint for the whole project, so it should satisfy all the key players' core visions of what's being produced. Having said that, the scriptwriter may need to complete several drafts of the script before the script can be used. Once the script is ready, the scriptwriter hands the script off to the director so the director can complete the storyboarding process. The scriptwriter also must ensure all participants have the up-to-date version of whatever scene is being filmed at the time. In summary, the scriptwriter will need to be in regular, close contact with the director so as to be sure they create a good, feasible product.

Director of Photography

The director of photography, or DP, is responsible for capturing the director's creative vision on film. The DP will use the storyboards as a guide for filming the necessary shots. To that end, the director of photography will need to have access to the necessary film equipment and will need to have a clear understanding of how to use the camera to capture the director's artistic vision. When finished filming, the DP will need to organize all of the footage for the editor to quickly access the desired shots and takes. This process will involve renaming the video files based on scene, take, etc., so the editor can access the files with maximum efficiency.

Cinematographer

The cinematographer is responsible for capturing the director's artistic vision, using the storyboards as a primary guide. The cinematographer will need to be knowledgeable in the application of the Rule of Thirds, the 180-Degree Rule, and the Golden Ratio. The cinematographer will need to be knowledgeable in the maintenance and operation of the camera, and must be able to be present whenever filming is to take place.

Editor

Films are told twice, it is said—once in front to the camera and again during the editing process. The editor is responsible for culling all of the footage for the best shots and putting them together to create a clean, cohesive whole. Good editing helps create a tempo for the story, moving the action along without either dragging it out or moving too quickly. A good editor must be able to identify what is necessary and be willing to cut what is not. An editor should be able to use the film the cinematographers give them to create a polished, professional-looking finished product. The editor will need to work closely with the director at this stage of the project.

Actors

These people will be responsible for filling the requisite character roles. If an actor is part of the class, then the actor must also participate in one of the other production capacities outlined above. Actors may be brought in from outside, however. Groups should cast appropriately, meaning that if a group needs a grandpa, that group should cast someone of the appropriate age, or if a character is a mom, the actor should be of an appropriate age as well. This is a great opportunity to work with students in the drama department as well as other talented actors. Bad casting can quickly kill the realism of a scene and pull the viewer out of the moment.

Connecting Classroom Learning to the Real World: Small-Group Project List

When I looked at life through the camera, I felt like I could finally see it.

—Katherine Howe, *The Appearance of Annie Van Sinderen*

One cannot truly understand film without participating in some way to make film. To suggest otherwise would be to suggest one could learn to drive without ever getting behind the wheel of a vehicle or that one could understand fishing without ever baiting a hook or casting a line. Such suggestions are inherently foolish.

That said, when it comes to filmmaking, there are quite a few options available to you to try with your students. The following are examples of the types of projects you may want to explore. Some work well for group projects while others work well as extra credit assignments. How you choose to use them is, of course, up to you.

Generally speaking, I assign one of these projects per quarter, and students work on them concurrently with whatever we are doing in class. Depending upon your students' access to and familiarity with the requisite technology, you may wish to adjust the number of projects you assign to suit your situation.

OPTION 1: FILM TRAILER OF MY LIFE

ASSIGNMENT: If someone were to make a film about your life, what would the trailer look like? Create a one-minute film trailer for that film.

RATIONALE: Trailers (or previews) are obviously an important part of the film-making process. In this case, the challenge is to tell the story in a much more concise format.

REQUIRED ELEMENTS: This trailer should include the title of the film, your name as the star, a soundtrack, and clips from scenes that would be included in your film. The trailer should be one minute long.

NOTE: *This assignment can be done with relatively little difficulty on a cell phone, and it makes a great introductory assignment. Students get to experience basic video editing, and you wind up with a finished product that helps you learn names and faces.*

OPTION 2: MUSIC VIDEO

ASSIGNMENT: Create a music video for a song that tells a story. Lyrics must be approved by the teacher and may not reference alcohol, drugs/drug use, or suicide.

RATIONALE: The story is already there—all that is left is to add the visual component. In theory, this assignment should be relatively easy because it is relatively short, and there is no need to write an original story. As a side note, alternate interpretations of the lyrics are acceptable.

REQUIRED ELEMENTS: The music video requires an understanding of the source text—in this case, a song—and the ability to convey that understanding via basic film techniques. As an option, if you are a musician, feel free to use your own original song.

NOTE: *This project is quite a bit more intensive than the introductory film trailer. Students are interpreting lyrics, managing a team of actors, and learning to edit longer sequences. This project is generally the first big project I assign.*

OPTION 3: MASHED-UP MOVIE TRAILER

ASSIGNMENT: Use video from one film and audio from another to make a misleading movie trailer—for example, a children's cartoon using a war film's audio track.

RATIONALE: This assignment helps students begin to take ownership of the process, which is key to telling original stories. Additionally, this project, perhaps more than any of the others, enables students to understand the importance of context as well as just how much power storytellers have to guide their audiences.

REQUIRED ELEMENTS: A "mash-up" is where one takes video clips from one film and sound from another to make a thirty-second movie trailer (think *Bambi* meets *300*). Cartoons work well for video clips, given that the mouths of the characters often do not match up exactly to their spoken words. A quick YouTube search will turn up some good examples.

NOTE: *I usually offer this project as an extra credit project, though it could certainly work as a standard one. Be aware the difficulty level is deceptive. Though the finished product will be short (I generally set a time length, whether 1:00, 1:30, or as much as 2:00), students must cull both footage and audio, a process that can be labor intensive.*

OPTION 4: SILENT FILM

ASSIGNMENT: Create an updated silent film. The story may be original, or it may be based on a published piece. The story must be approved by the teacher and may not reference alcohol, drugs/drug use, or suicide.

RATIONALE: Dialogue is a bit of a filmmaker's crutch. This assignment forces a reliance on the visual aspect of storytelling.

REQUIRED ELEMENTS: The silent film need not be completely silent; rather, it simply cannot include spoken words. There should, in fact, be sound, and both diegetic and nondiegetic sound is acceptable.

NOTE: *This project is the second large project I typically assign. The music video was relatively easy in the sense that the lyrics help drive the action. In the silent film, however, the story must be told in other ways. One cannot rely on dialogue but instead must use the various techniques we have covered in order to tell the story.*

OPTION 5: GENRE-BENDER MOVIE TRAILER

ASSIGNMENT: Make a "genre-bender" movie trailer.

RATIONALE: This project is a fun way to reinterpret film footage.

REQUIRED ELEMENTS: In this type of trailer, one takes a film, uses clips out of context, and, perhaps with the benefit of a voice-over, presents the film as belonging to a completely different genre. Think *The Shining* presented as a romantic comedy or *Edward Scissorhands* as a horror film.

NOTE: *This is another project I typically offer as an extra credit assignment, though again, this project could stand alone. The idea is similar to the movie trailer mash-up assignment. The difference—and this is important—is that the audio and video must come from the* same *film. In short, one must take clips from a given film out of context.*

OPTION OPTION 6: FILM REVIEW
ASSIGNMENT: You may go to see a new movie (must be within two weeks of its release), write a review (minimum of 500 words), and present your review to the class. Your score will be based on how thorough I feel you have been and how helpful I believe the review to be.
RATIONALE: This assignment is a great way to assess your thinking with regard to the films you have been studying. Are you beginning to understand how the elements work together to form a coherent whole? Can you evaluate the effectiveness of those techniques? Moreover, this assignment provides you with an excellent opportunity for authentic research, given that you will want to look into other films by that director, other performances by the actors, etc.
REQUIRED ELEMENTS: The review should be typed and at least 500 words long.
NOTE: This assignment works well as both a summative and a formative assessment. After all, having students put their thoughts in writing helps them organize those thoughts and enables the teacher to determine how well students understand what they have been studying. Based on the results, the teacher may then adjust instruction accordingly.

OPTION 7: TEN-MINUTE FILM PROPOSAL/PREPRODUCTION NOTEBOOK
ASSIGNMENT: Submit a proposal for a possible ten-minute film. The story must be approved by the teacher and may not reference alcohol, drugs/drug use, or suicide.
RATIONALE: This assignment represents the preproduction phase of the filmmaking process. Far from busywork, this assignment reflects the real-world process of making film.
REQUIRED ELEMENTS: This project will be presented in a three-ring binder and must include a 1,000-word treatment, a script, 50 storyboards (including shot list), shooting locations (including photographs of these locations), costumes (photographs and rationales), interior monologues (500 words each), a shooting schedule, and credits. As an alternative, the entire project may be done on a digital platform just as easily, depending on personal preference.
NOTE: I usually assign this as the third of four group projects. For longer film projects to turn out well, they must be planned well. Poor planning leads to poor filmmaking.

OPTION 8: FOLEY SOUND PROJECT
ASSIGNMENT: Given sample visual text, create the Foley sounds and add them to the video.

RATIONALE: Sound is massively important in film, and much of that sound is created in Foley studios. This project is designed to help you better understand the Foley process.

REQUIRED ELEMENTS: You will be provided a short film clip. After determining what sounds will be needed, film groups must create/re-create those sounds and add them to the video. Additionally, you must provide a video of the process you went through to add the sounds.

NOTE: The idea, of course, is to create, or re-create, the sounds produced in a short video clip. This assignment can be especially challenging when the sounds produced on-screen do not typically occur in nature. For example, no one knows how removing the lid of the Ark of the Covenant sounds. No worries! In Raiders of the Lost Ark, *Steven Spielberg used the porcelain lid of the water reservoir on the back of a toilet to get that heavy grinding effect!*

OPTION 9: SHORT DOCUMENTARY

ASSIGNMENT: Create a short documentary that addresses a topic of your choosing. The topic must be approved by the teacher.

RATIONALE: This assignment allows you to both address a topic that interests you and use the techniques we have covered thus far in the class regarding film techniques and how to impact audience perspective.

REQUIRED ELEMENTS: Documentaries are constructed in a specific way with specific components. Documentaries tend to include interviews, cutaways, cinéma vérité or live footage, process footage, and archival footage. The project will be assessed on the basis of the variety, effectiveness, and originality of the techniques you employed.

NOTE: This assignment gives students the opportunity to address topics that are important to them and, as a result, can be a rewarding experience. You will want to provide a time limit, of course; five to ten minutes should work nicely.

OPTION 10: TEN-MINUTE FILM

ASSIGNMENT: Create a ten-minute film (give or take thirty seconds) based on a previously published work (e.g., a song, short story, essay, novel, chapter from a novel, etc.). The story must be approved by the teacher and may not reference alcohol, drugs/drug use, or suicide.

RATIONALE: This assignment is the culmination of the class and represents an opportunity to explore the techniques covered in class to their full potential. Selected films may be eligible for entry into the film festival.

REQUIRED ELEMENTS: Genre and style are completely open. The ten-minute film may be stop-motion animation/photography, 2D animation, or live action. The project will be assessed on the basis of the variety, effectiveness, and originality of the techniques you employed.

NOTE: This assignment represents the culmination of the course. I require my students' films to be ten minutes long, but feel free to adjust that requirement as per your preference. I also showcase these films in an annual student film festival. Oscar-like statuettes are easy to find online, are relatively inexpensive, and make great mementos. We award ten or so of the most popular categories, from Best Editing to Best Production and Design to Best Director and Best Film.

Giving Credit Where Credit Is Due: Collaborative Assessment Philosophy

It's not important whether you worked hard or not. Ultimately it's about how the movie is. Nothing else matters.

—P. S. Arjun

Every student who has ever worked in a small group has experienced firsthand the difficulty of accurately assessing who did what. No one wants to be the member who did the lion's share of the work yet received the same grade as the group member who did little or nothing. The fact is, however, that for a variety of reasons, some students are simply more invested in the outcome of the assignment than others are.

Inevitably, for the teacher—who cannot possibly be present with every group every minute they are working—grading group projects poses problems. For example, what if one student winds up having to do most or all of the work? What if another student does not contribute at all? Should everyone receive the same grade? How is that equitable?

To satisfy all parties and to enable my students to feel a bit more invested in the process, I assess group projects as follows:

1. Each project will receive a score.
2. The score will be multiplied by the number of students who contributed to the project in order to determine a points total for the group.
3. Each group will meet, discuss peer and teacher feedback, and then determine just how much each group member contributed to the overall project. Once the group reaches consensus, the group will divide the points among

the group members. (In my own experience, while group members may easily misrepresent their contributions to the project to me, doing so with each other proves much more difficult. Those other group members were there; they know who did what—and who did not. As such, I almost never have students disagree when dividing points. Ultimately, however, if any group members *do* disagree, I ask everyone to write a "My Contribution to the Project" statement, after which I reserve the right to determine which group members should get which points.) Each group member may receive the same score if everyone worked equally; in the event the load was not evenly distributed, however, scores may vary within the group. In the end, students' scores should add up to the total number of points as determined in step 2.

4. Once students are in agreement the points have been distributed fairly, they should sign beside their individual scores. Signing indicates agreement. If students do not sign off on their scores, I will meet with the group to determine proper point distribution.
5. As the teacher, I am the final authority on grades, which means that I may adjust them as I see fit.

If there is ever a need to discuss the grade or the contributions (or lack thereof) of particular group members, groups (or individual students) may make an appointment to speak with me outside of class. If a student is not contributing to their group, they may be removed from the group at my discretion. Any students removed from groups for not contributing will be required to complete an alternative assignment in order to receive credit.

Obviously, how you assess your students is up to you. Personally, I like this strategy because students feel more ownership in the process and they are better able to hold their group members accountable. Do students always agree with their group members' assessment of their contributions? No, of course not. But the truth is that lying to me—the teacher—is easy. "Sure, I was there! I met with everybody! I did this and that. . . . Oh, absolutely!" And what do I know? I was not there. But lying to one's group members is much more difficult. In all honesty, when I have been clear about the grading process in advance, I rarely have any disagreement among group members. They all know how much or little they contributed.

So what happens when groups *do* disagree? As a bit of a safety net, before groups split up their points, I ask them to write a reflection on the process. How, specifically, did you contribute to your group's success? If a group cannot reach consensus, I read their reflections—which I keep confidential—before meeting with them. We talk about how the group worked together, and then I assign a grade based on what I learn from the reflections and group conversation. I'm all for student ownership, but my college degree has to count for something, right? I'm the teacher; I'm the final authority. Even directors have to answer to producers.

Sample Lessons

Now that we have covered the basic elements regarding the *how* and *why* of using film to build student literacy, you may wish to try a bit of film instruction with your students. Perhaps you teach English and want to incorporate more film into your instruction as a way to address nonprint media. Or perhaps you teach a Literature and Film class, like I do, and your whole year is devoted to reading and producing films as a way to teach students about audience and purpose and method, among other things.

In any case, what follows are twelve fully formed lessons you can use with your students. Each unit takes a slightly different approach to using film and helps students build on the skills they have learned along the way. This is, after all, an exercise in developing *skills*—skills students can use right away (I had a student who was hired by a local band to make music videos for them, for example) or perhaps down the road in a professional context (I have quite a few former students who now live in Los Angeles, Chicago, and New York who now use their skills professionally—from advertising executives and cinematographers to focus pullers, hair and makeup to independent filmmakers, and more). And at the beginning of every lesson, you will find a fully developed lesson plan—because, hey, I'm a teacher, too. I know how this sort of thing works. Feel free to adjust these plans, of course, as you see fit.

There is a great deal of educational "protein" regarding film instruction. In my two-and-a-half decades in the classroom, I have yet to encounter anything that can be taught from a print text that cannot be addressed using film. Film incorporates art, science, literature, and so much more. We discuss architecture, psychology, and philosophy. We discuss issues relevant to my students' lives. Film construction is a nexus of intellectual thought that requires a wide range of skills and abilities to be done well. There is room for an incredibly wide range of people at the table, and every student can find a way to contribute in a meaningful way.

Never forget that film is *fun*. And we should never underestimate the importance of fun in the educational process.

The Kuleshov Effect: Making Meaning through Juxtaposition

Lesson Plan

Essential Question
How does the juxtaposition of shots in film affect audience perception or understanding?

Objectives
1. Students will be able to analyze how the placement of images next to each other can impact audience perception.
2. Students will be able to demonstrate an understanding of the Kuleshov Effect via the creation of their own Kuleshov storylines.

Central Texts
Kuleshov Effect photo strips

Agenda

> STEP 1: Anticipatory Quickwrite
>
> STEP 2: Explore the Kuleshov Effect—Its Origin, What It Is, How It Works, Etc.
>
> STEP 3: Create Examples of the Kuleshov Effect
>
> STEP 4: Interpret the Kuleshov Storylines Created by Classmates
>
> STEP 5: Reflect on the Process

Differentiation
The idea here is to demonstrate an understanding of the Kuleshov Effect. That said, your students have a few options for how they may complete the assignment. Students may print off photographs and attach them to the template or

create a new template and insert the photographs digitally. If they would rather not use a printed template, they may choose to film their own sequences. If they film their sequences, they just need to be sure they will be able to share their work with their classmates.

Vocabulary

juxtaposition (n.)—the act of placing unlike objects/images side by side to create meaning or make a point

Resources

YouTube Video—"Hitchcock Explains the Kuleshov Effect to Fletcher Markle. 1964" by MediaFilmProfessor (https://youtu.be/96xx383lpiI)

"Kuleshov Effect/Effetto Kuleshov" by esteticaCC (https://youtu.be/_gGl3LJ7vHc)

"Rear Window Kuleshov Effect" by film kurgusu (https://youtu.be/HLxZcVETDDw)

"Kuleshov Effect – Alfred Hitchcock" by film kurgusu (https://youtu.be/4cfqkIFbyw4)

"The Kuleshov Effect" by Folding Ideas (https://youtu.be/Vy2Vhnqtu8I)

"The Kuleshov Effect – Everything You Need to Know" by No Film School (https://youtu.be/OVwKItbgd3s)

"THE KULESHOV EFFECT: the real magic of movie editing" by Movavi Vlog (https://youtu.be/rDTFwP_qcX0)

Suggested Timeline
Two days

Lesson 1

The Kuleshov Effect: Making Meaning through Juxtaposition

The job of the film director is *to tell the story through the juxtaposition of uninflected images*—because that is the essential nature of the medium.

—DAVID MAMET, *On Directing Film*

STEP 1: Anticipatory Quickwrite

How can the placement of film clips next to each other influence audience perception or understanding? Be prepared to share your thoughts with your classmates.

In the early 1900s, Russian filmmaker Lev Kuleshov had an interesting idea. He realized the power of film, or of the individual images that comprised film, lay in how the audience interpreted those images, which was in turn based on their relationship to each other. And long before Norman N. Holland, Stanley Fish, Wolfgang Iser, Hans Robert Jauss, or Roland Barthes, among others, set about defining the basics of reader-response criticism in the 1960s and 1970s, Kuleshov had already devised a means to demonstrate this phenomenon with film.

Filmmakers such as the Lumière brothers, Georges Méliès, Robert W. Paul, George Albert Smith, and Cecil Hepworth had already introduced audiences to moving pictures, sometimes with what audiences today would consider hilarious results. Most film students are aware of the story, for example, that when the Lumière brothers played "L'arrivée d'un train en gare de La Ciotat" for audiences in January of 1896, viewers nearly trampled each other in an effort to escape being run over by the train pulling into the station. Hellmuth Karasek—a German journalist, literary critic, novelist, and the author of many books on literature and film—pointed out in the German magazine *Der Spiegel* that the film "had a particularly lasting impact; yes, it caused fear, terror, even panic" (Karasek). Others, such as film historian Martin Loiperdinger, doubt the veracity of this often-told story (Loiperdinger). Even so, all agree there was a certain learning curve both for filmmakers learning to tell stories in new ways and audiences learning how to receive them. Enter Lev Kuleshov.

Kuleshov was fascinated with how audiences made meaning from film. And while the earliest films were comprised of single shots, Kuleshov experimented with cuts, thereby placing disparate images back to back. In order to study how audiences made meaning from these images, Kuleshov set up an experiment.

STEP 2: *Explore the Kuleshov Effect—Its Origin, What It Is, How It Works, Etc.*

In short, Kuleshov played a series of images back to back: a close-up of a man looking directly into the camera followed by a bowl of soup; a shot of the same man followed by a dead body; and a shot of the same man followed by a beautiful woman. Then he discussed with his audience what they saw.

What Kuleshov found was that his audience was blown away by the subtlety of the man's acting. They could see the hunger in his eyes in the first pair of images. In the second, they could see pain and remorse. And in the third, Kuleshov's audience could plainly see the man was attracted to the beautiful woman.

Kuleshov's audience did not realize the image of the man was the same in all three cases. He was not looking at soup, a body, or a beautiful woman; he was simply looking with a neutral expression at the camera. What Kuleshov was able to show was the meaning of the film lay in the conversation between the text and the viewer. By viewing the images back to back, the audience "understood" a particular relationship that did not actually exist. Kuleshov realized this process was the essence of storytelling in film, and it signaled the shift from short single-shot films to longer multi-shot films.

In order to better understand the process, consider the images in Figure 1.1.

FIGURE 1.1. Kuleshov's first example.

Interpretation: This is the first sequence Kuleshov showed to his audience. Notice how the man appears to be looking eagerly at a bowl of soup. Audience members swore they could see hunger in his eyes. Now look at Figure 1.2.

FIGURE 1.2. Kuleshov's second example.

Interpretation: In this second sequence, the man appears to be looking sadly at a dead body. Of course, you already know the shots of the man are exactly the same. Even so, audience members claimed to discern a deep sadness.

 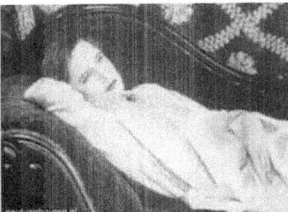 

FIGURE 1.3. Kuleshov's third example.

Interpretation: And this is the final sequence (Figure 1.3). Now the man appears to be looking longingly at a beautiful woman reclining on a couch.

The reality, unbeknownst to Kuleshov's audience, was that the man was simply looking at the camera. Any image edited between the two shots of the man's face would suggest the man was, in fact, looking at that subject.

Kuleshov's famous student Sergei Eisenstein, when examining the importance of structure to make meaning in film, posited that meaning was created as a result of the **juxtaposition** between shot A ("thesis") and shot B ("antithesis"), wherein a completely new idea ("synthesis") is created in the mind of the viewer (Springer).

Then, in 1964 on the CBC documentary *A Talk with Hitchcock*, Alfred Hitchcock expounded on the power of the Kuleshov Effect, calling this process "pure cinematics." Indeed, this is the process that makes modern feature films possible. And Hitchcock himself famously expanded Kuleshov's earlier experiment by changing his expression in the follow-up shot. Notice the implications in Hitchcock's sequences, Figures 1.4 and 1.5.

 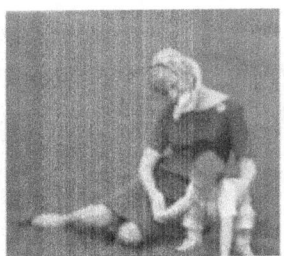 

FIGURE 1.4. Hitchcock's first example.

Interpretation: In Figure 1.4, Hitchcock is just a nice old man, smiling fondly as he watches a mother playing with her child.

FIGURE 1.5. Hitchcock's second example.

Interpretation: In this case, simply by changing the second image to a woman in a bikini, Hitchcock now appears to be a dirty old man. Meaning, it would seem, is created by how the viewer perceives the relationship of the images placed next to each other.

STEP 3: Create Examples of the Kuleshov Effect

As a way to wrap up the discussion on the Kuleshov Effect and have your students begin the process of influencing audience perception, have them create their own Kuleshov Effect storylines using the template provided.

STEP 4: Interpret the Kuleshov Storylines Created by Classmates

As an extension, have your students trade their storylines and interpret their partners' storylines (see Appendix 1A on p. 26). When students have finished creating their own storylines and then interpreting those of their classmates, they should take a few minutes to reflect on the process (see Appendix 1B on p. 27).

STEP 5: Reflect on the Process

What have you learned? How has this activity affected your understanding of the Kuleshov Effect? What does this process teach you about the process of editing? Be prepared to share your thoughts with your classmates.

Standards Addressed in This Unit

Key Ideas and Details
CCSS.ELA-LITERACY.CCRA.R.1

Craft and Structure
CCSS.ELA-LITERACY.CCRA.R.4
CCSS.ELA-LITERACY.CCRA.R.5
Integration of Knowledge and Ideas
CCSS.ELA-LITERACY.CCRA.R.7
Comprehension and Collaboration
CCSS.ELA-LITERACY.CCRA.SL.1
CCSS.ELA-LITERACY.CCRA.SL.2
Presentation of Knowledge and Ideas
CCSS.ELA-LITERACY.CCRA.SL.4
Production and Distribution
CCSS.ELA-LITERACY.CCRA.W.4
CCSS.ELA-LITERACY.CCRA.W.6
Research to Build and Present Knowledge
CCSS.ELA-LITERACY.CCRA.W.7

Appendix 1A

Directions for Student Reflection on the Kuleshov Effect Activity

The Kuleshov Effect	Name_____Pd_____	
Directions: Follow the directions on the template below in order to create your own version of the Kuleshov Effect. You will need to print out pictures to post in each frame. As an option, you may want to re-create this template on your computer and add the photographs digitally. Either way, save the interpretation line for a classmate to fill out.		
In this frame, place a photograph of yourself. Be sure to have a neutral expression. This photograph will be the same in each of the first boxes below.	In this frame, place a photograph of something you could be looking at or reacting to.	In this frame, you may either place the same photograph you used in box #1 or a photograph of you smiling, smirking, grimacing, or reacting in some other way.

Interpretation of the storyline presented above: _____
_____

Use the same photograph here that you used in the first box above.	In this frame, place another photograph of something completely different that you could be looking at or reacting to.	As an option, keep the second image the same and change this image instead.

Interpretation of the storyline presented above: _____
_____

Use the same photograph here that you used in the first box above.	In this frame, place another photograph of something completely different that you could be looking at or responding to.	As an option, keep the second image the same and change this image instead.

Interpretation of the storyline presented above: _____
_____

Appendix 1B

An Exemplar Reflection on the Kuleshov Effect for Modeling

The Kuleshov Effect EXEMPLAR

Directions: The following are three sample Kuleshov sequences.

Interpretation: I'm looking at a computer screen, probably working, nothing overly exciting. We come to this conclusion solely because the images are placed next to each other.

Interpretation: Maybe what I am doing is not much fun at all. In this case, all I changed was the final image, the response.

Interpretation: Maybe I am doing math, and it is really exciting. I used the same first image, of course, only with a different second and third image. Now the storyline is completely different from what we started with.

Kuleshov stumbled onto something really important here: the psychological process through which the viewer makes sense of film. Considered in isolation, each image means relatively little or nothing. As David Mamet would say, they are *uninflected images*. But by virtue of their placement next to one another, we infer a larger meaning. Compare this conversation between reader and text to reader-response literary criticism.

Intro to Film Study: Group Dynamics

Lesson Plan

Essential Question
Given the inherently collaborative nature of filmmaking, how should one construct small groups?

Objective
Students will be able to use what they learn about themselves and their classmates to form effective collaborative film groups.

Central Texts

"Build a Tower, Build a Team" by Tom Wujec for TED 2010

Explanations of various personality tests

Agenda

STEP 1: Anticipatory Quickwrite

STEP 2: Team-Building Activity #1—Marshmallows and Spaghetti

STEP 3: Team-Building Activity #2—One-Word Stories

STEP 4: Personality Test #1—The Five Shapes

STEP 5: Personality Test #2 (Optional)—Myers-Briggs Type Indicator (Personality Test)

STEP 6: Forming Small Groups

STEP 7: Movie Poster Tableau

STEP 8: Culminating Activity—Designing a Studio Logo

STEP 9: Reflect on the Process

Differentiation

Given that this unit is all about how an understanding of one's own strengths and weaknesses can be used to help form more effective collaborative groups, successful completion of this unit lays the foundation for all of the differentiation to follow.

Vocabulary

>tableau (n.)—a "freeze-frame" inspired by a text in which participants arrange themselves in order to convey character relationships or thematic elements

Suggested Timeline

One week

Lesson 2

Intro to Film Study: Group Dynamics

All film technique, I am convinced (and like many of my theories I am probably alone in adhering to it), originates in dreaming. We could dream slow motion before the moving camera was invented. In our dreams we could cut between parallel actions, we assembled montage shots long before some self-important Russian claimed to show us how. This is where film derives its particular power. It re-creates on screen what has been going on in our unconscious.

—WILLIAM BOYD, *The New Confessions*

STEP 1: Anticipatory Quickwrite

Why is an understanding of oneself as a learner beneficial when working in small groups? How can such an understanding affect how small groups function? Be prepared to share your thoughts with your classmates.

Begin where they are. This advice is all too familiar to us as teachers. Much as with a road trip, we cannot get where we want to go until and unless we first understand where we are. To that end, an anticipatory quickwrite is provided at the beginning of each unit. The idea is to assess what students know—or may need to know—in order to successfully complete the unit. Generally speaking, this process should take only two to three minutes, minus any discussion you may wish to pursue afterward.

Completing this step is very important. After all, it allows students both to predict the sort of activities they will encounter over the course of the unit and to hold you, the teacher, accountable for getting them there. To that end, once students have had their two minutes, have them conduct a think-pair-share, in which they share their quickwrites with their neighbors. Then, solicit responses from the whole group to be added to chart paper, which can then be posted on a wall for the duration of the unit.

Student responses may include, but almost certainly will not be limited to:

- How do we form groups?
- What are the elements common to all stories?

- How can understanding our personalities help us learn ways we can contribute in small-group settings?
- What is a tableau?
- How will group assignments be assessed?
- What film terms will we need to know?
- What are storyboards?
- What does *co-constructing* mean?
- How does one edit film footage?
- What can I use to edit film footage?

If students overlook any of these questions, feel free to add them to the chart paper, which should be posted where students can easily see it. After all, you may want to reflect with students periodically by asking them to add a sticky note beside the skills and concepts you have covered. Have them include the name of the activity on the sticky note. You may even consider using the chart to review the previous day's lesson before beginning new material. Ultimately, the entire list of skills and concepts should be addressed by the end of the unit.

STEP 2: Team Building Activity #1—Marshmallows and Spaghetti

Film is an incredibly collaborative process, and your students will need to feel very comfortable working in small groups. Thus, team-building activities become incredibly important to helping set the tone for your class for the year. Feel free to substitute other team-building activities, though note that the activities included here work particularly well.

This first activity works well with groups of four to five students. In order to group your students, have them first arrange themselves in order of height, shortest to tallest. Once they have managed to do so, the first four become your first group, the second four become the second group, and so on, until each group has at least four group members. There are quite a few variations of the Spaghetti Marshmallow Tower Challenge accessible online, and you may adjust the activity as you like. The process for this challenge is simple:

Step 1: Inform students they will receive a set of supplies with which to build a tower. The goal is to build the tallest possible free-standing tower using only the materials provided and within a set amount of time (twenty minutes).

Step 2: Give each group their supplies: twenty pieces of uncooked spaghetti, one yard of masking tape, one yard of string, and one marshmallow.

Step 3: Start the clock and let the groups work. If and when students have questions, refer them to the specific directions included in Step 1.

You will be amazed by the different variations your students come up with. Oh, and the tower must be able to stand on its own for at least thirty seconds before judging takes place!

Once everyone has finished, and a winner has been identified, reflect with your students on the process. Was there a leader? How did your group divide responsibilities? How did your group make decisions? What worked? What did not work? What would you do differently, if you did this activity again?

Should you choose, there is also a good follow-up video online entitled "Build a Tower, Build a Team" by Tom Wujec for TED 2010 available. Mr. Wujec discusses group dynamics and the decision-making process, and he also looks at how grouping people in different ways can lead to drastically different results. This video is generally a good discussion starter for the reflection process.

STEP 3: Team Building Activity #2—One-Word Stories

This activity also works well for groups of four to five students. This time, have students arrange themselves in order of their birthdays, from January 1 through December 31. The catch, however, is that students may not talk while doing so. The entire exercise must be completed in silence.

Once students have successfully arranged themselves, the first four become the first group, the second four become the second group, and so on.

Step 1: Before inviting students to present their own stories, review with them the four elements all stories share: setting, character(s), conflict, and resolution.

Step 2: Randomly invite groups to come up to the front of the classroom and stand before the class. Inform them that they will be composing a group story, but each person in the group may contribute only one word per turn, and each group member will present their word in order.

Step 3: The first person in the group begins the story, the next person adds the second word, and so on. The story is complete once the group has addressed all four elements (setting, character[s], conflict, and resolution). Have the audience keep track of which elements remain.

The idea is that each group must construct a story, but each member may only contribute one word at a time. Each team member adds a word, in order, without any individual knowledge of where the story is going. Instead, team members must work together to tell a complete story, including setting, character(s), conflict, and resolution. For example:

GROUP MEMBER 1: "One . . ."

GROUP MEMBER 2: ". . . day . . ."

GROUP MEMBER 3: ". . . in . . ."

GROUP MEMBER 4: ". . . June . . ."   *Now we know the time frame . . .*

GROUP MEMBER 1: ". . . an . . ."

GROUP MEMBER 2: ". . . old . . ."

GROUP MEMBER 3: ". . . man . . ."   *Now we have a character . . .*

GROUP MEMBER 4: ". . . wanted . . ."

GROUP MEMBER 1: ". . . to . . ."

GROUP MEMBER 2: ". . . go . . ."

GROUP MEMBER 3: ". . . fishing . . ."   *Now we have that character's motivation . . .*

GROUP MEMBER 4: ". . . but . . ."

GROUP MEMBER 1: ". . . something . . ."

GROUP MEMBER 2: ". . . happened . . ."   *Now we are getting into the conflict . . .*

The story continues until the group has addressed all four basic story elements, so some stories will go on longer than others. This is a great way to make sure students are familiar with these four elements. This activity also allows students to work together toward a common goal in a fun, often silly, way.

If you choose, you might have the audience keep track of each element. For example, divide the audience into quadrants, each listening for a particular thing. They begin by standing, but as they hear their element addressed, they sit down. In this way, audience members must actively listen for their assigned element.

STEP 4: Personality Test: The Five Shapes

Once students have broken the ice with each other, have them take a simple personality test to see what sort of group members they will likely be. A fun, rather short, test involves having students draw shapes and then prioritize them.

You can find one version of this test at Learning Mind or simply do a search for "shapes personality test." This personality test is not quite as scientific as, say, the Myers-Briggs Type Indicator personality test, but the results can be fun nonetheless. Regardless, the results are quite likely to spark some healthy introspection.

- Step 1: Have students draw the following five images on a clean piece of paper: a square, a rectangle, a triangle, a circle, and a zigzag line. The drawings need not be in any particular order, nor do they need to be any particular size.

- Step 2: Ask students to number the shapes in order of preference (1 = most like, 5 = least like).

- Step 3: Explain to students that their preferences say a great deal about their personalities. Share the characteristics of each shape. Some students will agree with their results; others may not. Either way, the results should get them thinking about how they can best contribute to their small groups.

Square

The tireless worker. Exhibits **hard work, diligence, perseverance**, and always strives for completion. **Patience and a methodical nature** make Squares skilled specialists. Squares collect information and have it neatly organized on their shelves, so they are able to quickly retrieve the desired facts and earn a deserved reputation for being a scholar in their field.

The Square refers to **left-hemisphere thinkers,** who are characterized by logical thought and mathematical mindsets. Squares **analyze and calculate answers to problems** rather than trusting instinct or inference.

The ideal of Squares is a planned, routine life where **everything is predictable**; they do not like the unexpected or surprises. In the business world, such people often become **good administrators and executives** but rarely succeed as managers because their constant need for additional decision-making information deprives them of their speed. In addition, their cold rationality often prevents Squares from connecting quickly with other people.

Triangle

This form symbolizes **leadership.** The main ability of Triangles is to **focus on goals and deeply and quickly analyze situations**. A Triangle is a very **confident person** who wants to be correct in everything. Triangles find it difficult to admit their mistakes, learn easily, and **absorb information** like a sponge. Their careers give their lives meaning.

Negative qualities: **excessive self-absorption.** Triangles are good at presenting the importance of their own work to senior management, can sense profitable business decisions from a mile away, and, while struggling for success, may "knock heads" with rivals.

Rectangle

The Rectangle is a transitional form from one shape to another. People who see themselves as Rectangles **are not satisfied with their lives** and are busy looking for chances to better their circumstances. The main mental state of a Rectangle is **a perceived sense of confusion**, bogged down by their problems and uncertainty.

Their most pronounced features are **inconsistent and unpredictable behavior and low self-esteem.** Positive qualities: **curiosity, inquisitiveness, a lively interest in everything, courage.** Rectangles try to do things that have never been done and ask questions that have never been asked.

Circle

The Circle is **a symbol of harmony**. Those who choose this shape are interested in **good interpersonal relations.** The highest value for the circle is **people and their well-being.** This is **the most benevolent of the figures**. The Circle is the glue that holds the team together. They stabilize the group and have a **high capacity for sympathy and empathy**.

They are **right-hemisphere thinkers,** not logical necessarily but creative and more emotionally charged. The processing of information in such people is not consistent and resembles a mosaic pattern. The main feature of their style of thinking is **a focus on the subjective aspects of the problem.**

Zigzag

The Zigzag is **a symbol of creativity**. The Zigzag focuses on imagery. The **right-hemisphere thinking** Zigzags are not fixated on the details, which simplifies the way they view the world; this allows them to construct a **holistic and harmonious conceptual view of the world,** to see its intrinsic beauty.

Zigzags cannot work in one place for a long time—such a commitment is boring and there are so many other interesting things to see and experience! The main purpose of the Zigzags is **the generation of new ideas and methods,** not their actual realization. Zigzags look to the future and are **more interested in possibilities than in reality**.

Source: www.learning-mind.com

You will no doubt have some students who agree with the results and others who do not. The important takeaway is not accuracy of the test as much as its ability to inspire introspection. You may even consider having your students get up out of their seats and move to a particular location you designate for each shape. That way, everyone can see how everyone else identifies.

STEP 5: Personality Test #2 (Optional)—Myers-Briggs Type Indicator (Personality Test)

If you are interested in conducting a more scientific personality test, have students take the Myers-Briggs Type Indicator personality test. If a guidance counselor is free and willing to administer the test to your students, you should certainly take advantage of the opportunity; guidance counselors are great resources for helping students understand their results. If not, students can still take the test for free online and see their personality descriptions.

STEP 6: Forming Small Groups

When it comes to setting up small groups, there are numerous, often competing strategies for how to do so. My personal belief is, whenever possible, teaching my students how to most effectively group themselves is preferable to either me placing them in groups or simply allowing them to work with their friends. I want my students to be successful in life long after school, so learning how to effectively set up and manage a collaborative work group is an invaluable skill.

First, consider the size of your small groups. Generally, I don't allow more than five people per group; as I discuss with my students, everything is a trade-off, even group size. Smaller groups have much more freedom but a bigger workload for each member. Larger groups are able to better share the workload but are much more bound by the strictures of extracurricular activities and work schedules. That said, groups of more than five people tend to become unwieldy. Five seems to be the tipping point—beyond this size, someone inevitably tries to become invisible and cash in on the work done by the rest of the group.

Second, consider skill sets. Some of your students will have had editing experience, and these people are incredibly valuable group members. Others will have access to camera equipment and know how to use it. These people, too, will be valuable additions to any group. Of course, pretty much everyone has a cell phone these days, and there are tons of apps that will allow for filming and editing. So, all things considered, I try to build small groups around editors.

Third, we go back to what we learned from the personality tests. Every group should have a creative thinker. Unfortunately, creative thinkers are not always the best at identifying the steps in the process, or, let's be honest, at finishing the "amazing" ideas they get started. Ultimately, each group will want a mix of shapes—creative thinkers, leaders, planners, doers, and those wonderful circles, who will work hard to ensure team unity and cohesion when life gets stressful and deadlines are looming.

All this taken into account, there really is no perfect way to group students; sometimes life gets messier than we might be led expect by a textbook. The important aspect is that students learn, and having to work with peers who possess a variety of skill sets and personalities can be a wonderfully messy, wonderfully informative process. Further, students need not work with the same group members on every project, so there is room to learn from past mistakes and do better the next time.

STEP 7: Movie Poster Tableau

Once students have selected their groups, you will want to do a quick team-building activity with them to help them get to know their partners better. In this case, have students begin by identifying a film everyone in their group likes. Once they have identified the film, give them five minutes to create a living **tableau** that conveys the basic idea of the film. In essence, they form themselves into a living movie poster.

Then have each group present their tableau to the class. After the class has had an opportunity to guess the film in question, have each student in the group explain their role in the tableau. "I represent (this character), and I am (doing whatever I am doing) because. . . ." You may even consider offering a prize for the best portrayal. You may want to take pictures to post on your class website—just be sure you have the proper photo release forms for your students signed before doing so.

STEP 8: Culminating Activity—Designing a Studio Logo

As a culminating activity, now that students have used what they have learned to sort themselves into small groups, each group should come up with a name for their production company. Once they have a name, each group will need to design a five-second clip to be placed at the beginning of their projects to introduce their studio.

You may choose to have them draw the logo and film it, or it could be a video clip, or it could be designed in a graphic design program. Encourage students to consider the screens they see at the beginning of films or at the end of television shows, as there is more than one way to design a logo.

At the end of each unit, it is important to take time to reflect on what the class has covered. Have students look over the poster the class made from the anticipatory quickwrite conducted at the beginning of the unit. The original question asked students to consider why an understanding of oneself as a learner is beneficial when working in small groups. How can such an understanding affect the way small groups function?

STEP 9: Reflect on the Process

What have you learned that will help with the filmmaking process? Be prepared to share your thoughts with your classmates.

Standards Addressed in This Unit

Comprehension and Collaboration
CCSS.ELA-LITERACY.CCRA.SL.1
CCSS.ELA-LITERACY.CCRA.SL.2
Presentation of Knowledge and Ideas
CCSS.ELA-LITERACY.CCRA.SL.5

3 Spec Scripts: Transforming a Classic for the Silver Screen

◎ Lesson Plan

Essential Question
What are the elements of a spec script?

Objective
Students will use their understanding of the elements of spec scripts to write a screenplay for a scene not currently included in Lorraine Hansberry's *A Raisin in the Sun*.

Central Text

A Raisin in the Sun by Lorraine Hansberry

Agenda

STEP 1: Anticipatory Quickwrite

STEP 2: Define the Five Basic Elements of a Spec Script

STEP 3: Rewrite an Excerpt from the Play in Spec Script Format

STEP 4: Identify the Five Elements of Spec Scripts in Students' Screenplays

STEP 5: Compose a Spec Script for a Scene Not Included in the Play

STEP 6: Reflect on the Process

Differentiation
The goal of this unit is to format a spec script correctly. To that end, there is more than one way to reach that goal. Some students may prefer to use a program like celtx.com to aid with formatting; others may prefer to type everything in a Word or Google doc. The goal is the product, not the process, so however a student gets to that point is fine.

Vocabulary

screenplay (n.)—a script written to be filmed and presented on-screen. There are two types of screenplays: (1) a spec script (written to be marketed) and (2) a shooting script (written for the filming process)

screenwriter (n.)—one who writes screenplays

shooting script (n.)—a script written by a filmmaker that includes details regarding the techniques the filmmaker wishes to use while making the film

spec script (n.)—a screenplay written with the objective of selling it to a filmmaker

Resources

celtx.com: A number of programs are designed to aid with correct screenplay formatting. Many require a fee, but celtx.com offers a free trial period. I often use this program with my students.

Drew's Script-O-Rama (http://www.script-o-rama.com): This website is a repository for thousands of scripts. Some are spec scripts, some are shooting scripts, but they are all labeled for easy identification. This is a great site to use when you want your students to see examples of professional screenplays.

IMSDb.com: This is another great site housing professional screenplays.

Suggested Timeline
Two ninety-minute class periods

Lesson 3

Spec Scripts: Transforming a Classic for the Silver Screen

I could be just a writer very easily. I am not a writer. I am a screenwriter, which is half a filmmaker.... But it is not an art form, because screenplays are not works of art. They are invitations to others to collaborate on a work of art.

—PAUL SCHRADER

STEP 1: Anticipatory Quickwrite

What must I know, or what must I know how to do, in order to successfully compose a spec script? Be prepared to share your thoughts with your classmates.

This unit walks you through an engaging way to extend your study of plays. That said, this unit does not present an alternative method for teaching plays; rather, it provides a way for students to deepen their understanding of the content and to transition more easily to a discussion of the screenwriting format. A **screenplay**, of course, is a script written to be filmed and then presented on-screen.

As English teachers, we are accustomed to teaching plays. And when we do, one step on the rung of the ladder of capability is always an overview of the elements of a play script and how to understand those elements. For example, when helping students learn to read plays, we point out the exposition that occurs sporadically throughout the play—the characters' names, the dialogue, and the stage directions (typically given in parentheses or in italics). Consider, for example, the following page of script from Lorraine Hansberry's *A Raisin in the Sun* (1959):

WALTER: Is he out yet?

RUTH: What you mean out? He ain't hardly got in there good yet.

WALTER: *(Wandering in, still more oriented to sleep than to a new day)* Well, what was you doing all that yelling for if I can't even get in there yet? (Stopping and thinking) Check coming today?

RUTH: They said Saturday and this is just Friday and I hopes to God you ain't going to get up here first thing this morning and start talking to me 'bout no money—'cause I 'bout don't want to hear it.

WALTER: Something the matter with you this morning?

RUTH: No—I'm just sleepy as the devil. What kind of eggs you want?

WALTER: Not scrambled. *(RUTH starts to scramble eggs)* Paper come? *(RUTH points impatiently to the rolled up* Tribune *on the table, and he gets it and spreads it out and vaguely reads the front page)* Set off another bomb yesterday.

RUTH: *(Maximum indifference)* Did they?

WALTER: *(Looking up)* What's the matter with you?

RUTH: Ain't nothing the matter with me. And don't keep asking me that this morning.

WALTER: Ain't nobody bothering you. *(Reading the news of the day absently again)* Say Colonel McCormick is sick.

RUTH: *(Affecting tea-party interest)* Is he now? Poor thing.

WALTER: *(Sighing and looking at his watch)* Oh, me. *(He waits)* Now what is that boy doing in that bathroom all this time? He just going to have to start getting up earlier. I can't be being late to work on account of him fooling around in there.

RUTH: *(Turning on him)* Oh, no he ain't going to be getting up no earlier no such thing! It ain't his fault that he can't get to bed no earlier nights 'cause he got a bunch of crazy good-for-nothing clowns sitting up running their mouths in what is supposed to be his bedroom after ten o'clock at night. . . .

WALTER: That's what you mad about, ain't it? The things I want to talk about with my friends just couldn't be important in your mind, could they?

Perhaps you study this play in your class, but even if you do not, the format is likely familiar. If you assign students to read parts, they know which parts they are to read because their character's name precedes the character's line. If information is included in parentheses, students know they are not to read these words aloud, and instead use that information to shape how they deliver the line, or to direct their actions while delivering the line.

Screenplays are not so different. They include virtually all of the same information, but the formatting is slightly different. To be clear, there are two types of film scripts—a **spec script** and a **shooting script**. A spec script is what a **screenwriter** writes in hopes of selling it to a filmmaker. A shooting script is adapted from the spec script and includes details on the types of shots to be used. In essence, a writer writes a spec script, sells it to studio, which solicits a director, and then the director develops a shooting script from it to use for filming. For our purposes, we will be working with spec scripts.

STEP 2: Define the Five Basic Elements of a Spec Script

As a way to get started, students should know that screenplays contain five basic elements: (1) the scene heading or slugline, (2) action, (3) character name, (4) dialogue, and (5) parentheticals. Fortunately, there are many websites and videos online that can help with spacing and formatting, including web-based programs that will format the writing automatically. The five elements are defined as follows:

1. **Scene Heading or Slugline:** This line informs the audience when and where the action is taking place, is left justified, and is written in all caps. The format of a scene heading is as follows: "INT" or "EXT" depending on whether the action is indoors or outdoors (interior or exterior), the place, and the time. The time, however, is usually written in fairly general terms (MORNING, TUESDAY, etc.) unless the specific time is relevant (9:00, NOON, etc.). Examples of scene headings may include:
INT – LIBRARY – MORNING
EXT – JONES HOUSE – EVENING

2. **Action:** Every scene heading must be followed by action. The action is left justified and aligned with the scene heading. The action is simply the explanation of what is going on and what the camera sees. For example: *The room is cramped and worn. There is a single window, through which the dingy yellow light of a Chicago morning seeps. The muffled sound of cars passing by can be heard, along with a distant train whistle. On the couch, a figure is sleeping.*

3. **Character Name:** The character's name should be written in all caps, centered. The names are not truly centered, though, but tabbed over to the center so the first letter of each name aligns.

4. **Dialogue:** This is what the character says. You should notice the margins for the dialogue are about an inch wider on either side than they are for the character names.

5. **Parentheticals:** This information, included in parentheses just below the character's name, lets the characters know what they are doing and how to deliver their lines. The margins for the parentheticals are about a half-inch wider than the character names.

STEP 3: Rewrite an Excerpt from the Play in Spec Script Format

As an exercise, try taking a page of script, such as the page from *A Raisin in the Sun*, and try writing it as a spec script. You should wind up with something that looks like this:

INT – THE YOUNGER FAMILY APARTMENT – MORNING

It is morning dark in the living room. TRAVIS is asleep on the makeshift bed at center. An alarm clock sounds from within the bedroom at right, and presently RUTH enters from that room and closes the door behind her. She crosses sleepily toward the window. As she passes her sleeping son, she reaches down and shakes him a little. At the window, she raises the shade and a dusky Chicago South Side morning light comes in. She fills a pot with water and puts it on to boil. Between yawns, she calls to the boy in a slightly muffled voice. TRAVIS, a sturdy, handsome little boy of ten or eleven, drags himself out of the bed and almost blindly takes his towels and "today's clothes" from drawers and a closet and then goes out to the bathroom, which is in an outside hall and which is shared by another family or families on the same floor.

WALTER
(O.S.)
Is he out yet?

RUTH
What you mean out? He ain't hardly got in there good yet.

WALTER
(Wandering in, still more oriented to sleep than to a new day)
Well, what was you doing all that yelling for if I can't even get in there yet?
(Stopping and thinking)
Check coming today?

RUTH
They said Saturday and this is just Friday and I hopes to God you ain't going to get up here first thing this morning and start talking to me 'bout no money —'cause I 'bout don't want to hear it.

WALTER
Something the matter with you this morning?

RUTH
No—I'm just sleepy as the devil. What kind of eggs you want?

WALTER
Not scrambled.

RUTH starts to scramble eggs.

                    WALTER (ctd.)
  Paper come?

RUTH points impatiently to the rolled up *Tribune* on the table. WALTER gets it and spreads it out and vaguely reads the front page.

                    WALTER (ctd.)
  Set off another bomb yesterday.

                    RUTH
(Maximum indifference)
  Did they?

                    WALTER
(Looking up)
  What's the matter with you?

                    RUTH
Ain't nothing the matter with me. And don't keep asking me that this morning.

                    WALTER
Ain't nobody bothering you.
(Reading the news of the day absently again)
  Say Colonel McCormick is sick.

                    RUTH
(Affecting tea-party interest)
  Is he now? Poor thing.

                    WALTER
(Sighing and looking at his watch)
  Oh, me.
(He waits)
  Now what is that boy doing in that bathroom all this time? He just going to have to start getting up earlier. I can't be being late to work on account of him fooling around in there.

>   RUTH
> (Turning on him)
> > Oh, no he ain't going to be getting up no earlier no such thing! It ain't his fault that he can't get to bed no earlier nights 'cause he got a bunch of crazy good-for-nothing clowns sitting up running their mouths in what is supposed to be his bedroom after ten o'clock at night....
>
>   WALTER
> > That's what you mad about, ain't it? The things I want to talk about with my friends just couldn't be important in your mind, could they?

STEP 4: Identify the Five Elements of Spec Scripts in Students' Screenplays

Once your students have finished rewriting the play script as a spec script, have them go back and identify each of the five elements as presented in the spec script version of the story.

It is worth noting to students that each page of script is equivalent to roughly one minute of screen time. Thus, this script excerpt would be about two minutes of film. By and large, most spec scripts average around 120 pages.

At this point, you might wish to have a conversation with your students regarding the considerations a writer must weigh when deciding whether to tell a story as a play or as a film. One of the biggest benefits a film offers is the freedom of the camera. An audience at a play views the entire story from their seats, which means that playwrights have to confine the action to a manageable number of sets. When it comes to film, a camera can go anywhere, even back in time or inside a character's mind.

STEP 5: Compose a Spec Script for a Scene Not Included in the Play

After discussing the limitations imposed upon playwrights, have your students go back through the play and make a list of scenes that were referenced but not shown to the audience. Think about the times the characters were out of the apartment—at school, at work, hanging out with friends. And while some of these moments are referenced in the play, others surely must have happened at some point regardless of whether they are specified or not—Beneatha talking with friends in her English class, Walter at a bar with friends, a flashback of Walter and Ruth dating, etc. These scenes are limited only by students' imaginations.

Once students have made a list of missing scenes, have them choose one and write a spec script for that scene including the five elements common to screenplays. Give them a time frame as well—perhaps a three- to five-minute scene—so that they will have a sense of how much to write. As you score their work, consider:

1. Does the script include a SCENE HEADING, ACTION, CHARACTER NAMES, DIALOGUE, and PARENTHETICALS?
2. Are the characters true to their personalities as presented throughout the rest of the play?
3. Does the action correspond thematically to the rest of the play?
4. Is the script long enough to cover the required time frame?

Your goal for this unit has been to help students understand how to write a properly formatted spec script. As an extension, feel free to allow students to film their scenes and share them with the class. And finally, once students have written their scenes, it is important to have them reflect on what they have learned.

STEP 6: Reflect on the Process

What have you learned about the process of creating a spec script? How does a proper play format compare with the spec script format? Be prepared to share your thoughts with your classmates.

Standards Addressed in This Unit

Conventions of Standard English
CCSS.ELA-LITERACY.CCRA.L.1
CCSS.ELA-LITERACY.CCRA.L.2
Vocabulary Acquisition and Use
CCSS.ELA-LITERACY.CCRA.L.6
Key Ideas and Details
CCSS.ELA-LITERACY.CCRA.R.1
CCSS.ELA-LITERACY.CCRA.R.2
CCSS.ELA-LITERACY.CCRA.R.3

Craft and Structure
CCSS.ELA-LITERACY.CCRA.R.4
CCSS.ELA-LITERACY.CCRA.R.5
Integration of Knowledge and Ideas
CCSS.ELA-LITERACY.CCRA.R.7
Range of Reading and Level of Text Complexity
CCSS.ELA-LITERACY.CCRA.R.10
Text Types and Purposes
CCSS.ELA-LITERACY.CCRA.W.3
Production and Distribution
CCSS.ELA-LITERACY.CCRA.W.4
Research to Build and Present Knowledge
CCSS.ELA-LITERACY.CCRA.W.9
Range of Writing
CCSS.ELA-LITERACY.CCRA.W.10

4

The Filmmaker's Toolkit: From Building Blocks to Works of Art

Lesson Plan

Essential Questions

How do directors use film techniques to guide an audience?

How do filmmakers plan out the shots they want to use in their films?

Objective
Students will be able to identify specific film techniques, as well as how those techniques can be used to guide an audience.

Central Text
Glossary of Film Terms (included in Appendix A)

Agenda

STEP 1: Anticipatory Quickwrite

STEP 2: Explore a List of Commonly Used Film Techniques, Paying Specific Attention to How and When Each Should Be Used in Order to Guide an Audience

STEP 3: Co-Construct Storyboards

STEP 4: Evaluate Sample Storyboards

STEP 5: Identify the Four Elements All Stories Share

STEP 6: Read a Sample Short Story and ID the Four Elements

STEP 7: Group Storyboard the Short Story

STEP 8: Determine How Many Shots We Should Have in Our Storyboard

STEP 9: Revise Storyboards

STEP 10: Have Students Work in Small Groups to Storyboard a New Story

STEP 11: Written Analysis of Shot Sequence—Why This Way?

STEP 12: Culminating Activity—"If My Life Were a Movie" Poster and One-Minute Trailer

STEP 13: Reflect on the Process

Differentiation

Some of your students are excellent artists, no doubt. Others may dread drawing anything. Students need not be fantastic artists to be fantastic storyboard artists, however. In this unit, students who do not wish to draw have the option to use their cameras instead. The end goal is still the same: to create a visual plan a cinematographer could follow to achieve the shots the director wants.

Vocabulary

back space (n.)—area behind a person's back when on-screen. Too much back space can send the subtle message that something is going to fill that space, and that something is usually bad. Thus, too much back space can send the message that a character is vulnerable

headroom (n.)—area above a person's head when that person is on-screen. Too much headroom can send the subtle message that something is going to fill that space, and that something is usually bad. Thus, too much headroom can send the message that a character is vulnerable

Resources

"Basic Filmmaking Techniques" (Google Prezi, Crisp, and the title)

Film Techniques quizzes (may be formative or summative) located in Appendix C at the end of this book

Kahoot! Links

"Film Techniques Review" (https://tinyurl.com/y7ajkbm7)

"Film Terms Review" (https://tinyurl.com/yc3h7kod)

"Name That Film Technique" (https://tinyurl.com/y8kojqeh)

Suggested Timeline

One week

Lesson 4

The Filmmaker's Toolkit: From Building Blocks to Works of Art

If you can film an idea in your mind, follow that film idea shot for shot, scene for scene and enjoy it, that idea is worth making for the world to see. It can change someone's life.

—CRAIG MAPP

STEP 1: Anticipatory Quickwrite

What techniques do directors use to guide an audience's emotional and intellectual responses to a film? Be prepared to share your thoughts with your classmates.

If the silver screen is the director's canvas, then the variety of film techniques at that director's disposal represents the palette. Good directors are quite familiar with how and when to use a wide range of techniques in order to induce a wide range of responses from an audience. Want to imply that a character is strong? Use a *low angle*. Need to convey the idea that the hero is hiding a secret? Try *side lighting*. What if all is not well, and things have suddenly taken a turn for the worse? Try a *Dutch tilt*. Audiences do not have to know *why* they feel a certain way, after all; the director's goal is simply to generate the feeling in them.

STEP 2: Explore a List of Commonly Used Film Techniques, Paying Specific Attention to How and When Each Should Be Used in Order to Guide an Audience

In all likelihood, most of your students will have a very limited background with regard to understanding basic film vocabulary. So you will want to walk through the variety of techniques detailed in the glossary of film terms included in the appendix. These terms are broken down by category.

There are a number of ways you can go over this material with your students, and as you explore these definitions, reinforce that while an understanding of the definition is important, an understanding of the effect of that technique is every bit as important. Filmmakers do not use different techniques simply because they have grown tired of other techniques; they use the techniques they know will engender the desired effect in their audience. Here are a few ideas to try:

OPTION 1: Try using an online platform such as Prezi to post definitions and examples. This way, students can access the presentation to study for assessments or to reinforce their understanding. Feel free to use the presentation I created for my own classes. All you need to do is create a free account, then search for presentations by author. If you'd like to access my presentations, search for Prezis that list Robert Crisp as the author. Alternatively, if you turn to the back of this book, you will find a glossary of film techniques that includes a QR code you can scan with your phone to access the Prezi I created that covers these basic techniques. Or simply Google "Basic Filmmaking Techniques Robert Crisp Prezi."

OPTION 2: As you go through the definitions with your students, stop after each section, call out random techniques from that section, and have students use their phones to take pictures utilizing the specified technique. If you have them show their screens to you once they are done, you can quickly assess whether they understand the technique correctly. As a follow-up, have students explain how and when they would use each technique you name. This will also tell you if your students are allowing too much **headroom** or **back space**, which you can then address.

OPTION 3: Sort students into groups and give each small group a set of images and sticky notes (manipulatives). Have each group discuss the images, write the techniques on the sticky notes, and attach the sticky notes to the appropriate images. Once they have finished, have them remove their sticky notes and trade images with another group, and then repeat the process.

OPTION 4: Create a Kahoot! to help students practice identifying the different techniques. If you would like to use one of the quizzes I created, feel free—you will need to create an account (I use the free version) and search for quizzes made by bcrisp. Again, these online options are great because your students will be able to use them to review and firm up their understanding of techniques. Not only that, you can also download and print your students' results to use for formative assessment purposes, enabling you to see which techniques your class understands and which you might want to cover in greater depth.

OPTION 5: Create scenarios for your students and ask them to determine which techniques would engender the desired effect on the audience. I have included scenarios in the back of this book immediately following the film technique definitions, divided by category (framing, lighting, movement, etc.), which you can use as either formative or summative assessments.

STEP 3: Co-Construct Storyboards

Now that your students have a basic understanding of some of the more commonly used techniques, the next step is to co-construct a few storyboards with them. If you have ever done co-construction with your students, you know how rewarding the process can be. The idea can feel a bit intimidating, though—the process requires you to be the point person on a classwide collaboration. Being the point person means you are in front, and your students are watching and evaluating every move you make. In this case, that role includes—gasp—drawing in front of your students!

If you're really antsy about it, you can always choose a student to take point. But by taking point yourself, you send a hugely important message, and you let your students see you be vulnerable. You show them that the assignment is worth doing—so worth it, in fact, that you're doing it, too. You show them that their art does not need to be perfect in order to be effective.

Another benefit of co-constructing is that the process allows you to think aloud with your students. Generally, teachers assess student work after the work has been done—that is, after the thinking has happened. Thinking out loud as you co-construct allows students to experience what the creative/reflective thought process should look like and provides them with a model for their own creative/reflective process moving forward.

As you get started, however, provide a few examples for your students. They will need to know, for instance, how to draw faces or to show movement. Fortunately, when it comes to storyboarding, drawing faces is easy: you draw a plus sign on the oval that represents the head. Where the lines intersect approximates the bridge of the nose. And for movement? Just draw arrows. Figures 4.1 and 4.2 are a few examples to get you started.

STEP 4: Evaluate Sample Storyboards (illustrations by Caroline Donnelly)

The goal of storyboarding is to help the filming process go as smoothly as possible. In writing terms, this would be part of the prewriting. The text next to each

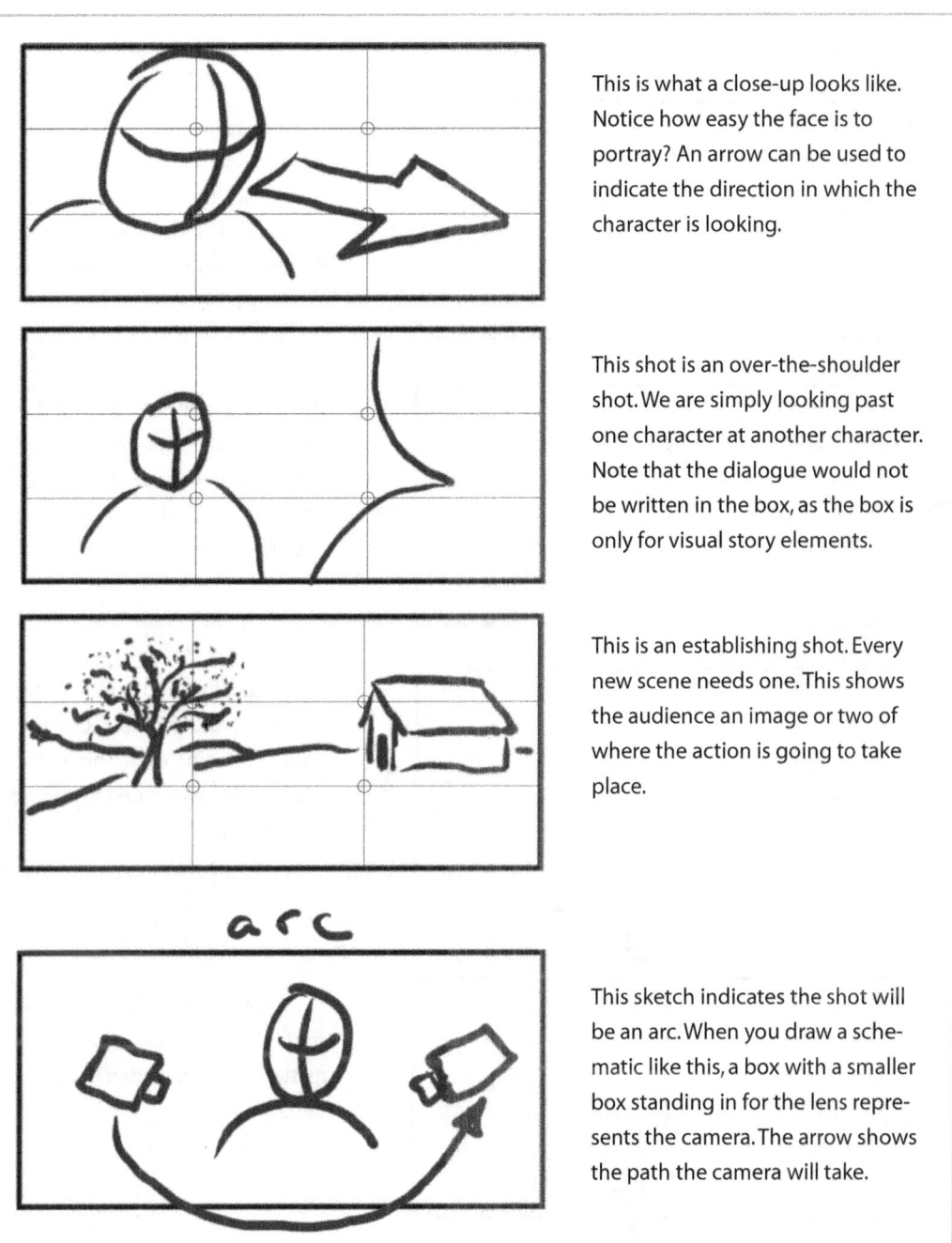

FIGURE 4.1. Model of how to create a storyboard.

The Filmmaker's Toolkit: From Building Blocks to Works of Art 55

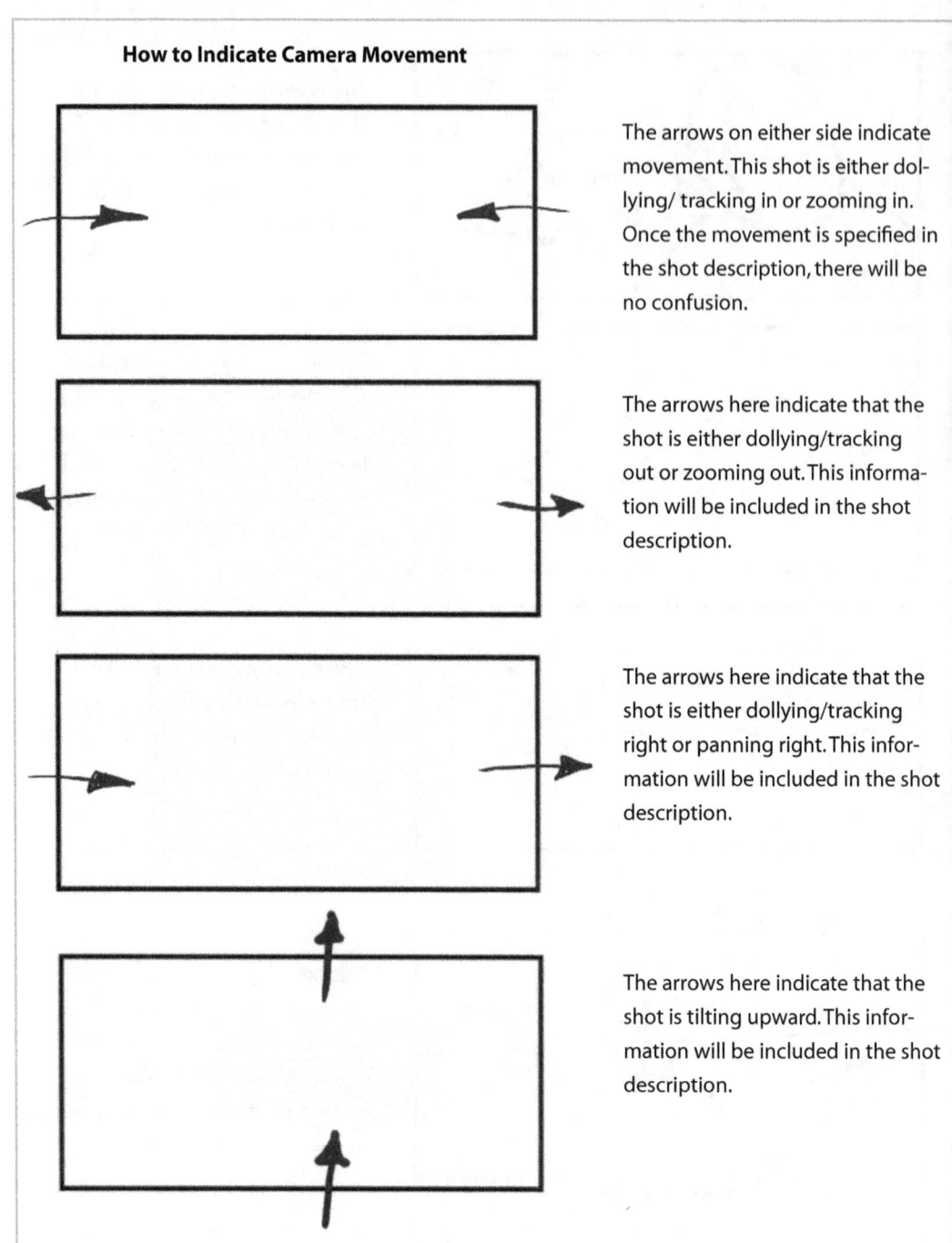

FIGURE 4.2. Model showing how to indicate camera movement.

shot is referred to as the shot list. It is okay if your artwork is not as good as Caroline's—she is really talented. Your goal is to give your cinematographer a clear idea of what you want to film. The less confusion, the smoother the process. See Figure 4.3 on page 60 for an alternate approach to creating a storyboard.

1. Shot #1
2. Composition: Alana, Mother of Iguanas, and her iguanas
3. Framing: close-up on an iguana, others (incl. Alana) in back
4. Angle: eye level (the point of view—POV—of Alana's classmates)
5. Movement: stationary
6. Lighting: high key lighting (classroom interior)
7. Sound: diegetic sound of iguanas, kids screaming
8. Editing Technique: cut to next shot

1. Shot #2
2. Composition: Caroline is painting a mural in the hallway

3. Framing: close-up on Caroline as she is painting
4. Angle: eye level
5. Movement: stationary
6. Lighting: high key lighting (school hallway)
7. Sound: nondiegetic peaceful music in background
8. Editing Technique: cut to next shot

1. Shot #3
2. Composition: Chuckie Chainsawhands, cowering in fear
3. Framing: close-up on Chuckie (reaction shot)
4. Angle: eye level
5. Movement: stationary
6. Lighting: high key, high contrast lighting
7. Sound: nondiegetic scary music
8. Editing Technique: cut to next shot

1. Shot #4
2. Composition: Jimmy the Fish makes his entrance
3. Framing: medium shot
4. Angle: POV of Jimmy's pantlegs and shiny shoes
5. Movement: tilt up to Jimmy's face
6. Lighting: high key lighting
7. Sound: nondiegetic sound of mob-themed music
8. Editing Technique: (ctd.)

1. Shot #4 (ctd.)
2. Composition: Jimmy the Fish smirks, waves at classmates
3. Framing: medium shot
4. Angle: eye level
5. Movement: tilt up from Jimmy's shoes
6. Lighting: side lighting (moral ambiguity, secrets, etc.)
7. Sound: nondiegetic sound of mob-themed music
8. Editing Technique: cut to next shot

Not so sure your art skills are up to par when it comes to drawing storyboards? No worries! Use action figures and your camera! Remember, your goal is to provide enough information so your cinematographer can capture the shots you want without any further explanation by you.

1. Shot #1
2. Cap and Carl talking
3. Long shot, two shot
4. Slight high angle
5. Stationary camera
6. High key lighting
7. Diegetic office sounds
8. Cut to…

         CAP
So, these clowns down at work, they want me to do the overtime, see? They just don't want to pay me. I hate that.

1. Shot #2
2. Cap and Carl talking
3. Knee shot, over the shoulder
4. Eye level
5. Stationary camera
6. High key lighting
7. Diegetic office sounds
8. Cut to…

         CARL
      (commiserating)
Ah, man, I hate it when they do that! I feel you, man.

1. Shot #3
2. Cap and Carl talking
3. Cowboy shot, over the shoulder
4. Eye level
5. Stationary camera
6. High key lighting
7. Diegetic office sounds
8. Cut to…

         CAP
     (getting wound up)
Right? I mean, they're all like, "Oh, Cap, save us! Cap, we need you! Blah! Blah! Blah!" I'm sick of it, you know?

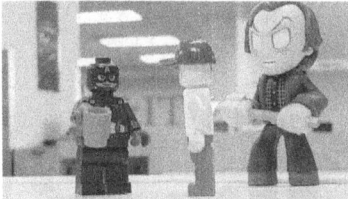

1. Shot #4
2. Cap and Carl, Tiny Jack appears
3. Long shot
4. Slight low angle
5. Stationary camera
6. High key lighting
7. Diegetic office sounds
8. Cut to…

        CAP (ctd.)
    (shaking his head, disgusted)
Ain't nobody got time for that.

1. Shot #5
2. Cap and Carl, Tiny Jack in BG
3. Medium shot, two shot
4. Eye level
5. Stationary camera
6. High key lighting
7. Diegetic office sounds
8. Cut to…

        CAP (ctd.)
I mean, am I wrong?

FIGURE 4.3. An alternate method for creating a storyboard sequence.

FIGURE 4.3. Continued.

1. Shot #6
2. Cap and Carl react
3. Long shot, two shot
4. High angle, Jack's POV
5. Trombone shot
6. High key lighting
7. Nondiegetic scary music cue
8. Cut to…

CAP (ctd.)
(shocked, in disbelief)
What in the Star-Spangled
Banner…?

1. Shot #7
2. Tiny Jack, breathing heavily
3. Medium shot
4. Low angle
5. Stationary camera
6. High key lighting
7. Diegetic sound of breathing
8. Cut to…

TINY JACK
(ragged heavy
breathing)

1. Shot #8
2. Cap and Carl flee in terror
3. Long shot
4. High angle
5. Stationary camera
6. High key lighting
7. Diegetic sound of screams
8. Cut to…

CAP & CARL
(shrilly in unison)
AAAAAAAGGGGHHH!!!

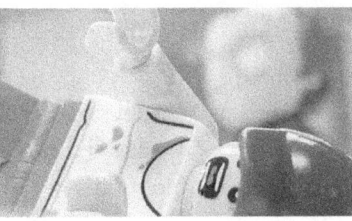

1. Shot #9
2. Tiny Jack watches, reacts
3. Medium close-up
4. Eye level
5. Stationary camera
6. High key lighting
7. Diegetic sound of screams
8. Cut to…

TINY JACK
Wait, hey guys! I just…
just…dang it! I just
wanted to know how to
get to Starbucks…

1. Shot #10
2. Carl falls, Tiny Jack looms
3. Medium shot across body
4. Low angle
5. Stationary camera
6. High key lighting
7. Diegetic sound of screams
8. Cut to black

CARL
(hyperventilating)
AAGHHKKGGGHHHH-!

FIGURE 4.4. Model for analyzing a single shot.

Analyzing a Single Shot (*illustration by Grant Eaton*)

Remember that filmmakers are always trying to guide their audiences. With that in mind, we can look at individual shots and identify techniques the filmmaker is using to do so. Consider the shot in Figure 4.4. In this case, it looks like Seamus may not be quite the upstanding candidate for class president he wants his classmates to think he is! Notice the lighting, implying that he has a dark secret? Or the angle from which he looks down on his classmates, like a predator surveying his prey? Or how he is signaling victory with one hand while crossing his fingers on the hand behind his back? These techniques all work together to reinforce a particular interpretation. Every shot should tell a story.

COMPOSITION

We see Seamus on stage, delivering a campaign speech to his classmates. We can see his classmates cheering; one holds a sign reading "SEAMUS 4 CLASS PREZ." Notice the smirk on our candidate's face, as well as the crossed fingers behind his back. Seamus, it seems, does not have the best of intentions.

FRAMING

Seamus is framed in what appears to be either a cowboy shot or knee shot. We are close enough to see his expression but far enough back to get a sense of the context, as well as a clear view of both his expression and his crossed fingers.

Angle

We are looking down from a high angle—usually used to indicate a character is weak or a victim. In this case, however, the purpose is slightly different. We see Seamus above his classmates in a more powerful position: a predator—a prey shot. Seamus, it seems, is going to take advantage of his classmates.

Lighting

Seamus is lighted from the side, which casts shadows across his face. Typically, side lighting is used to indicate that a character is hiding a secret or is morally ambiguous. It appears there is more to Seamus than meets the eye.

Next, this unit continues with the identification of basic story elements and scaffolds in complexity until students have the skills they need to successfully storyboard a sequence from a print text.

STEP 5: Identify the Four Elements All Stories Share

Every story has a setting. Without a "where" and a "when," every other element is simply floating in space. The reader has no context for what is happening, no framework for imagining the time and place of what is going on.

Likewise, every story must have at least one character, even if that character is not human. The character could be an alien, a creek pebble, or an angst-ridden orangutan, but you must have a character to experience the conflict and work toward some sort of resolution.

Further, there must be some sort of conflict, something that affects your character(s) and that your character(s) must deal with in some way. Without a conflict, your character is just twiddling their thumbs. (Does anybody actually do that anymore?)

And last, the problem must be dealt with or resolved in some way. Your character may not get what they want, but something has to happen as a result of your character grappling with the conflict.

STEP 6: Read a Sample Short Story and ID the Four Elements

Have students consider the following story. I wrote this story in response to a writing competition called "55 Fiction." The challenge was to write an entire story using only fifty-five words. The exercise was a lot of fun; you can actually find quite a few other examples published online or even as collections in book form. Best of all, these stories are great for quick storyboarding exercises.

The Snipe Hunt

"It's easy!" I say. "Just stand there."
"We'll drive them to you," chimes in Dell.
Maurice wonders what's so great about snipe anyway and why he has to stand in this ditch holding a bag.
Dell and I leave to round up the snipe.
Midnight.
Maurice waits.
No snipe.
No Dell.
No me.
Poor Maurice.

—Robert Bryant Crisp © 2001

Once students have read the story, have them identify the four elements as presented in the story. Be sure to have them identify evidence from the text to support their answers.

STEP 7: Group Storyboard the Short Story

Now that the class has a common text, use it to co-construct a storyboard sequence. You may have co-constructed essays with your classes in the past; when co-constructing essays, teachers typically act as the author, typing on a projector screen or even writing on chart paper, and students offer suggestions. The exercise works particularly well as it allows the teacher to use the think-aloud strategy to model the thought process for crafting an essay. "Okay, so I really like this sentence here, but I think I may need a better transition," or "Is this the word I really want here, or could anyone offer me a better one?" To be fair, the exercise does take time, and you may feel that you are "working without a net," so to speak, but few activities provide students with a better opportunity to experience how an expert thinks through a creative process.

In this case, rather than writing an essay, you will act as the class storyboard artist. Don't feel like your artistic skills are up to snuff? No worries! We aren't making art here. And given how nervous some of your students probably are about the prospect of drawing out their shots, this is your chance to show them they do not have to be perfect. In fact, I like to explain to my students that storyboarding is really just a way for a director to put ideas on paper so the cinematographer will know what to film. Nervous about stepping outside your comfort zone? We ask our students to do that every day (or we should, anyway). After all, how else do we grow? If your students see you are willing to try something challenging with them, they are less likely to see the assignment as busywork and are more likely to follow your lead. Worried you are not an expert storyboard artist? You can rely on what you *do* feel comfortable with: constructing stories. You are simply replacing nouns, modifying clauses, and action verbs with images. As you work through this part of the assignment with your class, you still know what elements of the story should be there.

The storyboarding process will probably be easier—especially during the revision process—if you sketch your shot ideas on 4" × 6" index cards and tape them to your board. As you sketch students' shot suggestions, the following questions will be helpful:

- Why should we include this shot?
- What information do we want the audience to have? Why?
- What information do we want to conceal? Why?
- How do we want the audience to feel? Why?
- Which angle would work best here? Why?
- How should the scene be lit? Why?
- If, for whatever reason, we couldn't get this shot, is there another shot we could use? Which shot is better? Why?
- Have we conveyed information about all four story elements?
- How many shots should we include in this sequence? How do we know?
- In terms of actual time, how long does this scene take to play out? How might our answer help us determine how many shots to use?

Don't lead students to the "right" answer—such a thing hardly ever exists—but instead lead them to an answer they can support. In her research study on dialogic learning, Clerehan (1996) argues that "the most important use of language is in stimulating dialogue." She goes on to point out that students "develop skills and gain knowledge not *from* talk, but *through* talk." Students learn best when, rather than being told which answer is correct, they are allowed to talk through their thoughts and thereby gain a better understanding of the process in question.

Every choice students make when it comes to filmmaking should be supported by careful thought and consideration. We want to move in for a close-up, for example, because we want to see the character's reaction to what just happened. We want to use side lighting on this character because she is hiding a secret. We want to use a low angle to convey this character's power. We should not use a particular technique because, well, we haven't used it in a while. Students should understand how to think through and weigh the different techniques at their disposal and not simply choose one technique over another at random.

STEP 8: Determine How Many Shots We Should Have in Our Storyboard

Students tend to underestimate the number of shots needed for this sequence. They pick out the most obvious "moments" in the story, and they then give each moment a frame. But filmmakers are more nuanced. They understand these moments must be connected with viscera—the shots that provide the details to make the moment feel real. A character will say something, and we get a shot of another character so we are able to see that character's reaction. Or maybe we shift to a character's hand, fiddling with a paperclip. Is the character nervous? Agitated? Afraid? Bored? The viewer is left to make an interpretation, and the interaction with the onscreen images is what creates engagement.

Fortunately for us, somebody somewhere researches everything. The number of shots filmmakers use per minute is no exception. Consider the chart in Figure 4.5 by Stephen Follows (2017). Have students examine the chart. What do they immediately notice? Why do they think different genres have varying numbers of shots per minute? What is the effect of many quick shots as opposed to fewer longer shots? Considering the genre of the short story they examined earlier, how many shots per minute should we expect in the film version? Given

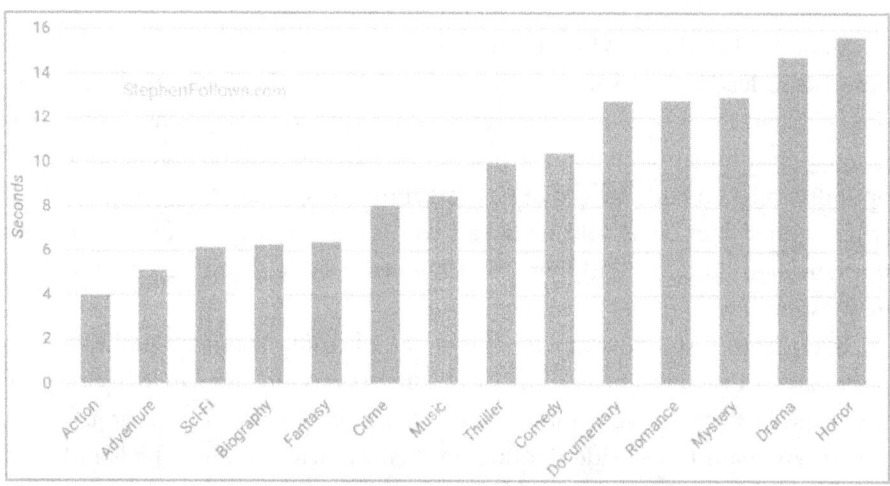

FIGURE 4.5. Average shot length in feature films released 1997–2016. (Graph by StephenFollows.com. Reprinted by permission.)

how long students decided the story takes to play out, you will now be able to determine a target number of shots to include.

Odds are, as mentioned earlier, your students will err on the side of drawing too few frames. So, what could they add to flesh out the scene? How will these additional frames affect audience perception?

STEP 9: Revise Storyboards

Most writers will attest that the revision process is a tremendously important part of the writing process. (English teachers make this argument all the time with varying degrees of success.) Ultimately, revision is every bit as important as the prewriting or writing phase. The same argument holds for filmmaking.

We have storyboards that connect the important notes in the story, but our sequence could be better, more fluid, more engaging. The question, of course, is how? We have already considered the number of frames, and while making sure our total number falls within the normal range for the genre will help, having a specific number of shots will not fix everything.

When writing, we generally pay special attention to transitions to ensure we connect our ideas smoothly, one to the next. The same is true for film. We don't want to simply throw all the big ideas of the story on-screen; we want to connect them smoothly, one to the next.

Moreover, going back to our original questions (with a few modifications) couldn't hurt, either:

- Are there additional shots we could include?
- Is there information the audience does not yet have but should? Why?
- Have we focused too much on any one thing? Why might we have done that?
- Does our storyboard convey the feeling we want it to? Why or why not?
- Are there different angles we could or should use? Why?
- How would the scene change if it were lit differently? Why?
- Do the shots we have work the way we want them to? Why or why not?
- Have we conveyed information about all four story elements?
- Does our new shot total fall within the range expected of our genre?

Just as with the editing and revision processes in essay composition, the goal is not to wind up with an entirely new piece but to create a more polished, effective piece.

STEP 10: Have Students Work in Small Groups to Storyboard a New Story

Now that you have co-constructed a storyboard sequence with your students, they should be more comfortable with the thought process. Have them create their own storyboard sequence based on different text. Feel free to use the text below or another of your choosing.

School Daze

"Do your homework," Mr. Haislip says.
"But—this is stupid. I'll never need this in life!" Sachit responds defiantly.
Mr. Haislip smiles at Sachit sadly. "You might be surprised."
Years pass. One day Mr. Haislip sees Sachit at lunch.
"It's good to see you, Sachit."
"You, too, Mr. Haislip. Would you like fries with that?"

—Robert Bryant Crisp © 2002

STEP 11: Written Analysis of Shot Sequence—Why This Way?

As with any assignment, a great deal of the actual learning process occurs or is solidified during the reflection process. Remember, these various film techniques are important not simply because they look different but because they convey different meanings. Good storytellers are good at guiding their audiences, and these techniques allow filmmakers to do just that.

At this stage, have students write a reflection on the process they went through when they chose to storyboard the story the way they did. Why use the two shot? Why the side lighting? Why move in for a close-up there?

This assignment does not have to be a full-on essay, though it certainly could be. The objective is to help your students solidify the idea that these techniques convey meaning and that choosing the proper techniques can go a long way toward helping the story have the proper emotional resonance. Further, should you choose to do so, expanding the activity into a full-on film analysis essay (whether of a short clip or an entire film) is a great way to challenge your students to employ in text skills they are acquiring while engaging with film.

Students should be prepared to discuss their reflections with their peers.

STEP 12: Culminating Activity—"If My Life Were a Movie" Poster and One-Minute Trailer

As a fun way to wrap up this unit, consider having your students make "If My Life Were a Movie" film posters and one-minute trailers. In short, have them consider the questions, "If someone were making a movie about you, what scenes would they include? What would the film be called? How would the poster look?" See the assignment in Figure 4.6.

Generally speaking, the concept for the poster is pretty straightforward and provides a great way for you to get to know your students better, as well as for them to get to know each other. These posters will also look great displayed on your classroom wall. The requirements are simple: (1) use 8½" × 11" computer paper; (2) align the poster vertically; (3) print the poster in color; (4) include the title of the film; (5) include "Starring [student's name],"; and (6) include a photograph, not a drawing, of the student's face.

The requirements for the film trailers are simple as well: (1) film horizontally, *not* vertically (after all, film screens are horizontal—we're not filming for a fast-food menu board here!); (2) include the title of the film; (3) include a "Starring [your name]" line; (4) include shots from the different "scenes" that would be included in your film (work, family, school, etc.); and (5) make your trailer exactly one minute long.

I generally require these trailers to be shot on students' phones, just to keep a level playing field. As for editing, if students have iPhones, they can use iMovie for free. I typically use either Video Maker or InShot—both are also free, and both work fine for assignments like this. And if you have students share these videos with you via Google Docs, you can easily play them for the class.

This assignment, in addition to helping me get to know names and faces, allows me to see if my students can do basic filming and editing and gives my students a chance to practice using the techniques we have covered. In terms of grading, as this is the first actual assignment involving filming and editing, I give completion credit provided they meet the basic requirements.

STEP 13: Reflect on the Process

What have you learned about the process filmmakers go through when planning their films? Why is this process important? Be prepared to share your thoughts with your classmates.

If My Life Were a Movie…

What would the poster look like? For your first homework assignment, create the movie poster for your life story. Your movie poster should meet the following requirements:

1. It should measure 8 ½" × 11" (computer paper).
2. It should be aligned vertically.
3. It should be in color.
4. It should include a title.
5. It should include the line: "Starring [Insert your first and last name here]."
6. It should include a photograph of your face, not a sketch. After all, these posters will help me get to know names and faces!

Beyond that, be creative and have fun!

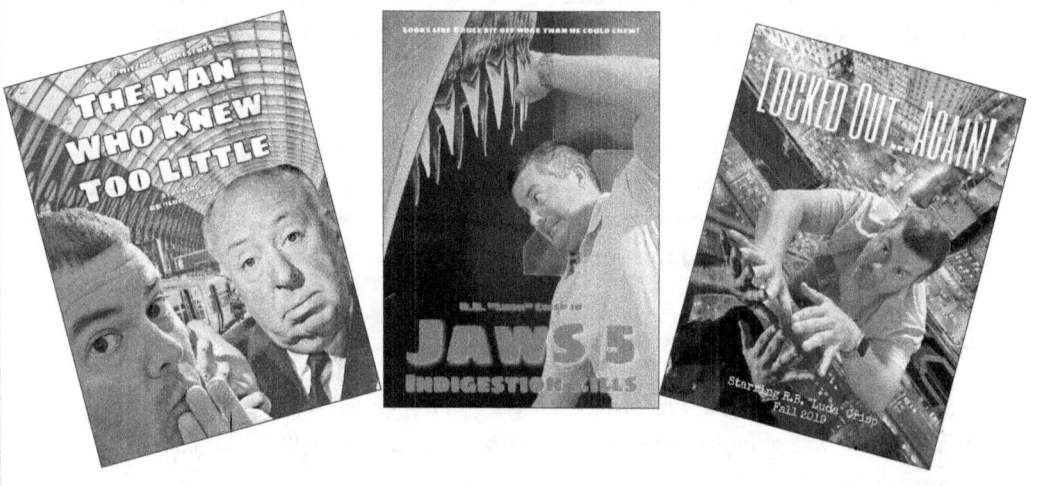

FIGURE 4.6. Instructions for the "If My Life Were a Movie" poster assignment.

Standards Addressed in This Unit

Knowledge of Language
CCSS.ELA-LITERACY.CCRA.L.3
Vocabulary Acquisition and Use
CCSS.ELA-LITERACY.CCRA.L.6
Craft and Structure
CCSS.ELA-LITERACY.CCRA.R.4
CCSS.ELA-LITERACY.CCRA.R.5
Integration of Knowledge and Ideas
CCSS.ELA-LITERACY.CCRA.R.7
Range of Reading and Level of Text Complexity
CCSS.ELA-LITERACY.CCRA.R.10
Comprehension and Collaboration
CCSS.ELA-LITERACY.CCRA.SL.1
CCSS.ELA-LITERACY.CCRA.SL.2
Text Types and Purposes
CCSS.ELA-LITERACY.CCRA.W.2
Production and Distribution
CCSS.ELA-LITERACY.CCRA.W.4
CCSS.ELA-LITERACY.CCRA.W.5
CCSS.ELA-LITERACY.CCRA.W.6
Range of Writing
CCSS.ELA-LITERACY.CCRA.W.10

5 *Edward Scissorhands*: Snow Globes, Visual Rhyming, and the Fine Art of Mise-en-Scène

Lesson Plan

Essential Question
How can directors make use of background elements to impact meaning or to affect audience perception?

Objective
Students will analyze a scene from *Edward Scissorhands* and identify background and compositional elements in order to explain how director Tim Burton uses mise en scène to make meaning and affect audience perception.

Central Texts

Edward Scissorhands (script excerpt) by Caroline Thompson

Edward Scissorhands (film excerpt) directed by Tim Burton

Agenda

STEP 1: Anticipatory Quickwrite

STEP 2: View and Analyze the Opening Credits with No Sound

STEP 3: Conduct a Think-Pair-Share Regarding the Score

STEP 4: Analyze Danny Elfman's Score

STEP 5: Examine the Script and Make Predictions

STEP 6: View and Analyze the Opening Scene

STEP 7: In Collaborative Groups, Students Select Their Own Five-Minute Film Clips to Analyze

STEP 8: Reflect on the Process

Differentiation

This activity examines the use of mise en scène, film scoring, and scriptwriting. As students become more familiar with these different elements of the filmmaking process, they will likewise come to better understand how they can use their own unique skill sets to contribute to the creation of a film project. Thus, this unit helps prepare students to find their interests and use them to more effectively contribute to their small-group film projects.

Additionally, you will have several options for assessment when you ask students, once they have experienced breaking down a scene as a class, to get into small groups and break down their own scenes. Some of your students may be most comfortable presenting their findings in writing; others may enjoy presenting their findings verbally. Still others may prefer to create a film analysis video similar to those found on YouTube channels such as "Every Frame a Painting," "RocketJump Film School," or "Lessons from the Screenplay." The method is not nearly as important as the act of breaking down the scene, so feel free to offer your students a bit of freedom in how they do so.

Vocabulary

color palette (n.)—the range of colors selected for a given shot or scene. Directors often select specific color palettes to convey meaning (e.g., Guillermo del Toro's use of color to differentiate the fairy world from the real world in *Pan's Labyrinth*).

magical realism (n.)—there is some disagreement regarding whether magical realism constitutes an actual genre, or if it might constitute a genre when in print but not in film. Regardless of how you stand on the issue, magical realism refers to a story that, for the most part, is realistic yet contains elements of magic. Think fairy tales for grown-ups or any of the Percy Jackson or Harry Potter films.

mise en scène (n.)—literally, "what's in the shot." This borrowed French term refers to the background details in a shot that serve to add meaning or to deepen audience understanding of the meaning of a particular shot and, by extension, of the scene and/or the film.

motivated camera movement (n.)—when the camera moves in response to on-screen movement (following a character or object, for example, as if the character or object is attached to the camera and pulling it along with them)

score (n.)—the music that accompanies a film

shooting script (n.)—the final iteration of the script that determines how the film is shot. Scripts typically undergo many changes as they progress from spec scripts to shooting scripts.

soundstage (n.)—a large, open building in which filmmakers rent space to build sets for filming

visual rhyming (n.)—when two shots or scenes look similar to each other, enough so as to draw a comparison or imply a connection

Resources

"Designing the World of Film: Crash Course Film Production #9" by CrashCourse (https://youtu.be/Q3BcS8Uwl9U)

"How to Speak Movie Part 2: Mise en Scène" by KyleKallgrenBHH (https://youtu.be/clBT7O3A3wI)

"Mise-en-scene (sic) | Introduction to Film Analysis" by Chris Gatt (https://youtu.be/3hfAkIEdxIA)

"Opening Shots Tell Us Everything" by Now You See It (https://youtu.be/CZhFtd1QZWc)

"Understanding Mise-en scene" (sic) by GripUp (https://youtu.be/TMb-Wa8sqQOg)

Suggested Timeline

Two days

Lesson 5

Edward Scissorhands: Snow Globes, Visual Rhyming, and the Fine Art of Mise-en-Scène

Making a film is like putting out a fire with [a] sieve. There are so many elements, and it gets so complicated.

—George Lucas

STEP 1: Anticipatory Quickwrite

How comfortable do you feel analyzing the techniques filmmakers use to elicit responses from their audiences? Which techniques do you feel most comfortable analyzing? Which techniques are most challenging for you to analyze? Be prepared to share your thoughts with your classmates.

The goals of a film class are, at their core, virtually identical to the goals of an English class: we want our students to be able to break down a complex text, examine the author's purpose, and analyze the techniques employed. The big difference, to make an obvious point, involves the medium. Many ELA teachers are hesitant to use film as a text primarily because we were trained to teach poetry, essays, novels, and short stories. Nonprint text is imposing because of our lack of familiarity with the medium and how it is composed. The purpose of this chapter is to walk you through how to break down a film clip in terms of imagery, symbolism, color symbolism, irony, genre, author's purpose, allusion, rhyme, archetypes, and character development—all of which will feel familiar, given our training as English teachers. In short, we are going to determine how to break down a film clip in much the same way we would break down a print text.

In this case, we will examine a scene from Tim Burton's classic film, *Edward Scissorhands* (1990). The story begins with a grandmother putting her granddaughter to bed on a snowy winter night. "Why is it snowing, Grandma? Where does snow come from?" the little girl asks. The story that follows is the answer to this deceptively simple question.

Virtually *everything* about this Tim Burton classic is deceptively simple. The sets, costumes, characters, and plot all feel as though we have tuned in to a routine fantasy film, a quirky and simplistic morality story. And yet, as he so often does, Tim Burton plays against our expectations.

STEP 2: View and Analyze the Opening Credits with No Sound

As you prepare to study this film, explain to students that we receive information from film in two ways: what we *see* and what we *hear*. Without giving students any background of the story, play the first few minutes of the opening credits without sound. (If any students have seen the film already, encourage them not to ruin the experience for their peers.) Stop as the camera ascends the cobweb-covered stairs. Ask students about their expectations regarding the film. What sort of story are they expecting? What genre do they think it is? What evidence supports these expectations?

Your students will point out the obvious, mostly along the lines of "Probably a horror movie, given all the spooky imagery." This is a good opportunity for you to point out the **color palette** Burton uses during this sequence and how all of that black and blue seems to support their reading.

STEP 3: Conduct a Think-Pair-Share Regarding the Score

What should the score sound like? Have students take a moment to quickwrite about the sort of music they expect here. If possible, have them identify the instrumentation, time signature, major or minor key, whether the music should be accompanied by human voices—whatever vocabulary they know to explain how the score should sound.

As students complete their quickwrites, have them share in small groups. Do other students share their expectations? Do their peers hear the music differently? Students should be prepared to share a few interpretations with the class.

STEP 4: Analyze Danny Elfman's Score

Once students have discussed their predictions, play the rest of the credits with the sound turned on. Does Danny Elfman's **score** fit their expectations? If not, how does his score differ? Which version do students prefer, their own or his, and why?

STEP 5: Examine the Script and Make Predictions

As the opening credits fade into a gentle nighttime snowfall, stop the film. Share with students the script for the opening scene. I should point out that the version I have included is not the **shooting script**, which is to say that the film will be a little different. Regardless, have students read the first few pages of the script. What details seem important? How would this scene translate to film?

Have students sketch a shot they expect to see. Encourage them to use their film vocabulary. What might the framing be? The angle? Will the camera move? What about the lighting? This is another good opportunity for students to share their shots with their peers.

Additionally, point out to students the (O.S.) notation that occasionally appears beside characters' names. This notation means "off-screen" and indicates the character is physically in the scene, though not in front of the camera. The notation (V.O.) indicates a "voice-over," in which the speaker is not an actual character within the scene.

EDWARD SCISSORHANDS
By Caroline Thompson

Story by Caroline Thompson and Tim Burton
Revised 2/22/90
BLUE

A1   TITLE SEQUENCE.   A1

SEVERAL SNOWFLAKE PAPER WEIGHTS

sit on a shelf. They've been shaken and snow swirls inside the plastic bubbles.

DISSOLVE

FROM ONE PAPER WEIGHT SNOW SCENE, MID-SNOWFALL, TO ANOTHER.

—A LOG CABIN in the woods. Its windows brightly lit.

—A horse-drawn SLEIGH pulled by a pair of blinkered chestnuts.

—A SNOWMAN.

—A FROZEN POND, tiny skating figures.

—A MOUNTAIN topped by a GOTHIC MANSION. In the swirling snow, the house with its dark spires almost seems a part of the craggy granite upon which it is perched.

AS WE PULL BACK

from the mountain, through the snowstorm, we realize that this scene is real.

TITLES END

as we continue to draw back through a WINDOW FRAME and turn with an OLD WOMAN who's been looking out into

1 INT. LITTLE GIRL'S BEDROOM. NIGHT. 1

Outside, it's snowing – but in here, where the old woman tucks her little GRANDDAUGHTER into bed, it is cozy and warm. Firelight makes the shadows big, the figures dim.

                  OLD WOMAN
Snuggle under now. It's cold out there.

                 GRANDDAUGHTER
Why is it snowing, Grandmommy? Where does it come from?

                  OLD WOMAN
That's a long story, sweetie pie.

                 GRANDDAUGHTER
I want to hear.

                  OLD WOMAN
                  (Voice tired)
Not tonight...

                 GRANDDAUGHTER
Why not? What's wrong?

                  OLD WOMAN
... Go to sleep.

GRANDDAUGHTER
I'm not sleepy. Tell me... Please...

The old woman sighs and sits on the edge of the bed.

OLD WOMAN
...Well, all right. Let's see... It would have to start with scissors.

GRANDDAUGHTER
Scissors?

OLD WOMAN
There are all kinds of scissors. And, once, there was even a man who had scissors instead of hands.

GRANDDAUGHTER
A man?

OLD WOMAN
Yes.

GRANDDAUGHTER
Hands scissors?

OLD WOMAN
No, scissor hands. Do you know the old mansion on top of the mountain?

GRANDDAUGHTER
It's haunted.

OLD WOMAN
(impatiently)
Do you want to hear this story or not?

The little girl nods.

OLD WOMAN
Okay then. A long time ago, an inventor lived in that mansion...

As the old woman speaks, we

MOVE OUT THE WINDOW.

> OLD WOMAN (O.S.)
> He made a lot of things, I suppose. He also made the man.... He gave him insides, a heart, a brain, everything. Nobody knows how, but he did it... He had just about finished covering him over with a delicate plastic that was exactly like skin—he only had the hands to go—when...

> GRANDDAUGHTER (O.S.)
> When what?

We glide through the snowfall OVER THE ROOFTOPS of the town and UP THE MOUNTAIN toward the MANSION on the peak.

> OLD WOMAN (O.S.)
> When he died. What the inventor should've invented was a new heart for himself...

> GRANDDAUGHTER (O.S.)
> Couldn't anybody help him?

> OLD WOMAN (O.S.)
> How? No one down here in town knew a thing about it... The man he'd created couldn't help. He tried to hold the inventor and he couldn't even do that because he still had long shears for hands.... Afterwards, he was all alone.

As we get closer to the mansion, the snow stops.

> GRANDDAUGHTER (O.S.)
> (full of pity)
> He didn't even have a name.

> OLD WOMAN
> Of course he did. We're talking about a man, aren't we? His name was Edward.

STEP 6: View and Analyze the Opening Scene

After students have discussed their expectations, show them the opening scene of the film. They will notice differences between the finished product and what they read in the script. This is a perfect opportunity to discuss these changes with students. What was Tim Burton's thought process? Why might he have wanted to make those changes? Explain to students that you will now examine the opening scene in terms of **mise-en-scène**, looking at the significance of all the details in the shot and how those details contribute to meaning.

This is a good time to point out to your students that *Edward Scissorhands* is an example of **magical realism**, a genre in which magic and reality merge, not unlike in a fairy tale. This genre relies heavily on symbolism, and it lends itself well to Tim Burton's directorial aesthetic.

You might also note to your students that while mistakes in the filmmaking process happen, students should understand that virtually everything they see in a given shot represents conscious decisions. In short, everything is there for a reason. And no, the uninitiated public will not "see" all of these things, but does that mean these details are not important?

On the contrary, a good storyteller must, in a sense, be a good psychologist. And these details, whether noted consciously or not, influence viewers' perspectives and expectations.

Notice, for instance, that the opening shot of the film looks a great deal like a snow globe. Why would Tim Burton not choose to make this community look more realistic? Surely he had the money and resources to do so. Yet we must assume the choice was deliberate.

Note, for instance, that authors will often agonize over the first lines of their work. *Good* first lines grab a reader's attention and help establish expectations; *great* first lines withstand multiple readings, even to the point of revealing new meanings once the reader has finished reading the story. Opening shots in films can be considered in these same terms.

In this case, the opening image resembles a snow globe. Why? Could it be Tim Burton is subtly alerting his audience that this story will take place in a fake world? Remember, this story is an example of magical realism. And where do fairy tales take place? Once upon a time, far, far away.... The snow globe imagery was a choice.

And that image makes sense on another level as well. Remember, the film is the answer to a very specific question: Where does snow come from? So, perhaps we should not be surprised that the wallpaper in the granddaughter's room contains a pattern that looks suspiciously like snowflakes.

As the camera pulls back and tracks along with the grandmother—this is called **motivated camera movement**, as the camera is pulled along with movement on-screen—we see the snow globes on the mantle. They have not gone away but were simply moved a bit in the narrative, and they further tie in to the concepts of snow and fake worlds.

Once the grandmother reaches the bed, we are presented with color symbolism, allusion, and **visual rhyming**. For starters, the little girl is wearing white. This one is easy; white represents innocence and purity, your students will point out, and she is a little girl, after all. So why, then, you may ask your students, does the grandmother wear red? Are we to see her as evil? Actually, as any student who has studied William Blake can tell you, red indicates experience. Grandma has been there and done that. She knows what she is talking about. We may even go so far as to say that the story she is about to relate comes from firsthand knowledge.

The allusion takes the form of the round knobs attached to the bedposts. One could argue they are globes, representations of fake worlds. The film is, after all, full of such representations. But an audience viewing this film in 1990 would also have been familiar with Disney's film *Bedknobs and Broomsticks*, in which a magical brass bedknob of roughly the same size and shape becomes a vehicle to a world of magic and adventure. Perhaps Burton is setting up his audience's expectations.

In addition to symbolism and allusion, Burton uses a technique called visual rhyming. Students will, of course, be familiar with the concept of rhyming in written text. The major difference with visual rhyming is that we are presented with similar-looking images rather than sounds. Take, for instance, the grandmother dressed in red, next to the bed, leaning over the little girl to her right, dressed in white. Now look at the bedside table to the left of the grandmother. On the table is a pitcher of red roses; above and to the left is a white teapot.

Or note the headboard, which looks exactly like the footboard. The only difference is that the headboard, like the grandmother and the roses, is above and to the left of the footboard. Or notice the doll at the foot of the bed, positioned much like the little girl in relation to the headboard behind her. Like Shrek's onion or Donkey's parfait, there are layers of meaning here.

And while we are at it, notice how large everything in the room is in relation to the little girl. The bed is massive, as are the squares on the comforter, pulled up nearly to the little girl's neck. But for the tight spotlight trained on her—primarily to illuminate her white nightgown—the little girl could almost be mistaken for another doll. The juxtaposition of large and small in the scene helps support the idea that the fabric of reality is warped, that magic is afoot. And what better environment for the telling of fairy tales, underscored by the fireplace in the corner and the snow falling outside, than a night at grandmother's house?

As the camera shifts to behind the bed, you might want to point out to your students that this film was shot on a **soundstage** rather than in a real house and that movie sets are designed to be moveable. The wall we saw earlier is no longer there.

As the grandmother settles in to tell her story to the little girl, the old woman's hands begin to move with her words as if shaping the story out of thin air. Note that hands will be important in this story (hence, the title).

But then, as the grandmother begins the story, the camera floats across the bed, across the grandmother, and to the window through which the grandmother was staring initially, filling the screen. The interesting thing about this window is that the pane dividers, unlike most dividers, form a cross.

Maybe this is an accident, but it is still worth exploring. Given the unusual shape, especially one so loaded with meaning, could Burton have been sending his audience a message?

This is a good place to discuss with your students the concept of archetypes—character types that recur throughout literature. Perhaps your students will be able to supply examples, such as the absent-minded professor, the bad boy, the chosen one, or the damsel in distress. They may also have heard of the Christ figure.

Christ figures share a handful of specific characteristics: (1) a miraculous birth; (2) unusual or supernatural powers or abilities; (3) an innocent or sinless nature; (4) suffering/dying literally/figuratively for the sake of others; and (5) dying "up" or ascending (though this trait seems to be more suggestion than requirement). Examples of Christ figures include Aslan from The Chronicles of Narnia, Harry Potter, Gandalf from The Lord of the Rings, and John Coffey from *The Green Mile* (notice the initials?). As for the fifth characteristic, you might consider Herman Melville's Billy Budd, who dies by hanging aboard his ship. This particular hanging is carried out by Billy's crewmates taking hold of one end of the rope strung over the yardarm and walking. Thus, unlike a more typical hanging, Billy dies as he ascends.

Could Burton be telling his audience that Edward is a Christ figure? If so, there should be other indications throughout the film. At this point, you may want to draw your students' attention back to the snowflake wallpaper. Perhaps they will notice that the "snowflakes" seem to contain crosses or that their overall shape seems to resemble traditional depictions of the Star of Bethlehem. Encourage your students to look for other indicators along the way to see if they can support this archetype.

As the camera passes through the window, you may want to point out that what seems like one shot is actually two. The transition occurs as the camera reaches the window and tilts downward, at which point the screen goes black. At this moment, the first shot dissolves into the second shot, which begins just under the edge of the large platform holding the scale model of the community. The camera then flies over the town, veering from Dutch tilt to Dutch tilt. Again, the artificial community serves to remind the viewer that we are viewing a fairy tale.

The shot progresses until we see the mansion on top of the mountain at the end of the cul-de-sac. We then cut to a shot from inside the mansion, which slowly pulls back to reveal we are looking over the shoulder of the character who, based on the grandmother's story, we can reasonably assume to be Edward. This shot serves as the bookend of the introductory story. Notice, for instance, how the shot is framed the same way the first shot was framed, another example of visual rhyming. The indication is that the two characters are connected, though we do not yet know how.

We should also note there is something missing in this shot—specifically, the snow. The conclusion we can draw from this is that we have entered the flashback portion of the story. *Edward Scissorhands* is, after all, a frame story: a story about someone telling a story. Note that as we look down at the community, we can see only the one loop. Everything beyond is blackness. The community itself can be seen as a metaphorical snow globe.

Now we have covered roughly the first six minutes and thirty seconds of the film, a process that generally takes around ninety minutes to teach. We are only halfway through the process, however; everything so far was designed to walk students through an interpretation of a short film text. The next step helps solidify this process.

STEP 7: In Collaborative Groups, Students Select Their Own Five-Minute Film Clips to Analyze

This step is hugely important, as this is when students put into practice what you have just taught them about interpreting a short film text. The idea is to have students work in small groups to break down a film text of their choice. I prefer to have them work in their collaborative filmmaking groups, which allows the activity to function as a bonding experience as well.

Students will need time to work in small groups; if they are already in groups for their film projects, I prefer to keep them in those same groups. I think keeping the same kids together helps them bond. Either way, the idea is to have students find a five-minute film clip to analyze. YouTube is a great resource for that. And at this point, as the teacher, you have options. Have students discuss the clip in their small groups first. Then, once they have had a few minutes to break down everything they see:

OPTION 1: Have students write a film analysis essay in which they dissect the techniques, effects, and, if possible, director's style as evidenced in the clip they have chosen.

OPTION 2: Have students present their findings to the class, focusing on the techniques, effects, and director's style as evidenced in the clip.

OPTION 3: If students are comfortable with video production (or if they just do not want to present to their classmates), have them create a film analysis essay. They should focus on the same elements they would if they had chosen options one or two, but they instead create a video similar to what one might find on a YouTube channel that specializes in film analysis, such as "Every Frame a Painting," "RocketJump Film School," or "Lessons from the Screenplay."

You will probably want to give your students time in class to work on this assignment, regardless of which option you choose, but you will want to make sure they understand they will be working on this assignment outside of class as well. Given all the platforms available to us these days, including Zoom, Google Docs, FaceTime, etc., students should have little difficulty collaborating with their small groups.

STEP 8: Reflect on the Process

Having now analyzed a clip as a class, then breaking down another in your small group and presenting your findings to your classmates, what have you learned? What goals do you have moving forward? Be prepared to share your thoughts with your classmates.

Standards Addressed in This Unit

Conventions of Standard English
CCSS.ELA-LITERACY.CCRA.L.1
CCSS.ELA-LITERACY.CCRA.L.2
Vocabulary Acquisition and Use
CCSS.ELA-LITERACY.CCRA.L.6

Key Ideas and Details
CCSS.ELA-LITERACY.CCRA.R.1
CCSS.ELA-LITERACY.CCRA.R.2
CCSS.ELA-LITERACY.CCRA.R.3
Craft and Structure
CCSS.ELA-LITERACY.CCRA.R.4
CCSS.ELA-LITERACY.CCRA.R.5
CCSS.ELA-LITERACY.CCRA.R.6
Integration of Knowledge and Ideas
CCSS.ELA-LITERACY.CCRA.R.7
CCSS.ELA-LITERACY.CCRA.R.9
Range of Reading and Level of Text Complexity
CCSS.ELA-LITERACY.CCRA.R.10
Comprehension and Collaboration
CCSS.ELA-LITERACY.CCRA.SL.1
CCSS.ELA-LITERACY.CCRA.SL.2
Presentation of Knowledge and Ideas
CCSS.ELA-LITERACY.CCRA.SL.4
CCSS.ELA-LITERACY.CCRA.SL.5
Text Types and Purposes
CCSS.ELA-LITERACY.CCRA.W.2
Production and Distribution
CCSS.ELA-LITERACY.CCRA.W.4
CCSS.ELA-LITERACY.CCRA.W.6
Range of Writing
CCSS.ELA-LITERACY.CCRA.W.10

Looking like You Know What You're Doing: Avoiding Bathroom Selfie Cinematography

Lesson Plan

Essential Question
What techniques can cinematographers use to compose quality shots?

Objective
Students will be able to use the Rule of Thirds in order to compose shots.

Central Texts
Various photographs taken using the Rule of Thirds

Agenda

> STEP 1: Anticipatory Quickwrite
>
> STEP 2: Study Examples of Photographs Using the Rule of Thirds
>
> STEP 3: Take Six Photographs Using the Rule of Thirds
>
> STEP 4: Expand on What We Have Learned by Exploring Other Approaches
>
> STEP 5: Reflect on the Process

Differentiation
This unit introduces a very popular framing technique: the Rule of Thirds. This technique is not the only framing technique, however; there are other approaches, including techniques such as geometrical shot composition or Golden Ratio composition. But the goal is for students to be able to use an approach to capture better images, and while the Rule of Thirds is not necessarily the best framing technique, it is one of the easier techniques to grasp. If, however, students prefer to use one of the other approaches and can explain their reasoning, by all means, let them explore that preference.

Vocabulary

geometrical shot composition (n.)—an approach to organizing a given shot using geometrical principles, including shapes and symmetry

Golden Ratio shot composition (n.)—an approach to organizing a given shot within the parameters of the Fibonacci spiral

Rule of Thirds (n.)—an approach to framing images that divides the image into thirds both horizontally and vertically

shot composition (n.)—the process of organizing the image within the frame

Resources

"8 IMPORTANT Composition Tips for Better Photos" by Jamie Windsor (https://youtu.be/VArISvUuyr0)

"Rules of Framing and Composition" by Motion Array Tutorials (https://youtu.be/fM64ycm7tz4)

"Start Taking BETTER PHOTOS TODAY! The Rule of Thirds—Photography Composition Tutorial" by Joshua Cripps Photography (https://youtu.be/IpEuYp4_iSg)

"The Rule of Thirds in 5 minutes | Creating More Dynamic Framing" by Julian Discovers (https://youtu.be/HMjvvltQpmw)

"The Rule of Thirds in Art" by Drawing & Painting - The Virtual Instructor (https://youtu.be/sQyquPmATww)

"The Rule Of Thirds | What is it? Filmmaking & Photography Training" by Learn Online Video (https://youtu.be/A7wnhDKyBuM)

Suggested Timeline
Two ninety-minute classes

Lesson 6

Looking like You Know What You're Doing: Avoiding Bathroom Selfie Cinematography

Professional cinema image-taking should integrate, interest, serve, and enhance the story.

—Haskell Wexler

STEP 1: Anticipatory Quickwrite

What techniques do you know for composing your shots? How do these techniques affect the quality of your images? Be prepared to share your thoughts with your classmates.

Lesson one: if you are using your phone for a camera—which is completely fine—for the love of all things good and holy, turn your camera sideways. We have all seen the shots, the ones in which the subject/photographer is standing in front of a bathroom mirror, the flash is going off, the camera is turned at about a thirty-degree angle (quite the rakish angle), and the subject is doing their best to make their lips look as though they are being held together by an invisible clothes pin. Those are the shots we are going to *avoid* with all of our hearts. In case you feel as though you are being judged . . . you are.

Lesson two: audiences will judge you hard. Filmmaking is not a participation trophy sport. If you make a film, you can safely assume your audience has seen many, many films, some good and some bad. Audiences do not have to be educated in order to know what they like. Filmmakers, however, need to know what they are doing and why they are doing it. Making a film is all about guiding an audience, and the best directors do it without the audience realizing what is happening. This means filmmakers must be very intentional about their craft.

Take, for instance, the fact that one's camera should be aligned horizontally. Ever see a movie in a theater where the screen is aligned vertically instead of horizontally? Me, neither. Ever see those film segments on the news—the ones shot by viewers—in which the image is in a narrow vertical band and the sides of the screen are blurred out? Me, too. They look bad, right? Like, it-was-shot-by-an-amateur bad. Those segments were shot vertically. The blurry, out-of-focus images on either side are simply screen fillers. If you want to shoot like a pro, start by aligning your camera correctly. Then, once you have mastered horizontal camera alignment, there are a few additional tricks you can use to help your **shot composition**.

STEP 2: Study Examples of Photographs Using the Rule of Thirds

One helpful trick is to use the **Rule of Thirds**. To take advantage of this technique, go into your camera settings and select the grid that looks like a tic-tac-toe board (see Figure 6.1). Once selected, the grid will appear in your viewfinder but not on the actual photograph. The idea is to use those grid lines to align your shot. In short, the two vertical lines should be aligned with whoever is in the frame. The two horizontal lines are for aligning the horizon. The four intersections are generally the most important positions in the frame. The upper two are the power points and typically align with a character's head when that character is strong, confident, or otherwise in control. The two lower intersections are weaker points and are often aligned with a character's head when that character is weak, isolated, or vulnerable.

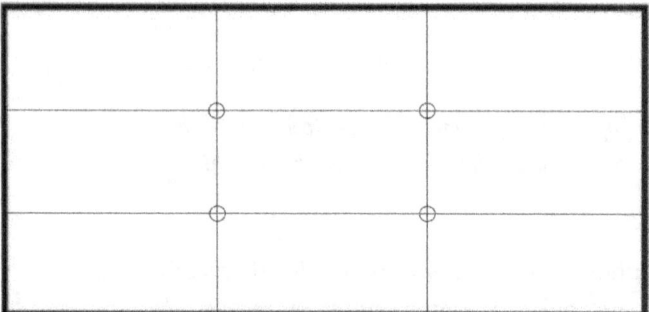

FIGURE 6.1. Camera setting grid for determining the Rule of Thirds.

To be fair, there are certainly other methods of composing your shots, whether you frame symmetrically, use geometrical shapes, or follow the Golden Ratio. The Rule of Thirds, however, is the easiest way to begin thinking about shot composition. Consider the examples in Figure 6.2, each of which is composed according to the Rule of Thirds.

STEP 3: Take Six Photographs Using the Rule of Thirds

Now that you have seen examples of framing using the Rule of Thirds, take six photographs utilizing this approach. Be prepared to share your work with the class.

The **Rule of Thirds** is not the only way to frame your shots (sometimes it's not even the *best* way), but it generally works well and is a great way to begin contemplating shot composition!

FIGURE 6.2. Sample images framed using the Rule of Thirds.

Continued on next page

FIGURE 6.2. Continued.

STEP 4: Expand on What We Have Learned by Exploring Other Approaches

If you feel comfortable using the Rule of Thirds and want to try your hand at other approaches to shot composition, consider researching other methods such as **geometrical shot composition** or the **Golden Ratio** (Fibonacci spiral), then try taking photographs using these methods.

STEP 5: Reflect on the Process

Now that you have had the chance to explore the Rule of Thirds and possibly other framing techniques as well, what have you learned? How will this new knowledge affect your cinematography? Be prepared to share your thoughts with your classmates.

Standards Addressed in This Unit

Vocabulary Acquisition and Use
CCSS.ELA-LITERACY.CCRA.L.6
Craft and Structure
CCSS.ELA-LITERACY.CCRA.R.5
Integration of Knowledge and Ideas
CCSS.ELA-LITERACY.CCRA.R.7
Comprehension and Collaboration
CCSS.ELA-LITERACY.CCRA.SL.2
Presentation of Knowledge and Ideas
CCSS.ELA-LITERACY.CCRA.SL.4
CCSS.ELA-LITERACY.CCRA.SL.5
Production and Distribution
CCSS.ELA-LITERACY.CCRA.W.4
CCSS.ELA-LITERACY.CCRA.W.6
Research to Build and Present Knowledge
CCSS.ELA-LITERACY.CCRA.W.8
Range of Writing
CCSS.ELA-LITERACY.CCRA.W.10

7 Casey for the Win: Exploring Director's Prerogative

◎ Lesson Plan

Essential Question
What is directorial freedom, and how and why do filmmakers utilize this freedom?

Objectives
1. Students will be able to exercise directorial prerogative by reinterpreting "Casey at the Bat" by Ernest Lawrence Thayer via a film treatment, changing one of the four basic elements common to all stories.
2. Students will be able to conduct research to plan a faithful adaptation of the story of Jackie Robinson based on the screenplay for the film *42*.

Central Texts

"Casey at the Bat" by Ernest Lawrence Thayer

42 (script excerpt) by Brian Helgeland

Agenda

STEP 1: Anticipatory Quickwrite

STEP 2: Review What We Know about the Elements All Stories Share

STEP 3: Explore a Print Text with an Eye toward Making It Our Own

STEP 4: Write the Treatment

STEP 5: Translate Treatments into Scripts

STEP 6: Translate Scripts into Storyboards

STEP 7: Reflect on the Process (Part 1)

STEP 8: Explore the Ramifications of Being "Based on a True Story"

STEP 9: Examine a Scene from *42*, the Story of Jackie Robinson

STEP 10: Research the "Truth"

STEP 11: Use Our Research to Storyboard a Faithful Adaptation

STEP 12: Evaluate a Scene from *42* for Historical Accuracy

STEP 13: Discuss the Ethics of Storytelling

STEP 14: Reflect on the Process (Part 2)

Differentiation

This activity encourages students to adapt a text with consideration given to their own interests and skill sets. Thus, students are invited to interpret a print text in a way that means something to them as opposed to interpreting a print text the way their teacher says they should. The important thing here is the message, the idea. Everything else is just window dressing that does not matter much. If the poem is about the dangers of hubris, there are lots of ways to tell that story, even for nonbaseball people. Likewise a work about disappointment. And keep in mind that the resolution may be changed as well. Perhaps the story becomes one of redemption or of digging down deep and delivering your best effort when people are counting on you. Regardless, this assignment takes full advantage of the various lenses through which our students see the world around them.

Vocabulary

faithful adaptation (n.)—a transformed text, such as a film made from a print text, that stays close to the original source material

shot list (n.)—a list of the relevant details a cinematographer will need in order to achieve the shot the director wants

storyboard (n.)—an image drawn in a box the approximate shape of a movie screen that indicates what the director wants to see on-screen

Resources

"Director Choices" by The FilAM Film Collective (https://youtu.be/sYqPaqfXBSU)

"Film vs. Novel: What Makes Them Different?" by Now You See It (https://youtu.be/F3QsUx0x_4w)

"How a Director Stages and Blocks a Scene" by Filmmaker IQ (https://youtu.be/9FBnSmbafC8)

"How to Adapt a Book to a Movie" by Tyler Mowery (https://youtu.be/7ybqNio5ci8)

"The Art of Adaptation" by Story Arts Centre (https://youtu.be/N4VsGUCdIIs)

"The Case for Book-to-Film Adaptations | Signature Views Mini-Doc" by Signature Views (https://youtu.be/0az32iTWo68)

"Tips for Beginner Directors" by DSLRguide (https://youtu.be/R3fVUNVDhdw)

Suggested Timeline
Two weeks

Lesson 7

Casey for the Win: Exploring Director's Prerogative

A filmmaker has almost the same freedom as a novelist has when he buys himself some paper.

—STANLEY KUBRICK

STEP 1: Anticipatory Quickwrite

How much freedom do directors have when adapting a film from previously published print texts? Be prepared to share your thoughts with your classmates.

At its core, from an English teacher's perspective, film is about the transformation of text. Film is, if we allow that the film in question was adapted or inspired by a print text, an exercise in telling the same story "another way." The caveat to this is that one must first understand the original story. The deep interaction with the original text that is required lends itself to a more thorough understanding of that same text. That close interaction with text is the English teacher's dream, and it certainly does not happen with round-robin reading.

Consider, for a moment, Ernest Lawrence Thayer's classic poem, "Casey at the Bat." In a traditional English class, we would discuss the elements common to poetry, such as rhyme scheme, meter, and other structural elements. In terms of content, we could talk about how Thayer establishes the setting and conflict or how he sets expectations and builds suspense. We could discuss complicating actions. We could examine the theme or how the conflict is resolved. We could take a historical/biographical approach and consider the importance of baseball in American culture at the time of the poem's writing. We could take a deconstructionist approach, examining the use of particular words and/or phrases. Or we could examine the piece through a feminist lens. At the end of the day, any and all of these approaches would be valid. In a film class, however, we take a bit of a different angle.

In every one of the approaches above, Thayer retains ownership of the poem. He wrote the poem, the poem is his, and the poem is what it is. There is a constant and immutable gulf between sender/author and receiver/audience. The student never experiences ownership of the text. This unit will seek to bridge that divide by exploring the process of converting a print text into a film and thereby creating the experience of ownership for the filmmaker.

STEP 2: Review What We Know about the Elements All Stories Share

Have students read the poem silently. The purpose is simply to get a feel for what is going on. To that end, once students have finished reading, have them write a brief summary of the action.

After students have written their summaries, have them share with partners and listen for discrepancies between their summaries. This particular poem is pretty straightforward, so there are not likely to be many.

After students have shared their summaries, ask them if they are aware that all stories are comprised of four elements. *New Times* of San Luis Obispo, in their guidelines for their annual "55 Fiction" short story contest (a fantastic classroom resource, by the way, the winners of which are available in a series of books), explains those four elements this way:

1) **SETTING**: All stories have to take place somewhere, so be sure your story has a setting.

2) **A CHARACTER OR CHARACTERS**: You also need some characters. Again, this sounds obvious, but it's sometimes lacking, especially when writers mistake a poem for a story. Characters don't have to be people, of course. They can have infinite variations: animals, rocks, microbes, ghosts. Anything.

3) **CONFLICT**: To be effective, a story also needs conflict. The word itself can be misleading; conflict doesn't mean that your story needs a war or people fighting in the streets. It simply means that something has to happen in your story. The lovers argue. The deer flees. The alien is perplexed by the creatures below him on that strange, blue planet. Even in this last example, something is happening, even though our alien isn't moving or talking. There is conflict; a tension is present in the narrative.

4) **RESOLUTION**: This leads us to the outcome of the story, also known as resolution. This doesn't necessarily mean that the story has to have a moral (Justice is its own reward; in the end, love triumphs, etc.), or even that the conflict itself is resolved. It may or may not be.

But what it does mean is that when the story ends, someone has to have learned something: He found out his wife wanted to kill him and grind him up in the garbage disposal; the star troopers successfully eluded the alien armada when they thought they'd been discovered; Jim was shown to be as much of a liar as his father; whatever.

The characters in your story don't necessarily have to have learned anything. But if they don't, then the reader must. The story's resolution is what creates its impact and meaning, giving readers a sense of completion and satisfaction.

("Rules for 55 Fiction")
https://www.newtimesslo.com/sanluisobispo/55FictionHowtoEnter/Page

STEP 3: *Explore a Print Text with an Eye toward Making It Our Own*

Once students are comfortable with these four elements, have them identify in writing the four elements from "Casey at the Bat." Then have students compare their observations with those of their classmates. Again, given the straightforward nature of this particular poem, students should have little difficulty identifying any of these four elements. The SETTING is a baseball game on a field in or near Mudville on a bright and sunny summer day. The CHARACTERS are a combination of baseball players (some of whom have been named), the plate umpire, and the faceless crowd in the stands. The CONFLICT is that Mudville is trying to beat a rival team. Casey is at bat, and everything comes down to whether he can drive in the winning run. The RESOLUTION is that Casey strikes out and Mudville loses the game.

Next, have students identify one aspect of the poem they would like to change, whether the setting, character(s), conflict, or resolution. As directors, students have creative license, meaning they may choose to make changes to those same elements. I like baseball, and I have no issue with the characters, nor do I dislike the choice of focusing on the climactic at bat. I do, however, dislike the fact that Casey strikes out. Like the Mudville fans, I want Casey to crush that baseball; unlike the Mudville fans, I have the power to make him do it. In my director's version of the story, Casey hits that ball a mile. There would be joy in Mudville.

This step is perhaps the most critical. We English teachers teach English because we are good at breaking down the written word. We engage closely with written text; it comes alive for us. We already have a sense of literary buy-in that many students (okay, perhaps *most* students) do not have. Changing textual elements—exercising directorial prerogative—helps create that sense of buy-in for students. Now the story is theirs. Examples of student "takes" on the poem could include:

- Casey is a star basketball player. Her team is down by one, and the clock is counting down. She can win the game if she makes a shot. Supremely confident, she passes up several open looks, opting instead for the dramatic buzzer beater. Five seconds ... four ... three ... Casey pulls up, but her shot is contested. She misses the shot, and her team loses.

- Casey plays football. He is the star quarterback. His team is down by four, and the clock is ticking. First and goal on the three-yard line. The defense is expecting a quarterback sneak. Casey just kneels. Second down. Once again, Casey kneels. Third down, eight seconds left. Casey kneels. Fourth and goal, two seconds left. Casey sets his jaw, grinds his teeth. The game comes down to this. And Casey gets stopped at the one-yard line.

- Casey is an artist. There is an upcoming art competition. She has won this competition the past three years. She is supremely confident. Everyone else works on their entries, but Casey relaxes. Why should she worry? She spends her time shopping, hanging out with friends. Her entry? She hasn't started yet, but she isn't concerned. She'll think of something. The due date approaches. Everyone has been working for weeks but not Casey. She realizes she should put something together. She finally starts working, staying up all night for two days straight. She realizes she should have started sooner, but no time for that now. In the end, she does not do her best work. Embarrassed, she drops out of the competition at the last minute.

- Casey runs cross-country. He has never won, but he has worked hard and shown a lot of improvement. His biggest competition will be Brad, who runs for the rival school. Brad always wins. The day of the meet arrives, and Casey has a plan. During the race, he runs well enough to secure second place but does not try to overcome Brad. Supremely confident, Brad runs fast enough to stay in first, but he does not overly exert himself. He smiles and waves at the spectators along the trail. Casey bides his time. Finally, the last straightaway comes into view. Brad is blowing kisses at the crowd when Casey makes his move. Brad does not realize Casey has passed him until it is too late. Brad gives everything he has, but Casey has been working hard, and his training pays off. Casey wins.

The preceding synopses are useful to understand the concept of transforming text, though students should write out the story in a bit more detail than what I have provided above. Whether you provide time in class or assign the story as homework, every student must have a text in order to proceed to the next step.

Casey at the Bat
by Ernest Lawrence Thayer

The Outlook wasn't brilliant for the Mudville nine that day:
The score stood four to two, with but one inning more to play.
And then when Cooney died at first, and Barrows did the same,
A sickly silence fell upon the patrons of the game.

A straggling few got up to go in deep despair. The rest   5
Clung to that hope which springs eternal in the human breast;
They thought, "If only Casey could get a whack at that—
We'd put up even money now, with Casey at the bat."

But Flynn preceded Casey, as did also Jimmy Blake,
And the former was a lulu and the latter was a cake;   10
So upon that stricken multitude grim melancholy sat,
For there seemed but little chance of Casey's getting to the bat.

But Flynn let drive a single, to the wonderment of all,
And Blake, the much despised, tore the cover off the ball;
And when the dust had lifted, and men saw what had occurred,   15
There was Jimmy safe at second and Flynn a-hugging third.

Then from five thousand throats and more there rose a lusty yell;
It rumbled through the valley, it rattled in the dell;
It pounded on the mountain and recoiled upon the flat,
For Casey, mighty Casey, was advancing to the bat.   20

There was ease in Casey's manner as he stepped into his place;
There was pride in Casey's bearing and a smile lit Casey's face.
And when, responding to the cheers, he lightly doffed his hat,
No stranger in the crowd could doubt 'twas Casey at the bat.

Ten thousand eyes were on him as he rubbed his hands with dirt;   25
Five thousand tongues applauded when he wiped them on his shirt;
Then while the writhing pitcher ground the ball into his hip,
Defiance gleamed in Casey's eye, a sneer curled Casey's lip.

And now the leather-covered sphere came hurtling through the air,
And Casey stood a-watching it in haughty grandeur there.   30
Close by the sturdy batsman the ball unheeded sped—
"That ain't my style," said Casey. "Strike one!" the umpire said.

From the benches, black with people, there went up a muffled roar,
Like the beating of the storm-waves on a stern and distant shore;
"Kill him! Kill the umpire!" shouted someone on the stand; 35
And it's likely they'd a-killed him had not Casey raised his hand.

With a smile of Christian charity great Casey's visage shone;
He stilled the rising tumult; he bade the game go on;
He signaled to the pitcher, and once more the dun sphere flew;
But Casey still ignored it, and the umpire said, "Strike two!" 40

"Fraud!" cried the maddened thousands, and echo answered "Fraud!"
But one scornful look from Casey and the audience was awed.
They saw his face grow stern and cold, they saw his muscles strain,
And they knew that Casey wouldn't let that ball go by again.

The sneer is gone from Casey's lip, his teeth are clenched in hate, 45
He pounds with cruel violence his bat upon the plate;
And now the pitcher holds the ball, and now he lets it go,
And now the air is shattered by the force of Casey's blow.

Oh, somewhere in this favoured land the sun is shining bright,
The band is playing somewhere, and somewhere hearts are light; 50
And somewhere men are laughing, and somewhere children shout;
But there is no joy in Mudville—mighty Casey has struck out.

A Brief Note as I Consider My Treatment

Now I must consider how I might convert this print text into film. We know that all stories, whether print text or film, contain the following four elements: setting, character(s), conflict, and resolution. If I wish to stay true to the source material—the poem—I will compose what is referred to as a **faithful adaptation**. However, in this case, I do not choose to go that route.

As the director, I have creative license, meaning I may choose to make changes to any of the story elements as I see fit. I like baseball, I have no issue with the characters, and I like the choice to focus on the climactic at bat. If I want Casey to hit a home run, then in my story, that is what he does. Or if I want my son to be the pitcher who strikes him out, well, I can make that happen as well. It's my story now. See Figure 7.1 for a form to help you keep track of your ideas.

SCCR Graphic Organizer   Name_____

Premise: *In Ridley Scott's film* Alien *(1979), the main character, Ripley, was originally supposed to be a man. Consider how drastically that one decision altered the franchise! What if the lighthouse keepers in* The Lighthouse *(2019), directed by Robert Eggers, had not been in a lighthouse at all but were squatting in someone's attic? What if Hester Prynne, the main character of Nathaniel Hawthorne's novel* The Scarlet Letter, *had been a man? Or what if Atticus Finch in* To Kill a Mockingbird *had been a racist lawyer in an otherwise progressive and happily integrated town?*

Directions: *Use this graphic organizer to keep track of your observations and plan for your own version of the story. Remember: make the story your own by changing one or two elements!*

Title_____Author_____

	Something I would change:	Impact on the story:
SETTING: When and where does the story take place?		
CHARACTERS: Who are the characters?		
CONFLICT: What is the central issue with which the characters must deal?		
RESOLUTION: How is the conflict resolved?		

FIGURE 7.1. Graphic organizer for planning your film story.

STEP 4: Write the Treatment

Once filmmakers find an idea, they must secure funding for it. After all, Christopher Nolan, Michael Bay, David Fincher—they don't pay to make their own films. They secure funding from a production company. So, how does that process work? This is where the film treatment comes in.

A film treatment gives a potential producer a big idea in a manageable form. In essence, it is a written synopsis of the story, including notes on style, etc. Interestingly, there is no real standard for how long a treatment should be. In fact, some go on for sixty pages or more. For the purposes of our class, I modify the assignment a bit.

First, we write treatments for short stories I assign. These short stories might run anywhere from fifty-five words to several pages. As we read the story, I ask students to identify the setting, characters, conflict, and resolution. Then we look for something to change.

The reason I ask my students to change one or two elements of the stories we read is that I want them to approach text differently than the way they approach text in a typical English class. Generally speaking, when students read texts in an English class, they are asked to identify the author's intent. They are asked to analyze the tone or the theme. They are asked to examine the literary devices or rhetorical tools the author uses. But they are never asked to take ownership of the text. Changing an element of the story forces them to take ownership of the story. The story is now theirs.

Thus, instead of considering the thought process the author might have undergone to create a text, students go through that process themselves. Within the framework of the original story, they now have to make decisions about what happens next, and how, and what the outcome will be. In this way, they begin to better understand the thought process of an author—not from behind glass the way a museum patron might examine a particular display but instead as an author. They make the transition from art critic to artist. The thought process is as follows: (1) read the text; (2) change one or two elements; and (3) write down how your version would play out on-screen.

Writing a treatment will be, for many students, difficult at first. A treatment is not an essay; it has no thesis statement or five-paragraph structure. A treatment is a written plan for a film. For the purposes of my class, I provide the following parameters:

- **All treatments must be typed.** At some point, we will likely want to do other things with these treatments—trade them, revise them, etc. Having them typed and saved ensures we can do so with minimal difficulty.

- **Treatments must be at least five hundred words in length.** I am fine with longer treatments, but I won't accept anything shorter than five hundred words. Shorter treatments are an indication the author has not spent the kind of time and energy developing the story that I want to see. A five hundred-word minimum implies at least a modicum of depth of thought.
- **All film terms should be in bold.** This is certainly not "industry standard." Bolding our film terms simply provides a vehicle for me to help my students focus on using those terms. If they are thinking in terms of their film techniques, then they are already developing interesting shot sequences and reinforcing their understanding of those techniques.
- **Each treatment should cover the entire assigned story, unless otherwise noted.** I want to know the entire story arc, beginning to end. There are times, of course, when we may write a treatment for an excerpt, such as a paragraph or a stanza, but by and large, treatments should cover the entire story.

That said, how would I write a treatment for "Casey at the Bat"? What would I change? What would I keep? Consider the following examples (I have included my thoughts for the sake of clarity):

Sample Treatment 1

I am a huge baseball fan, so I would keep the baseball element. It is a context I know well and feel I can therefore translate well on-screen. My biggest gripe with Thayer's poem has always been that Casey struck out. I want him to get a hit and win the game; however, letting Casey get a hit is too easy. My son is a college pitcher, so I think I will write the story so that rather than Casey being cocky and losing, the pitcher is clever and wins.

Casey at the Bat

The story opens with **establishing shots** inside the Mudville baseball park. We are among a throng of people, most moving to find their seats or grab something from a souvenir stand, others standing in small groups discussing the game. Lots of **diegetic** crowd noise here (and throughout), with subtle **nondiegetic** mood music helping create the feeling of a warm summer day at the ballpark. The camera (**Steadicam**) follows a dad and his young son as they grab a couple of hot dogs and drinks from the concession stand and begin working their way through the crowd toward their seats. They approach, and the camera **pans** as they walk past before we lose them in the crowd. I want the camera always to be moving, never static, so as to add a bit of energy to the scene. That way, in the most intense moment as the film approaches its climax and the camera stops moving, the audience will feel the intensity of the moment.

We **cut** to inside the stadium as fans find their seats. We have a brief montage of shots showing couples on dates, parents with children, and groups of friends, many of whom are wearing their respective team's logo and colors: burgundy and white for the hometown boys, navy and gold for the visiting Royals.

The PA announcer welcomes fans to the game. As the players' names are announced, we **track** along just inside either baseline, getting a **medium shot** of each player as he takes his place. We **cut** to the view from the pitcher's mound toward home plate, behind which a local high school chorus sings "The Star-Spangled Banner." **Cut** to various **close-ups** of players, hands over their hearts, some mouthing the words, some quiet and introspective. Warming up in the Royals' bullpen, number 39, the starting pitcher for today, pauses, removes his hat, and stands at attention.

The anthem done, we **cut** to the players on the field, warming up. We **track** along the first-base line, watching the players go through the motions. **Cut** to **long shots** of players fielding ground balls and catching pop flies. Then the game begins.

Much of the game will be shot as a **montage**, **dissolving** from one good play to another. We see the occasional player thrown out at first, a line drive over second, a deep fly to right. Players take the field, players leave. **Cut** occasionally to reaction shots from the crowd. As the innings play out, we **track** left to right across an old green baseball scoreboard plastered with advertisements for local places of business.

We can see that Mudville has kept it close with the visiting Royals, but heading into the bottom of the last inning, they are down four to two. The first batter for the home team grounds out. **Cut** to the second batter, who hits a long fly ball to the fence in left. Then we **cut** to a long shot of left field. The fielder is there and catches it with his back against the wall. **Cut** to various crowd shots as a number of fans have given up and are heading toward the exits. With two outs, they have given up hope.

We **cut** to a crowd reaction shot when suddenly we hear the unmistakable crack of a well-struck baseball. A number of fans stand in disbelief. We **cut** to the reverse-angle **POV** shot from the crowd's perspective as we see the base runner heading down the line. **Cut** to a wide-angle shot at ground level, just behind first base, as the shortstop makes an uncharacteristic bobble, and the runner makes it safely before the ball. **Medium shot** of the crowd cheering, offering high fives to each other. Some return to their seats. Others stand where they are to watch. The next batter takes the count to three balls and one strike, and then sends a hard grounder just out of reach of the diving first baseman. Runners on first and second, two outs, and Mudville's best batter steps to the plate. This is where the game gets personal.

We **cut** to a **medium shot** of Casey, hometown favorite, stepping into the box, resplendent in his burgundy-and-white uniform. Casey should be filmed from a **low angle**. The first of Mudville's runs was scored earlier when Casey hit a double to the fence, driving in the runner who had been on second. The second run was scored when Casey hit a home run. Casey grins at the catcher, taps his bat on the plate, and goes through his pre-swing routine.

The Royals' coach calls time-out and walks to the mound for a conference. The camera **arcs** slowly through the stands, focused on the drama unfolding below. We watch from the crowd's **POV** as the umpire approaches to break up the mound visit.

Then we **cut** to a **medium two-shot** of the visiting pitcher talking with his coach. "I can do this. You've seen this guy swing—I know what I have to do. Besides, you know Diekman did that thing to his arm. There's no way he can close." The coach looks hard at the young man, and then we **pan** as he turns to look at the bullpen. The bullpen catcher, seeing the look and understanding the implied question, shakes his head.

"All right, but you better not screw this up," the coach says to the young man just as the umpire arrives at the mound. Umpire and coach turn and leave as one.

Cut to a **medium shot** of the pitcher, a young unknown who has managed to keep his pitch count low over the course of the game. He has only given up three hits over nine innings, but the triple and home run were both Casey's. Ordinarily, he would have been pulled in favor of the Royals' closer, but he has impressed the coach today, who rewarded him with the opportunity to finish. Besides, their closer had been spotty recently, as he recovered from a mild muscle strain, and given the bullpen catcher's reaction, he didn't have it today, either.

Cut to the catcher's **POV** as the first pitch comes in: a curveball, starting out toward the batter but dipping in for a strike. Casey never takes the bat off his shoulder. The crowd boos, but Casey holds up his hand and smiles. "Swing at a breaking ball on the first pitch? That ain't my style." **Close-ups** on Casey and the pitcher as the two consider each other. The next pitch is a cutter, low and outside. The umpire calls the strike, and the crowd goes wild. Casey nods, holds his hand up to quiet the crowd. He knew what was coming next. He's seen every pitch this kid could throw. In a **medium close-up**, Casey sneers at the young pitcher, adjusts his helmet, and steps deliberately back into the box. "Bring it," he mouths at the pitcher.

Cut to **close-up** of the pitcher, now from a slightly **lower angle**. **Cut** to **over his shoulder** as the pitcher receives the signs from his catcher. He shakes off the first, then the second. The catcher pauses, looks over at the dugout, then back to the pitcher. His fingers flash the sign.

Cut to catcher's **POV**. For the first time, the camera is completely static, reflecting the players' concentration. As the pitcher begins his delivery, everything goes to **slow motion**. **Extreme close-up** on Casey's hands gripping the bat, then back to the **POV** shot.

It was the one pitch Casey had not seen all day, the one pitch young number 39 had not thrown in a game all season, the one pitch he'd been working on for this moment. The camera **follows** as the knuckleball flutters aimlessly toward the plate. The crowd, as one, is on its feet. Casey realizes his mistake. He swings as hard as he can, but the ball flutters unmolested into the soft leather confines of the catcher's mitt. We see a small cloud of dust erupt from the pocket of the mitt as the ball slaps leather. Everything is silent—no **nondiegetic** music and only the muted **diegetic** sound of the ball hitting the mitt. For a moment, everything is silent. Then the crowd goes wild.

(1,373 words)

Okay, at 1,373 words, my treatment ran a bit long, at least in terms of this assignment. Honestly, as I got into telling my story, I found stopping at five-hundred words to be extremely difficult. And yes, my son is number 39; he is the young pitcher who strikes out Casey. I can do that, if I want to—after all, it is my story!

Sample Treatment 2

For this version, I'd like to do something a bit different: no baseball this time around. Looking back over my notes, I like the cross-country example. And given the context, as well as my intended outcome, "Casey at the Bat" will not work as a title, so I'll change that, too.

Not Today, Karen

We begin with **establishing shots** of a high school track stadium, and then **cut** to **medium shots** of runners milling around, stretching, getting ready for their events. As one athlete comes into view from the left side of the frame (left-to-right movement indicates progress), another calls her by name. "Hey, Casey! You running soon?" The athlete we now know as Casey nods and grins at her friend. She rolls her shoulders, trying to stay loose. Realizing her shoe is untied, she kneels down to tie it. **Cut** to Casey's **POV** of her hands tying her shoe.

A shadow falls across Casey. **Cut** to **high-angle POV shot** of Casey kneeling with her hand shading her eyes. **Cut** back to Casey's **POV** as we see her competitor standing there, **backlit**, the sun directly behind her head like a halo. "You sure you want to do this?" a voice sneers at Casey. We cannot get a clear view of the speaker's face. Cut back to **POV** of Casey, shielding her eyes and squinting. She does not answer. "Cat got your tongue, loser? Don't worry, save your strength. You're gonna need it." The voice has an edge to it. Casey's competitor walks off, laughing. **Cut** to **close-up** of Casey's reaction.

Then, over the intercom, we hear the announcer call Casey's event. We hear the **diegetic** sounds of a track meet in progress—crowd noise, an announcer, starting gun, running spikes on the track. Casey and her fellow competitors head toward the starting blocks in preparation for their event. **Cut** to **medium shot** of the starter. As the starter raises his pistol, we **track** back across the track, revealing the racers in the foreground on the right side of the screen. **Cut** behind the runners as the starter's pistol fires, and they head off down the track.

Casey's start is not great. She finds herself fourth of six as she makes her way down the front stretch. She fights the urge to panic—she has four laps to get into position. **Cut** to **medium shots** of Casey, her competitors around her, as she waits to make her move.

Casey slips ahead of one after another of her competitors. It is the final lap. Only one more runner in front of her: Karen, the girl who tried to intimidate her before the race. Karen, who always seems to win. Karen, for whom winning is not enough; she has to make everyone else feel like they lost. **Cut** to **medium close-up** of Casey as she remembers her training. We **flashback** as she remembers all those hours she spent preparing for this moment. She glances to her right, and we see a **POV** shot of her mom standing at the turn in her accustomed spot with a big poster board sign she made for the occasion. **Cut** back to a **close-up** of Casey's face, her brow furrowed in determination.

Cut to **long shot** from the finish line at track level of the runners making the final turn. Karen and Casey have pulled away from the pack. **Cut** to **medium shot** of Karen, smiling triumphantly, waving at the crowd. She does not realize Casey has managed to stay with her.

Suddenly, Casey makes her move. **Nondiegetic** triumphant sports music begins, softly at first, then growing in intensity. **Arc** slightly to Karen's side as we see Casey dig deep and give it everything she has. **Cut** to **close-up** of Karen's face as she finally realizes Casey is passing her and has the momentum with only yards remaining. **Cut** to **low-angle tracking shot** as the girls race the final yards. Casey is giving it everything she has, and Karen can't respond quickly enough. **Cut** to **eye-level tracking shot** from in front of the girls as Casey breaks the finish line first. **Medium close-up** on Casey. She is breathing heavily as her friends surround her. She grins, looks around, taking in the moment. "Not today, Karen. Not today."

(657 words)

Even without a baseball field, you can see the influence of Thayer's poem on this version of the story. Sure, Casey is female, and yes, baseball has been replaced with a track meet, but we still have Thayer's original admonition that pride goes before a fall. Of course, in this version, the stumbling block is not Casey's pride but Karen's. Casey is simply there and prepared to take advantage of that weakness. Karen has, in essence, switched places with Thayer's Casey.

And at 657 words, I wrote this one a bit closer to that 500-word mark. Notice the difference in detail; when you assign treatments, you will need to have in mind how much you want your students to write. Hopefully, these two examples will give you a good sense of how you'd like your students to structure their treatments. They should provide you with a measure of how in-depth you want them to go. Remember, the idea is to provide a synopsis of the story and a general idea of how the story will play out on-screen. Later your students will use these treatments to write scripts.

STEP 5: Translate Treatments into Scripts

The next step in the process is to have your students exchange treatments in preparation for translating one another's treatments into scripts. Exchanging treatments shows your students just how much detail they need to include for others to understand their creative vision. No conversations are allowed; every important detail must be on the page. Your students may be surprised when the script version of their story varies from the treatment they wrote, and they will eventually get to see what their classmates have done, which will provide a great moment for formal or informal reflection.

When it comes to writing these scripts, students should understand they still have creative freedom. Granted, they should honor the framework of the treatment they were given—scriptwriters will not be making wholesale changes—but those treatments, as a rule, allow a writer lots of room to flesh out the story. Scriptwriters will need to add dialogue, for instance. And most of that dialogue, aside from benchmark comments, will not be in the treatment.

Remind students we are writing spec scripts, and there are five elements they need to include (see Lesson 3, "Spec Scripts: Transforming a Classic for the Silver Screen"):

1. **Scene Heading or Slug Line**: This line informs the audience when and where the action is taking place.
2. **Action**: The action is simply the explanation of what is going on and what the camera sees.
3. **Character Name**: Yeah, you've got this.
4. **Dialogue**: This is what the character says.

5. **Parentheticals**: This information lets the actor know what they are doing and how to deliver the line.

To be fair, establish a limit as to how much script you want your students to write. Two to four pages, for example, is plenty and should not overwhelm your students. I also allow my students, who are scripting only two to four minutes of the story, to begin at whatever point they choose. Once they have finished their scripts, have them exchange the scripts once more.

STEP 6: Translate Scripts into Storyboards

At this point, we have progressed from inspiration ("Casey at the Bat" by Ernest Lawrence Thayer) to treatment to script. The next iteration in the process is the creation of storyboards. When I have my students storyboard, we actually combine two elements: **storyboards** and the **shot list**.

Technically, the storyboard is simply an image. The storyboard artist begins with an empty box the same size and shape as the movie screen. Then the artist draws the shot, sometimes including arrows to indicate camera movement but not writing any dialogue inside the box. The storyboard artist draws only what the audience can see on-screen.

The shot list refers to the technical information that enables the cinematographer to achieve the shot in question. Typically, there are eight details included in a shot list (see Lesson 4, "The Filmmaker's Toolkit: From Building Blocks to Works of Art"): (1) shot number, (2) composition, (3) framing, (4) angle, (5) camera movement, (6) lighting, (7) sound, and (8) the editing technique used to get to the next shot. I have my students do the storyboards and shot list together, in part because my students who feel they have no artistic ability often find a measure of comfort in being able to explain what is in the shot they just drew.

As an option, consider having your students do these steps separately with the shot list first. Then they will be able to see if they are describing the images adequately.

STEP 7: Reflect on the Process (Part 1)

Now that you have gone all the way from inspiration to treatment to script to storyboards, what was surprising to you? What was the most fun? What was most challenging? What did you do well? What will you do differently next time? What have you learned? Be prepared to share your thoughts with your classmates.

STEP 8: Explore the Ramifications of Being "Based on a True Story"

While "Casey at the Bat" was inspired by baseball in the late 1800s, the story itself is not true. Consequently, a director should not feel obligated to retell the story in a specific way. Ultimately, the poem is a morality play in verse form: *Don't let your pride be your downfall.* Want Casey to play basketball instead of baseball? No harm, no foul. But what happens when films are made to reflect actual events? How obligated should a director feel to stay close to actual historical events?

We have all seen films that are "the untold story" or "based on real events" or "inspired by a true story." But what does that actually mean? The truth is these phrases are nothing but marketing gimmicks. There are precious few, if any, actual rules about how and when a director may use these lines. They are effective, though, in helping audiences suspend their disbelief and buy into a story. Consider how much scarier horror films become, for example, when you believe the events really happened. *If it happened to her*, you can tell yourself, *it could happen to me!* "Casey at the Bat" might as well be said to be "based on a true story," as I have no doubt people played baseball in the late 1800s, and that at some point, a gathered crowd was disappointed by a star player striking out. But when the story really did happen, when real people were involved, how obligated should the filmmaker be in reporting the truth?

Different directors obviously have different perspectives when answering that particular question. *The Greatest Showman* (2017), for example, directed by Michael Gracey, was based on the life story of P. T. Barnum. The main character goes by the same name, and many of the events are recognizable facsimiles of events in P. T. Barnum's life. Yet the film takes tremendous liberties with historical facts. *The Revenant* (2015), directed by Alejandro G. Iñárritu, presents the thinly documented true story of Hugh Glass, yet it fails to adhere to the accuracy of what facts are known. *Braveheart* (1995), directed by Mel Gibson, is another great film that also happens to be a veritable train wreck of historical inaccuracies. All of these films present "true" stories that are radically different from documented fact.

On the other hand, *Psycho* (1960), directed by Alfred Hitchcock, was based on the novel *Psycho* (1959), written by Robert Bloch. The novel, in turn, was based on the true story of killer Ed Gein. Yet the main character's name was different, and many of the events of Gein's life were greatly altered. Neither the novel nor the film pretended to be a true story. *The Patriot* (2000), directed by Roland Emmerich, was loosely based on the real stories of several American Revolutionary War patriots, with a few fictional British atrocities thrown in for good measure. The main character had a completely original name and backstory, and the film did not present itself as a true story. *Jaws* (1975), directed by Steven Spielberg, was based on the novel by Peter Benchley (1974). While the film was also influenced by a series of shark attacks that occurred off the coast of New Jersey in 1916, the novel was shaped more by an article in a newspaper recounting the story of a 4,500-pound great white shark caught by Frank Mundus in 1964 off the coast of Long Island. Neither the novel nor the film pretended to be anything more than fiction, however.

Then there are films of historical importance, films that, if the facts were altered, doing so would be considered a grave disservice to the story. Consider the public outcry when Michael Bay added a love triangle to his version of *Pearl Harbor* (2001), perhaps thinking the general public would be unable to find anything that might otherwise hold their attention in the shocking sneak attack that propelled the United States into war in the Pacific. Not every director makes this mistake, of course. *Apollo 13* (1995), directed by Ron Howard, *12 Years a Slave* (2013), directed by Steve McQueen, and *Selma* (2014), directed by Ava DuVernay, are all considered quite historically accurate. Along these lines, *42* (2013), directed by Brian Helgeland—the story of how Jackie Robinson became the first African American to play in Major League Baseball—is likewise a notably accurate portrayal of actual historical events.

Branch Rickey's decision to sign Jack Roosevelt Robinson to the Brooklyn Dodgers in 1947 signaled a watershed moment not only for baseball but for the country as well. Robinson's jersey number, 42, remains the only number to be retired across all of Major League Baseball to this day. No new players may wear the number, save on April 15 each year, the day Jackie Robinson broke the color barrier in baseball, when everyone on every team dons number 42 in his honor. No one else in baseball—not Cy Young, not Ted Williams, not Babe Ruth—is honored in this way. Suffice it to say, Jackie Robinson's story is suitably powerful that any sort of embellishment or alteration would not only be unnecessary but also disrespectful to his memory.

STEP 9: Examine a Scene from 42, the Story of Jackie Robinson

To that end, let's take a look at a scene that occurs early on in the film, when Jackie Robinson was playing for the Kansas City Monarchs against the Birmingham Black Barons, both teams in the Negro League.

42
Written by
Brian Helgeland

2   EXT. RICKWOOD FIELD – BIRMINGHAM, ALABAMA – NIGHT   2

The big Birmingham Black Barons CATCHER behind the plate as Kansas City Monarchs JOHN SCOTT stands at bat. The catcher's attention on the RUNNER DANCING off first. Stomping a foot, feinting, hard to see clearly in the glare of the lights.

>   CATCHER
>   Where'd you learn to move like that, runner?!
>   At dime a dance night?! Stay quiet!

INSERT: <u>Birmingham, Alabama. April 8, 1945</u>.   *

On the first pitch the runner takes off. The catcher fires to second. See it from his POV as the runner slides in "SAFE!"
A foot on the bag, the runner dusts off, heckles the catcher:

>   RUNNER
>   Is that the best you got?! Huh?! I'm going to steal nine,
>   ten bases today! You better start counting!

The catcher frowns. Standing, we see he is a big, big man.

>   CATCHER
>   (Alabaman)
>   Where's your shortstop from?

>   JOHN SCOTT
>   (Louisianan)
>   California.

>   CATCHER
>   He's got a mouth on him.

Shaking his head, the catcher gets back in his crouch, signals the PITCHER. On the wind-up, the Runner is off again. The catcher fires to THIRD: "Safe!"

>   RUNNER
> You got a rag arm, catcher!
>
>   CATCHER
> Steal home! You'll find out what kind of arm I got!
>
>   RUNNER
> Okay, I'm coming!

The Catcher looks over at Scott who chuckles.

>   CATCHER
> California, huh?
>   (Scott nods)
> Well California here he goes, if he comes down here.

The Catcher gets back down in his squat. Signals the pitcher: fastball. Scott digs in, ready. The runner dancing off third. Here comes the wind-up…

The Runner takes off even as the pitcher fires it in. The Birmingham Catcher receives it. As the Runner slides –

The Catcher intentionally drives his glove, the ball and both hands into the runner's face – WHALLOP! Sound drops as we're knocked flat senseless along with the runner.

ON HIM now as he tries to push himself up from the dirt. A close look at JACK ROOSEVELT ROBINSON. A born battler, he shakes out the cobwebs, finally lurches to his feet, looks to the UMPIRE. He never heard the call.

>   JACK
> What was I?

The umpire passes one hand over the other: *Safe*.

The scene is included in order to show Jackie's prowess on the baseball field. After making it to first base, he steals second base, third base, and finally home, much to the opposing catcher's chagrin. The dialogue may or may not be historically exact, but it is certainly indicative of the sort of conversations in which Robinson would often engage with opposing players.

The scene occurs just before the five-minute mark, plays out over twenty-three shots, and clocks in at just under forty-nine seconds long. It is an action sequence, which accounts for the high number of shots per minute. Before watching the scene, have your students read the excerpt from the script. As they read it the first time, have them imagine what the scene looks like as it plays out in their minds. Once they have an idea of how the scene looks, let them know they will be asked to storyboard ten shots from the scene.

STEP 10: Research the "Truth"

Given that we are committed to a historically accurate portrayal, before students can storyboard the scene, they will need to do some research, just as actual art departments, costume designers, set designers, and directors have to do. As you will eventually view this scene with your students and analyze its historical validity, they should not simply look up shots from the film. Instead, help them develop a list of details they will need to research. Feel free to have them use the handout I have provided with any additions you feel appropriate (see Figure 7.2).

STEP 11: Use Our Research to Storyboard a Faithful Adaptation

The next step is to plan a few shots (see Figure 7.3). Have students storyboard three shots they would use during this sequence, including shot list information. As they consider which shots to include, encourage them to compose shots that include some of the historical details they found. Including such details helps ground the story in its time and setting for the audience and reinforces the idea for your students that they are creating a faithful adaptation.

STEP 12: Evaluate a Scene from 42 for Historical Accuracy

Once students have read the script and developed their shots, let them see the film version. The scene in question occurs just before the five-minute mark and is very short, so you can show the scene more than once, should you wish. Showing scenes like this one at least three times allows students to watch first for understanding and then for analysis and evaluation.

When students have finished conducting their research and analyzing the clip, have them write an essay to evaluate the historical accuracy of the scene.

Historical Research for *42*   Name_____

Directions: *You are to conduct research regarding the historical context of the film* 42, *which looks at the events surrounding how Jackie Robinson broke Major League Baseball's color barrier. To ensure that you plan a scene that is as historically accurate as possible, you will research a series of relevant questions. You will want to create a series of Google Slides to display your findings. Whenever possible, include multiple pictures for each question.*

1. In what year does this scene take place?
2. What did the Kansas City Monarchs' uniform look like?
3. What did the Birmingham Black Barons' uniform look like?
4. What sort of protective gear did batters wear during this time?
5. What sort of gear did catchers wear during this time?
6. What would a catcher's mitt of this time look like?
7. What would a fielder's glove of this time look like?
8. What gear did umpires wear/use?
9. What did the fields where Negro League teams played look like?
10. What did the stands where Negro League teams played look like?
11. What did baseballs of this time look like (modern red stitches or the older red-and-blue stitches)?
12. What did the bases look like?
13. Would there have been lights at a baseball field during this time?
14. Who would have attended a Negro League baseball game?
15. How many fans would have been in attendance?
16. What sort of snacks would patrons have eaten at a game?
17. What time of day would games have been played?
18. What did Jackie Robinson look like?
19. What did John Scott look like?

Once they have found the answers to the questions you gave them, you may have your students create Google Docs or Slides that include photographs of their findings. Once students have a clear understanding of these questions, only then will they be able to accurately plan out a shot sequence. And while some of these details may not even make it onto the screen, a good filmmaker must always be prepared.

FIGURE 7.2. Assignment to help students conduct historical research about the film *42*.

Story:_____ Name:_____

Screenwriter:_____

Shot#_____   Shot#_____   Shot#_____

_____   _____   _____
_____   _____   _____
_____   _____   _____
_____   _____   _____
_____   _____   _____
_____   _____   _____
_____   _____   _____
_____   _____   _____

Notes on shot selection
Did the director use any of my shot ideas? Any really interesting shots? Any surprises? Any shots I wish they'd used? etc.

Notes on historical accuracy
Did I see historical details I found in my research? Were any details different from what I discovered? Was anything left out?

FIGURE 7.3. Planning sheet for shot descriptions.

Remind them that they are to make specific claims about the portrayal supported by specific evidence from the scene and followed by an explanation of that evidence. I have provided a rubric for this purpose if you like (see Figure 7.4).

That sense of creativity and freedom should, of course, extend to you, the teacher, as well. Should you prefer, have your students write on a different but related topic. For example, have students write about the ethics involved with telling a "true" story about the lengths directors must go to in order to get historical details right, or even about what the standard should be for historical accuracy in order for a film to be advertised as "based on a true story."

As a resource, you may also want to check out the YouTube channel "History Buffs." This channel is devoted to a close examination of the accuracy in historical films, and it might help your students understand what it means to examine a film's historical credibility. Be aware, however, that the host's language can occasionally get a bit rough, so you may want to preview the videos before showing them to your class.

STEP 13: Discuss the Ethics of Storytelling

We now find ourselves at the perfect point to discuss an incredibly important topic relative to our field of study: the ethics of storytelling. Right or wrong, many people's sense of history is shaped by the stories they see play out on-screen. They know they are viewing constructs, but even so, they tend to attach a certain credibility to these stories, whether these appear on the silver screen, on a television show, or in a commercial. All too often, audiences believe that "based on a true story" means the story they are seeing is fact. And as storytellers, we cannot expect our audience to conduct the relevant research beforehand, thereby dismissing our own responsibility regarding historical accuracy. Take the opportunity to discuss with your students why changing elements of the narrative of a poem can be drastically different from changing elements of actual historical events, especially when the story is this important.

STEP 14: Reflect on the Process (Part 2)

Having explored the idea of directorial prerogative, what responsibility does a director have, if any, in terms of accuracy to the source material? Are there situations in which directors should feel obligated to tell a story a certain way? And if so, does that sense of obligation leave room for creativity? How, if at all, will this unit affect the way you choose to tell your own stories? Be prepared to share your thoughts with your classmates.

Film Analysis Essay Rubric   Name_____

Film/Scene:_____

Directions: *Use the following descriptors to determine how well you addressed the prompt.*

Introduction				
The introduction grabs the reader's attention and presents a clear thesis.	The introduction is mostly solid, and the thesis is okay but not clear and compelling.	The introduction is topically relevant but lacks a clear thesis.	The introduction is largely underdeveloped and lacks a thesis.	The introduction is missing.
Body				
The essay does a masterful job of making specific claims, providing clear evidence from the film, and offering an analysis of that evidence.	The essay makes good claims and does provide evidence in support of those claims, but the explanation of that evidence could still be stronger.	The essay does a decent job of making claims, but the claims may be fairly obvious or unsupported by evidence.	The essay makes weak or very obvious claims and lacks supporting evidence or explanation.	The essay makes specific claims and provides evidence from the film, but the analysis is weak or lacking.
Conclusion				
The essay has a strong conclusion that leaves the reader with no doubt as to the author's stance on the issue.	The conclusion is mostly solid, but it is not clear and compelling.	The conclusion shows promise but has not been fully developed.	The conclusion is largely underdeveloped and lacks clarity and focus.	The conclusion is missing.
Grammar and Mechanics				
The essay demonstrates a strong mastery of correct grammar and mechanics.	The essay demonstrates a good mastery of correct grammar and mechanics.	The essay demonstrates a moderate mastery of correct grammar and mechanics.	The essay demonstrates a weak mastery of correct grammar and mechanics.	The essay demonstrates little or no grasp of proper grammar and mechanics.

FIGURE 7.4. Potential rubric for the essay on film analysis.

Standards Addressed in This Unit

Conventions of Standard English
CCSS.ELA-LITERACY.CCRA.L.1
CCSS.ELA-LITERACY.CCRA.L.2
Knowledge of Language
CCSS.ELA-LITERACY.CCRA.L.3
Vocabulary Acquisition and Use
CCSS.ELA-LITERACY.CCRA.L.6
Key Ideas and Details
CCSS.ELA-LITERACY.CCRA.R.1
CCSS.ELA-LITERACY.CCRA.R.3
Craft and Structure
CCSS.ELA-LITERACY.CCRA.R.4
CCSS.ELA-LITERACY.CCRA.R.5
CCSS.ELA-LITERACY.CCRA.R.6
Integration of Knowledge and Ideas
CCSS.ELA-LITERACY.CCRA.R.7
Range of Reading and Level of Text Complexity
CCSS.ELA-LITERACY.CCRA.R.10
Comprehension and Collaboration
CCSS.ELA-LITERACY.CCRA.SL.1
CCSS.ELA-LITERACY.CCRA.SL.2
Presentation of Knowledge and Ideas
CCSS.ELA-LITERACY.CCRA.SL.4
CCSS.ELA-LITERACY.CCRA.SL.5
CCSS.ELA-LITERACY.CCRA.SL.6
Text Types and Purposes
CCSS.ELA-LITERACY.CCRA.W.2
CCSS.ELA-LITERACY.CCRA.W.3
Production and Distribution
CCSS.ELA-LITERACY.CCRA.W.4
CCSS.ELA-LITERACY.CCRA.W.5
CCSS.ELA-LITERACY.CCRA.W.6
Range of Writing
CCSS.ELA-LITERACY.CCRA.W.10

Othello: Getting More from the Moor of Venice

⊚ Lesson Plan

Essential Question
Given the same source text, how can different directors adapt that text to tell the same story in completely different ways?

Objective
Students will develop a plan for the production of a scene from *Othello*, by William Shakespeare, and then evaluate their choices in comparison with several film versions of the same scene.

Central Texts
Several different film versions of a pivotal scene from *Othello*

Agenda

STEP 1: Anticipatory Quickwrite

STEP 2: Read the Excerpt from *Othello*, Act V, Scene 2, in Which Othello, Believing His Wife Desdemona to Have Been Unfaithful, Kills Her

STEP 3: Work in Small Groups to Translate the Script into Modern English

STEP 4: Research What a Moor during This Period Would Likely Have Worn

STEP 5: Design the Set in Which This Scene Plays Out

STEP 6: Provide the Stage Directions Shakespeare Left Out

STEP 7: Analyze at Least Two Film Versions of This Scene

STEP 8: Write an Evaluation of the Different Film Versions

STEP 9: Reflect on the Process

Differentiation

Depending on the time frame in which you are working, you could combine steps two through six and have students complete these steps in a jigsaw format, each small group being responsible for one step. If you choose this option, then you may also have each group observe and evaluate only the portion of the presentation on which they worked while viewing and comparing the different film versions. For example, the group that designed sets could evaluate the set design, and the group that researched Moorish clothing might only observe and evaluate Othello's costume.

If you assign these groups, ensure that each group has a comparable number of students. If you allow students to form their own groups, you can observe which part of the production process individual students enjoy most, which may allow you to create groups later, should you like.

If your students have already split off into production groups, you may simply choose to have them work in those groups, using this activity as yet another team-building exercise, as the members of the group will each be responsible for a different aspect of the filmmaking process when working on their small-group film projects. Ultimately, these choices are your prerogative.

Resources

While you could certainly adapt this unit to fit a different play, Shakespeare's writings work particularly well, given the lack of stage directions and the availability of multiple versions of pretty much every play. Should you stay with *Othello*, consider using any of the following (be aware that some of these performances have drawn criticism for having white actors portray people of color):

O (2001), directed by Tim Blake Nelson, starring Mekhi Phifer as Odin "O" James and Julia Stiles as Desi Brable

Othello (1995), directed by Oliver Parker, starring Laurence Fishburne as Othello and Irène Jacob as Desdemona

Othello (1965), directed by Stuart Burge, starring Laurence Olivier as Othello and Maggie Smith as Desdemona

Othello (1951), directed by Orson Welles, starring Orson Welles as Othello and Suzanne Cloutier as Desdemona

Otello (1986), directed by Franco Zeffirelli, starring Plácido Domingo as Otello and Katia Ricciarelli as Desdemona

Othello (2001 TV movie), directed by Geoffrey Sax, starring Eamonn Walker as John Othello and Keeley Hawes as Dessie Brabant

Othello (1981 TV movie), directed by Jonathan Miller, starring Sir Anthony Hopkins as General Othello and Penelope Wilton as Desdemona

YouTube video resources:

"Macbeth. Compare and Contrast: Opening scenes from five adaptations" by Jacquie Sexton (https://youtu.be/UWyegNZOqQE)

"Othello: Iago's Soliloquy" by Robert Dukes (https://youtu.be/teMAAkG66Vk)

Suggested Timeline
One week

Lesson 8

Othello: Getting More from the Moor of Venice

Entertain, but also, give the viewer something to think about.
—Abhijit Naskar, *The Film Testament*

STEP 1: Anticipatory Quickwrite

When comparing multiple stage or film versions of the same story, what makes one version better than another? What is the relationship between interpretation and accuracy? Be prepared to share your thoughts with your classmates.

Plays, by and large, are meant to be experienced rather than read. Such is the assertion of Sir Ian McKellen. "It's not what ordinary people should have to bother with. That's for the actors to do. The plays weren't written to be read, they were written to be spoken out loud and acted and for us as an audience to watch" (Moreland). And yet so many of us, as teachers, take the approach that to truly appreciate the work, students must read it rather than view it. And if we do show "the" film version, we do so as a way of rewarding students for staying conscious while we read it in class. For their part, many times students are just happy to know "what it's supposed to look like."

McKellen contends that "[t]oo many of us are put off Shakespeare at school by having to stare at pages of blank verse wondering what it's all about." By the time we finish struggling through the reading and prepare to view the film or play, the experience has been ruined. "The idea of any children in their early teens with a teacher who has not quite worked out how to do this, so that it just comes down to reading and reading, perhaps speaking it out loud, maybe even standing up and acting out a little bit. . . . [I]t worries me that you might easily be put off Shakespeare for life if that's how you start out" (Moreland). And indeed, some students have felt this way.

Certainly, Shakespeare was written to be experienced rather than read. Audiences did not fill the Globe Theatre to experience the exquisite joy of deciphering printed text en masse. Yet when introducing students to Shakespeare's work, what alternative remains?

Using film to build student literacy presents twenty-first-century educators with interesting opportunities. Students are used to being the audience. *Here is the story. These are the characters. This is what happens. This is why that happens.* But film allows students to take the role of storyteller. This paradigm shift lets students engage with text in entirely new ways.

This unit invites students to engage with Shakespeare's *Othello*—a great choice, given that Shakespeare is notoriously skimpy with stage directions. In this unit, as always, the emphasis is on the audience. What do we want the audience to think, feel, or expect? What connections do we want them to make? And what can we do to ensure that these processes happen? See Figure 8.1 for a director's form that can help students think through their vision.

STEP 2: Read the Excerpt from Othello, Act V, Scene 2, In Which Othello, Believing His Wife Desdemona to Have Been Unfaithful, Kills Her

Shakespeare is a great choice to use for this activity because he provides very little in the way of stage directions. Should the actor stand here? Should the actor deliver the line just so? Such considerations are left to those presenting the story. And these choices combine to send messages—some subtle and some not so subtle—that serve to shape the audience's experience of the piece in terms of both understanding and enjoying it.

Our objective is to enable students to plan out a scene and present to an audience the same way professional film directors do. To achieve this, we are not interested in reading the entire play. Instead, we want our students to take a section of the print text—in particular, text that proves difficult for most traditional English students to decipher—and plan a nonprint presentation of that text to better enable an audience to understand what is going on and why (see Figure 8.2). Every choice students make will have meaning and will therefore serve to shape audience perception.

STEP 3: Work in Small Groups to Translate the Script into Modern English

If students are to make directorial choices, they must have a basic understanding of what is going on, and the art of translating the text into modern English is a valuable experience to achieve that. Students may not get every nuance of expression, as most students are struggling just to figure out what is happening. Only after they grasp this can they begin to appreciate the finer points of nuance, implication, and double entendre. And at that point, students are ready to begin shaping the perceptions of their audience.

TEXT:_____ NAME:_____
DATE:_____

DIRECTIONS FOR STEP 1: Given a sample text, think about how you would film it. Then write your ideas in the appropriate boxes below:

Versions to Be Compared	Actions/Gestures *How would your character move? What gestures would you have your character make? What expressions would the audience see on your character's face?*	Vocal Inflection *How would your character deliver the lines in question? Would your character speak loudly, softly, angrily, sadly, quickly, slowly, etc.?*	Costumes/Props *Even a character's costume can have meaning, so what will your character be wearing? What message do you want your character's costume to convey?*	Music/Sound Effects *What music or sound effects should accompany this scene? Be as specific as possible—sound is a powerful tool when it comes to influencing your audience.*
VERSION 1: My Interpretation				
VERSION 2:				
VERSION 3:				
VERSION 4:				

DIRECTIONS FOR STEP 2: Now that you have had the opportunity to compare these different versions, you have undoubtedly noticed some differences. Go through your chart and circle the interpretation you prefer for each of the four categories (Actions/Gestures, Vocal Inflection, Costume/Props, Music/Sound Effects). Be prepared to discuss your ideas.

FIGURE 8.1. Director's form for planning a scene.

Othello Act V, Scene 2

Directions: *In the respective columns, note how the actors should deliver their lines in terms of vocal inflection and volume, as well as any actions, gestures, or facial expressions they should use.*

VOCAL INFLECTION, VOLUME	TEXT	ACTIONS, GESTURES, FACIAL EXPRESSIONS
	Othello It is the cause, it is the cause, my soul,— Let me not name it to you, you chaste stars!— It is the cause. Yet I'll not shed her blood; Nor scar that whiter skin of hers than snow, And smooth as monumental alabaster. Yet she must die, else she'll betray more men. Put out the light, and then put out the light: If I quench thee, thou flaming minister, I can again thy former light restore, Should I repent me: but once put out thy light, Thou cunning'st pattern of excelling nature, I know not where is that Promethean heat That can thy light relume. When I have pluck'd the rose, I cannot give it vital growth again. It must needs wither: I'll smell it on the tree. [*Kissing her*] Ah balmy breath, that dost almost persuade Justice to break her sword! One more, one more. Be thus when thou art dead, and I will kill thee, And love thee after. One more, and this the last: So sweet was ne'er so fatal. I must weep, But they are cruel tears: this sorrow's heavenly; It strikes where it doth love. She wakes. **Desdemona** Who's there? Othello? **Othello** Ay. Desdemona. **Desdemona** Will you come to bed, my lord? **Othello** Have you pray'd to-night, Desdemona? **Desdemona** Ay, my lord. **Othello** If you bethink yourself of any crime Unreconciled as yet to heaven and grace, Solicit for it straight. **Desdemona** Alas, my lord, what do you mean by that?	

FIGURE 8.2. Excerpt from *Othello* to help students model thinking like a director.

VOCAL INFLECTION, VOLUME	TEXT	ACTIONS, GESTURES, FACIAL EXPRESSIONS
	Othello Well, do it, and be brief; I will walk by: I would not kill thy unprepared spirit; No; heaven forfend! I would not kill thy soul.	
	Desdemona Talk you of killing?	
	Othello Ay, I do.	
	Desdemona Then heaven have mercy on me!	
	Othello Amen, with all my heart!	
	Desdemona If you say so, I hope you will not kill me.	
	Othello Hum!	
	Desdemona And yet I fear you; for you are fatal then When your eyes roll so: why I should fear I know not, Since guiltiness I know not; but yet I feel I fear.	
	Othello Think on thy sins.	
	Desdemona They are loves I bear to you.	
	Desdemona That death's unnatural that kills for loving. Alas, why gnaw you so your nether lip? Some bloody passion shakes your very frame: These are portents; but yet I hope, I hope, They do not point on me.	
	Othello Peace, and be still!	
	Desdemona I will so. What's the matter?	
	Othello That handkerchief which I so loved and gave thee Thou gavest to Cassio.	
	Desdemona No, by my life and soul! Send for the man, and ask him.	
	Othello Sweet soul, take heed, Take heed of perjury; thou art on thy deathbed.	
	Desdemona Ay, but not yet to die.	

VOCAL INFLECTION, VOLUME	TEXT	ACTIONS, GESTURES, FACIAL EXPRESSIONS
	Othello Yes, presently: Therefore confess thee freely of thy sin; For to deny each article with oath Cannot remove nor choke the strong conception That I do groan withal. Thou art to die. **Desdemona** Then Lord have mercy on me! **Othello** I say, amen. **Desdemona** And have you mercy too! I never did Offend you in my life; never loved Cassio But with such general warranty of heaven As I might love: I never gave him token. **Othello** By heaven, I saw my handkerchief in's hand. O perjured woman! Thou dost stone my heart, And makest me call what I intend to do A murder, which I thought a sacrifice: I saw the handkerchief. **Desdemona** He found it then; I never gave it him: send for him hither; Let him confess a truth. **Othello** He hath confess'd. **Desdemona** What, my lord? **Othello** That he hath used thee. **Desdemona** How? Unlawfully? **Othello** Ay. **Desdemona** He will not say so. **Othello** No, his mouth is stopp'd; Honest Iago hath ta'en order for't. **Desdemona** O! my fear interprets: What, is he dead? **Othello** Had all his hairs been lives, my great revenge Had stomach for them all.	

VOCAL INFLECTION, VOLUME	TEXT	ACTIONS, GESTURES, FACIAL EXPRESSIONS
	Desdemona Alas! he is betray'd and I undone. **Othello** Out, strumpet! weep'st thou for him to my face? **Desdemona** O, banish me, my lord, but kill me not! **Othello** Down, strumpet! **Desdemona** Kill me to-morrow: let me live to-night! **Othello** Nay, if you strive— **Desdemona** But half an hour! **Othello** Being done, there is no pause. **Desdemona** But while I say one prayer! **Othello** It is too late. [*He stifles her*]	

STEP 4: Research What a Moor during This Period Would Likely Have Worn

Othello, like many of Shakespeare's plays, is a retelling of a much earlier story. Scholars tend to agree that the primary source for *Othello* was the novella *Hecatommithi*, written in 1565 by the Italian author Cinthio. Leo Africanus's *A Geographical History of Africa* also served to help Shakespeare flesh out his version of the story (Mabillard). Additionally, that novella may have been based on even earlier events.

If we consider the play to be set in Venice during the mid- to late 1500s and accept the political climate between Venice and Turkey of the time, then we at least have parameters to help fuel our research. Much as today, however, not every Moor would have dressed the same way. Students must weigh their options and make choices, understanding that costumes are one of the first visual cues audiences get and therefore help them begin to form opinions about the characters on-screen.

STEP 5: Design the Set in Which This Scene Plays Out

What does Desdemona's bedchamber look like? Does the scene take place in a castle? Is it in some sort of mansion or villa? This room will go a long way toward helping the audience understand the historical context of the play. Potentially, the design could also help the audience understand the mood of the scene and could allow for some creative cinematography.

STEP 6: Provide the Stage Directions Shakespeare Left Out

Considering what the characters are saying, how might they have sounded? In the margins of the text, have students write notes about how the actors' voices should sound. Does Othello whisper? Does he shout? Does he sound angry or sad? How does Desdemona respond? Is she offended? Afraid? Confused? In all likelihood, there will be variation. Have students write their observations next to the text in question on the template provided.

This is one of the most emotionally charged scenes in the play. Even so, the characters will not be yelling at each other the entire time. There will be ups and downs, just as in any conversation. The volume will change; the pitch will change. Even the tempo at which the characters speak will change. Each character will progress through a range of emotions, and this progression will serve to keep the audience engaged. And as Shakespeare did not generally include stage directions, students must make choices based on their understanding of what the characters are saying.

How do the characters behave? Is Othello standing or sitting? How is Desdemona responding? How does each character move? How do their facial expressions change?

As the characters speak, they are unlikely to simply stand there facing each other. Their facial expressions will change as they react to what the other has just said. They may pace, walk over to look out a window, sit down, stand up—the choices are myriad. Even the climax offers a choice: How does Othello "stifle" Desdemona?

STEP 7: Analyze at Least Two Film Versions of This Scene

There are quite a few versions of nearly every Shakespeare play, so students can and should view and analyze multiple versions of the same scene. Many students look at "the" film as the definitive version of a play, but by viewing and analyzing multiple versions, they can begin to understand that each director is simply presenting their vision, highlighting different aspects of the characters' personalities, establishing subtly different moods, and making different allusions. While viewing each version, students should use the observation template to take notes regarding each director's choices.

As students observe different takes on the scene, they will notice each version has a distinct personality. The actors dress differently, move differently, and deliver their lines differently. Even the sets vary greatly. So, which version is the definitive take on what Shakespeare intended? The truth is none of them is. Or maybe all of them are. We cannot ask Shakespeare, so we cannot know. Instead, which version do your students prefer?

As they begin to pick out what distinguishes each version from the others, have your students identify which version's set they like best. Have them do the same with the costumes, the vocal delivery, the blocking, and anything else they notice. In which version are the costumes the best? In which version are the vocal inflections best? How does the blocking change, and which approach is most effective? What is the cumulative effect of these differences? How would audiences perceive each version differently?

Experience has shown that while students may prefer one version over another, they often do not choose that version as the best for every category. For example, students may prefer the vocal delivery in one version but the costuming in another. Such differentiation is clear evidence of critical thinking.

STEP 8: Write an Evaluation of the Different Film Versions

Having now assessed multiple film versions for actions/gestures, vocal inflection, costume/props, and music/sound effects, students should begin to see that these versions do not represent "truth" but simply different interpretations or impressions of who the characters are and what is happening. Thus, students should also begin to see that their own interpretations have merit, too. Reader response criticism would argue that meaning lies in the conversation between audience and text. Having thus broken down the scene, consider having students pursue a written scene analysis. What is Shakespeare saying here, for example, and how might a director underscore Shakespeare's message via the proper use of these staging elements at their disposal?

Which version, overall, was most effective? Which director came nearest to achieving the playwright's creative vision? As a side note, you may want to have students discuss their ideas in small groups before committing their thoughts to writing. These small-group discussions might help students form and evaluate their opinions before writing about them, thus becoming part of the prewriting process and perhaps even providing some validation should others in their group share similar opinions.

In any event, wrapping up the unit by students putting their thoughts in writing gives them a framework in which to make up their minds about the scene they have studied. The goal, of course, is to create a more informed audience, one who will henceforth evaluate print text with a more critical eye.

To save you some time and give you a heads-up as to what your students may observe, *O* is a modern take on the play. Othello becomes Odin "O" James, a star basketball player. This version would be akin to using the 1996 version of *Romeo + Juliet*, directed by Baz Luhrmann. The dialogue—and obviously the context—are quite different from what Shakespeare wrote. This version is interesting primarily for showing students how directors can make changes to the print texts on which they base their films.

Oliver Parker's 1995 version has Laurence Fishburne in the title role. Othello wears silks, has a shaved (and tattooed) head, and wears gold jewelry. He is incredibly refined and worldly, and while he believes he must kill Desdemona, the decision quite clearly breaks his heart. As the scene ends, Othello smothers Desdemona with her pillow. Your students will notice that while Desdemona puts up a fight to live, she still caresses his cheek before dying.

Stuart Burge's 1965 version is actually a filmed stage version with Laurence Olivier as Othello. Laurence Olivier, you should be aware, plays the role in full-body makeup that makes him appear to be an odd shade of brownish-green. Your students may even notice some of the makeup seems to rub off on Desdemona's sheets during the murder scene. In this version, Othello wears what appears to be an undertunic—perhaps his bedclothes—and jewelry that comes off more as shackles, as if Othello is a slave to circumstance.

Orson Welles cast himself as Othello in his 1951 version. In this black-and-white rendition, Othello wears heavy furs and a thick, chain-like necklace. This Othello, it would seem, is more bestial than refined. He comes across as more angry and determined than heartbroken. Students may also notice the high-contrast lighting, a vestige of the German Expressionist–inspired style of his 1941 *Citizen Kane*. As an added bonus, the "deathbed" in which Desdemona finds herself does, in fact, resemble a burial crypt. And as the scene resolves, Othello kills Desdemona by placing her sheet over her face before leaning in to kiss her. Either the sheet is enough to suffocate her, or Othello actually sucks the air from her lungs. Either way, she dies as they embrace.

If you are looking for another scene to compare, the scene in which Iago attempts to kill Cassio is interesting in this version. Due to logistical problems, the costumes were delayed, which made filming problematic. Welles eventually decided to have his actors (including the extras) swipe the robes from their hotel rooms. He then filmed the scene in a Turkish bathhouse. It was a brilliant solution and saved him quite a bit of money.

Plácido Domingo's 1986 version is an opera. Consequently, this version has quite a different feel from the others. As with *O*, it may prove useful when illustrating just how much freedom directors have when telling their stories.

Geoffrey Sax sets his 2001 version of the story in modern-day London. Again, if you are looking for a faithful adaptation, this version is *not* it. The language, along with the setting, has been modernized, something that some like and others hate. To be fair, the reviews of this film are all over the place. Some feel the modern context and language make it more accessible while others argue the text has been dumbed down or that the modern context makes Othello's flaws much more difficult to stomach.

Jonathan Miller's 1981 version bypasses James Earl Jones (originally intended for the title role) in favor of Anthony Hopkins. While Hopkins is decidedly a fantastic actor, some viewers feel his performance in this film (which is ten years earlier than his iconic turn in *The Silence of the Lambs*) is not his best. Would this man truly have been a career military man? Moreover, partly due to her age, Penelope Wilton can come across as not quite right in the role of Desdemona. And as for the costuming. . . . Well, see what you think about the costume Richard Hughes designed for Othello.

In the end, what's important is students have the opportunity to see that a filmed version of print text is "a" version rather than "the" version. Think of it this way: even siblings, when discussing events they both experienced, will tell their stories in slightly different ways, emphasizing slightly different points or remembering slightly different details. The versions are different, but both are true in their own way to what the storyteller remembers. By comparing the creative visions of several filmmakers, students can begin to understand the validity of their own interpretive processes.

STEP 9: Reflect on the Process

Now that you have gone through the scene, made notes as to how you would direct the actors, and then compared several film versions of this scene, what have you learned? Has this process been helpful in terms of understanding a complex print text? Be prepared to share your thoughts with your classmates.

Standards Addressed in This Unit

Conventions of Standard English
CCSS.ELA-LITERACY.CCRA.L.1
CCSS.ELA-LITERACY.CCRA.L.2

Knowledge of Language
CCSS.ELA-LITERACY.CCRA.L.3
Vocabulary Acquisition and Use
CCSS.ELA-LITERACY.CCRA.L.4
CCSS.ELA-LITERACY.CCRA.L.5
CCSS.ELA-LITERACY.CCRA.L.6
Key Ideas and Details
CCSS.ELA-LITERACY.CCRA.R.1
CCSS.ELA-LITERACY.CCRA.R.2
CCSS.ELA-LITERACY.CCRA.R.3
Craft and Structure
CCSS.ELA-LITERACY.CCRA.R.4
CCSS.ELA-LITERACY.CCRA.R.5
CCSS.ELA-LITERACY.CCRA.R.6
Integration of Knowledge and Ideas
CCSS.ELA-LITERACY.CCRA.R.7
CCSS.ELA-LITERACY.CCRA.R.9
Range of Reading and Level of Text Complexity
CCSS.ELA-LITERACY.CCRA.R.10
Comprehension and Collaboration
CCSS.ELA-LITERACY.CCRA.SL.1
CCSS.ELA-LITERACY.CCRA.SL.2
Presentation of Knowledge and Ideas
CCSS.ELA-LITERACY.CCRA.SL.4
CCSS.ELA-LITERACY.CCRA.SL.5
CCSS.ELA-LITERACY.CCRA.SL.6
Text Types and Purposes
CCSS.ELA-LITERACY.CCRA.W.2
Production and Distribution
CCSS.ELA-LITERACY.CCRA.W.4
Research to Build and Present Knowledge
CCSS.ELA-LITERACY.CCRA.W.7
CCSS.ELA-LITERACY.CCRA.W.8
CCSS.ELA-LITERACY.CCRA.W.9
Range of Writing
CCSS.ELA-LITERACY.CCRA.W.10

9 From the Stars to the Silver Screen: A Technical Analysis of the Opening Scene of Spielberg's *E.T. The Extra-Terrestrial*

Lesson Plan

Essential Question
How do directors use framing, angles, lighting, pacing, and music to guide their audience's emotions and perceptions?

Objectives
1. Students will create three storyboards to demonstrate an understanding of the structure of a spec script.
2. Students will use the jigsaw strategy to identify specific techniques a given director uses in a sample scene and analyze the effects those techniques have on an audience.
3. Students will be able to engender particular feelings/emotions in an audience through the use of specific film techniques.

Central Texts

E.T. The Extra-Terrestrial (shooting script excerpt) written by Melissa Mathison

E.T. The Extra-Terrestrial (film excerpt) directed by Stephen Spielberg

Agenda

STEP 1: Anticipatory Quickwrite

STEP 2: Read Script Excerpt, Paying Attention to Format/Structure

STEP 3: Sketch Three Shots to Include in the Film

STEP 4: In Small Groups, Analyze the Opening Scene

STEP 5: Write an Original Character Introduction Scene

STEP 6: Storyboard the Scene

STEP 7: Reflect on the Process

Differentiation

One of the compelling characteristics of filmmaking is just how many different ways there are to contribute to the finished product. This activity can help students understand how they might best be able to contribute—whether through art direction, writing, cinematography, lighting, or scoring the film. As students learn how to think about each of these elements independently, they can better understand how they work together to create a coherent whole. Further, this understanding could prove invaluable when students form small groups. The most effective groups will contain students with a wide variety of skill sets.

Vocabulary

film language (n.)—the style or specific mix of techniques a filmmaker uses to tell a story. For example, John Ford preferred never to move his camera, as he felt it disrupted the audience's immersion in his story. Guillermo del Toro, by contrast, prefers to have the camera moving always, if sometimes only slightly. Some directors like crash zooms while others prefer to use only techniques the human eye can replicate. Some directors gravitate to particular lenses, some directors prefer longer takes, and so on.

shooting script (n.)—the script the director uses for filming, a production document

spec script (n.)—a screenplay written with the objective of selling it to a filmmaker

Resources

"ET Key Scene 1 Opening" by Emma Sey (https://youtu.be/zn1j-vF1QyA)

"Spielberg: How to Introduce Characters" by Entertain the Elk (https://youtu.be/iQLJDxp2FEI)

"Steven Spielberg's techniques and themes" by Steven Benedict (https://youtu.be/-uCBYFHRHU0)

Suggested Timeline

One week

Lesson 9

From the Stars to the Silver Screen: A Technical Analysis of the Opening Scene of Spielberg's *E.T. The Extra-Terrestrial*

E.T. began with me trying to write a story about my parents' divorce.

—STEVEN SPIELBERG

STEP 1: Anticipatory Quickwrite

What tools are available to filmmakers for making meaning? How do these different tools work together to create meaning? Be prepared to share your thoughts with your classmates.

For this activity, the idea is to observe how directors use a variety of techniques to influence or guide audience expectations. Good filmmakers are skilled at guiding their audiences, but how do they do it? Part of the key to understanding how directors succeed is to look at those techniques in isolation.

STEP 2: Read Script Excerpt, Paying Attention to Format/Structure

Have students read the excerpt from the **shooting script** (see Figure 9.1). You may want to point out that a shooting script delineates specific shots used in the filming. Compare this script with the **spec scripts** included elsewhere in this book, for example, to note the structural differences.

STEP 3: Sketch Three Shots to Include in the Film

Once students have read the script, have them sketch three shots they would include in their film version (see Figure 9.2). Then have students compare and explain their shots with the shots their neighbors sketched. Sketching the shots first will result in students watching the film more closely to determine if any of the shots they envisioned made it into the film.

REVISED – 8/31/81

E.T.
The Extra-Terrestrial

by
Melissa Mathison

1   The BLACK SCREEN becomes a NIGHT SKY as one by one, stars   1
        begin to poke through and come to life in the darkness.

        BEGIN TITLES

        PAN across the SKY, creating the illusion of moving deeper into SPACE. This illusion is shattered
        with the intrusion of a familiar CRESCENT MOON.

        The MOON drops behind a gnarled TREE LIMB and the LIMB pulls away to reveal the pointed
        treetops of a REDWOOD FOREST.

        A SOFT LIGHT is visible through the heavy camouflage of TREES. The VIEW MOVES toward
        this LIGHT, up and over the TREES and finally comes to rest on a freak clearing, a barren
        meadow, nestled among the towering trees.

        It is here that we see the SPACESHIP.

        The SHIP gently floats, anchored to the earth by a beam of lavender light.

        END TITLES   X

2   EXT. THE LANDING SITE – NIGHT   2

        The SPACESHIP is not large. It slightly resembles a reflective, hot-air balloon, a Christmas
        tree ornament, inscribed with a delicate gothic design. An open hatch door stretches down to
        the grassy landing site. Soft pastel light spills from the interior of the SHIP, and in this light, we
        make out the movements of CREATURES.

        The CREATURES are short, stocky, humanoid, but our distance and the misty atmosphere
        prevent any close identification of features. The CREATURES are banded together, working
        with strange, antiquated tools, probing the Earth. Their jerky movements and their reaction to
        the slightest sound – an owl hooting, a bird flying, the rustle of leaves – reveal their hesitancy
        and fear.

        A smoky, white, camouflaging mist seems to emanate from the CREATURES themselves, on an
        inhale-exhale rhythm, as if their hot breath was consolidating in the cool night air, blanketing
        their tracks with fog.

        An OWL HOOTS. THE CREATURES FREEZE. The danger passes. Work is resumed.

FIGURE 9.1. Excerpt of the shooting script from *E.T. The Extra-Terrestrial*

FIGURE 9.1. Continued.

| 3 | INSERT: HANDS | 3 |

A STRANGE PAIR OF HANDS – four-fingered, long and slender, delicate. The hands dig into the soil and pull a flowering herb from the ground.

| 4 | LONG SHOT: A CREATURE | 4 |

ONE CREATURE walks toward the open hatch door, carrying the same flowering weed. FOLLOW him up the gangplank and into the SHIP.

| 5 | INT. SPACE SHIP – NIGHT | 5 |

A soft-white den of mist. We HEAR clearly now the unique breathing pattern of THE CREATURE as we see his obscured form move through the ship.

| 6 | INT. SHIP'S GREENHOUSE – NIGHT | 6 |

The mist clears and we are in a greenhouse – a Gothic cathedral of a structure. Heavy precipitation drips from the decorative fanning roofline. THE CREATURE places the HERB in a basin filled with a thick liquid.

| 7 | INSERT: THE HERB | 7 |

It takes root in this liquid and straightens with life. It is then spotlit by a shaft of pastel light.

| 8 | PULL BACK: THE BASIN | 8 |

The basin is filled with plants – plants which reflect the tropics of Earth: orchids, cactus, a baobab tree. All plants are being systematically nurtured by orchestrated shafts of pastel lights.

| 9 | EXT. LANDING SITE – NIGHT | 9 |

The CREATURE descends the gangplank and walks past the group of his FELLOW CREATURES. HE comes to the edge of this slightly raised field and looks out toward the trees. THE CREATURE carefully descends the rocky incline surrounding the field and disappears into the tall grass which marks the entrance to the forest.

| 10 | REVERSE: A FELLOW CREATURE | 10 |

One FELLOW CREATURE stops his work. A RED LIGHT begins to glow in his chest – as if a deeply buried heart were shining and the red glow was seeping through thin, translucent skin.

| 11 | EXT. TALL GRASS – NIGHT | 11 |

THE CREATURE reappears from out of the TALL GRASS. He faces the ship. HIS HEART also begins to shine through, and the ruby glow pinpoints him: a small awkward creature, alone in the gigantic Redwood Forest under a starry sky.

| 12 | REVERSE: A FELLOW CREATURE | 12 |

The FELLOW CREATURE resumes his work.

FIGURE 9.1. Continued.

| 13 | HIGH ANGLE: THE CREATURE | 13 |

THE CREATURE. Still lit by his own conscience, turns and looks up at a towering fir tree. The RED LIGHT goes out. HE walks into the forest.

| 14 | EXT. FOREST – NIGHT | 14 |

THE SOUNDS of the forest rise: birds, babbling brooks, the twitter of insects. THE CREATURE moves deeper into the forest.

| 15 | AT HIS FEET: A TABLEAU | 15 |

A perfect tableau – wildflowers, ferns and moss.

| 16 | PULL BACK: THE CREATURE | 16 |

THE CREATURE sinks to his haunches and reaches out to take one thing – a sapling – a miniature REDWOOD, a perfect bonsai, growing at the feet of its elders. As THE CREATURE RISES, he is momentarily silhouetted in a glimmer of light, coming from the far side of the forest.

THE CREATURE turns and looks in the direction of his ship. Then, he looks back in the direction of the strange light. THE CREATURE begins to walk toward the unidentified light.

| 17 | EXT. HILL/LOOKOUT – NIGHT | 17 |

To the SOUND of heavy BREATHING and an awkward tread, we SEE the CREATURE'S HAND reach out and pull back a leafy limb.

| 18 | THE VIEW: THE SOURCE OF LIGHT | 18 |

THE SOURCE OF LIGHT – a suburban neighborhood, edging up against the base of the mountains and the border of the forest.

| 19 | WIDER: THE CREATURE | 19 |

THE CREATURE innocently steps out onto the road and crosses to the far side.

| 20 | HIGH ANGLE: THE CREATURE | 20 |

THE CREATURE stands, silhouetted on a ragged bluff. A sea of yellow house lights lies below him. Faint sounds of civilization intrude on the soft noises of the forest.

| 21 | CLOSER: THE CREATURE | 21 |

We cannot see THE CREATURE'S face, but the stillness and the constancy of his stare and the way his grip tightens on his small tree, reveal his fascination, curiosity and fear.

We see one red light come on in the distance. The light is seen by THE CREATURE. Suddenly, THE CREATURE turns his head to look down the road. Following his reaction, we hear the SOUND of a MOTOR and with no further warning, harsh, blinding white lights streak around the corner. THE CREATURE throws himself to the ground, sliding down the embankment on the wrong side of the fire road.

FIGURE 9.1. Continued.

22	CLOSE: THE SAPLING	22

The sapling rolls away from the curb and into the road.

23	WIDER: THE APPROACHING CAR	23

The approaching car pulls to a stop. A tire crushes the small redwood under muddy rubber.

24	THE CREATURE'S POV: THE CAR DOOR	24

The car door opens and a man steps out. Seen only from the waist down are: dark pants, heavy boots and a huge ring of KEYS hanging from his belt.

The KEYS make a tremendous racket, displacing all other sounds of the night.

25	REVERSE: THE CREATURE	25

THE CREATURE slides under cover just as his RED LIGHT COMES ON. We see a glimmer of it through shrubbery. His hand moves in to cover it.

26	WIDER: MORE CARS	26

More cars converge on the scene. We SEE bright HEADLIGHTS and HEAR slamming doors, muffled voices. Then we HEAR THE CREATURE break a branch from a shrub. He holds it against his chest. The SOUND OF KEYS.

The sudden shafts of flashlight beams encircle the road and shoot out into the trees.

THE CREATURE moves unnoticed along the hillside. He crosses the road.

27	EXT. RAVINE – NIGHT – LONG SHOT	27

We see shadows of men jumping the ravine and heading into the forest. THE CREATURE hides in the near end of the shallow ravine.

KEYS is the last to jump.

The SOUND of KEYS is hideous.

28	CLOSE ON: THE CREATURE	28

We SEE THE CREATURE's trembling form, and HEAR a sharp inhalation of breath as KEYS jumps.

Behind the camouflaging branch, we SEE THE CREATURE's heart throb violently.

29	EXT. THE LANDING SITE – NIGHT	29

The SHIP is dark. All hands are on board.

The silence of this spot is broken by the distant shouts of men. The FELLOW CREATURE remains in the door opening, his heart light sending frantic signals into the dark forest.

FIGURE 9.1. Continued.

30	EXT. THE FOREST – NIGHT	30

THE CREATURE moves quickly but awkwardly through the forest. His breathing is heavier now.

Flashlight beams scour the forest.

The CREATURE bursts past human legs, zig-zagging invisibly through the tall grass. The rush of movement almost topples one human searcher, and there are sudden, amazed shouts of discovery. THE CREATURE'S ruby-red beacon is all that can be seen. KEYS jangle horrifically as the phalanx of men moves forward.

31	EXT. THE LANDING SITE – NIGHT	31

The hatch door lifts.

The last image from the interior of the ship is the FELLOW CREATURE's RED LIGHT, as the ship's petal-door spirals to a close and we HEAR a panicked group breath.

32	EXT. TALL GRASS – GRASS	32

THE CREATURE emerges from the trees and dives into the tall grass.

33	EXT. THE LANDING SITE – NIGHT	33

The ship hovers, then departs quickly, spinning above the treetops and disappearing into the night sky.

34	CLOSER: THE CREATURE	34

THE CREATURE stands on the deserted landing site. The grass is flattened where the ship once stood. THE CREATURE reaches his arm into the sky and cries out – a SOUND of desperation, disbelief and fear. The SOUND of KEYS RISES.

35	EXT. EDGE OF THE FOREST – NIGHT	35

THE CREATURE dashes back into the forest. His RED LIGHT fades out. We see only a dim shadow now.

This is E.T. He is stranded on EARTH.

                                                                           FADE OUT

Story:_____ Name: _____
Author:_____ Date: _____ Pd.:_____

Directions: *Sketch three shots as you envision them from the text provided. In the next box, use your film terms to describe the shot. Then write a rationale for the shot, explaining the effect you wish to create.*

SHOT 1:	SHOT 1 Description:
Rationale/Intended Effect:	
SHOT 2:	SHOT 2 Description:
Rationale/Intended Effect:	
SHOT 3:	SHOT 3 Description:
Rationale/Intended Effect:	

FIGURE 9.2. Form for sketching director's shots.

STEP 4: In Small Groups, Analyze the Opening Scene

Before viewing the film, however, explain that the goal of this portion of the activity is to examine, in isolation, the techniques the director uses to guide his audience, as well as the intended effects of those techniques. These techniques are only actually important in terms of the response they engender in the reader/viewer; otherwise, they have no real purpose. Have students number off, then assign each number a single film aspect to observe as follows:

- **Group 1:** This group should observe the **FRAMING**. Is the camera primarily close to what is being filmed, or is it far away? On what details does the camera concentrate? What point of view does the camera employ? When do we see mostly long shots? When do we get close-ups?
- **Group 2:** This group should pay attention to **ANGLES**. When do we get eye-level shots? When do we look up or down? How do the angles we see affect our interpretation of what we see?
- **Group 3:** This group should pay attention to the **LIGHTING**. How are the shots lit? How are the characters lit? What are the sources of light?
- **Group 4:** This group should pay attention to **PACING**. What do you notice about the duration of the shots? Are there places where the shots are faster? Slower? Do you notice a pattern to when the duration of individual shots changes?
- **Group 5:** This group should pay attention to the **MUSIC/SCORE**. How does the score reflect what we see happening on-screen? How does the score affect audience perception/expectation?

As students watch this opening sequence, they need not write notes for every shot but should instead observe tendencies. What techniques are used most often? Does the pattern change at any point? Might there be some predictable intention behind the techniques used? How are we, the audience, being guided by these techniques? Taken as a whole, these various techniques and their patterns of usage by a given director are referred to as a **film language**. Each director's film language or style of storytelling is as unique as a fingerprint. The graphic organizer (Figure 9.3) will help students keep track of their observations and provides a space to record what they learn from other groups' observations as well.

Once students know what they are supposed to observe, play the opening sequence from just after the introductory title cards through the shot where the spaceship has left, E.T. has begun his trek toward the city below, and the men are combing the hillside with flashlights looking for clues (approximately eight

Name:_____ Date:_____
Film Title:_____ Director:_____

Directions: *Use the following chart to record your observations.*

FRAMING	ANGLES	LIGHTING	PACING	SCORE

Reflection: How do these techniques work together to guide the audience expectation? How might this scene have played out differently without the techniques you observed?

FIGURE 9.3. Observation chart.

minutes into the film). When you stop the film, allow students a few minutes to write down what they remember seeing. Writing *after* viewing allows students the opportunity to pay attention to the film and not miss any details by attempting to write simultaneously with viewing.

Students will notice lots of different things, of course, but to ensure their observations are in the ballpark with what you want them to see, note the following:

- **Group 1 (FRAMING):** This group may pick up on the fact that there are lots of different framing choices here. We have close-ups on alien hands; long shots (or full-body shots) as the aliens pause, nervous and glowing, after the owl hoots; close-ups on the one man's keys; establishing shots both outside and inside the spaceship; and long shots of one alien walking through the trees. Students should discuss why these particular choices were likely made. The long shot of the aliens, nervous and glowing, tends to convey the idea that these aliens are closely related, are emotionally connected, and are reassuring one another. The long shot of the lone alien (who turns out to be E.T.) looking so tiny while walking through the giant redwoods likely was intended to convey the idea that these aliens are isolated, out of place, and pose no real threat.

- **Group 2 (ANGLES):** This group will notice that the aliens seem to be shot primarily from their own eye level. The humans, on the other hand, are generally shot from low angles or from the aliens' eye level. The choices to film the aliens from their own eye level was likely made so the audience can see the unfolding action the way the aliens do, thereby creating a connection between them. The humans, on the other hand, are shot from angles that make them appear larger, dangerous, and perhaps threatening. The audience should definitely feel the difference in terms of the humans' more imposing presence.

- **Group 3 (LIGHTING):** The use of light throughout this scene is interesting. We begin with the shot of the starry night sky, eventually progressing down to Earth and the brightly lit grid of what we assume to be Los Angeles. Perhaps these lights are intended to be a symbolic juxtaposition of the aliens' home vs. the humans' home. Further, the aliens' chest cavities light up when they are afraid, also demonstrating the strong connection among the aliens. On the other hand, the headlights of the trucks and the flashlights the humans carry come across as probing, intrusive, almost weapon-like. As the men run, notice how they shake their flashlights back and forth, adding to the sense of chaos.

- **Group 4 (PACING):** This group should quickly pick up on the idea that not all of the shots are the same length. In fact, their duration varies widely. Early in the scene, before the humans arrive, the shots move slowly and the cuts are more spread out. Once the action picks up, however, the camera moves more quickly and the cuts happen much more quickly. We can feel the intensity picking up, and the more the action builds, the quicker the shots come at us. By the end of the scene, they have once again slowed down.

- **Group 5 (MUSIC/SCORE):** This group may notice how composer John Williams uses music to provide emotional cues. They may point out how the music feels mysterious and calm with a quiet energy. They will certainly notice when, as the action builds, the score complements the action. As Stanley Kubrick once pointed out, "A film is—or should be—more like music than like fiction. It should be a progression of moods and feelings. The theme, what's behind the emotion, the meaning, all that comes later" ("Screenwriting Wisdom from Stanley Kubrick," Screencraft). The score is, then, our emotional road map.

After a few minutes, play the clip again. Have students look for any details they may have missed the first time. Then, once they have recorded their observations, have them meet with their groups and compare notes. Did they notice the same things? More important, how might the techniques they noticed serve to guide audience perception? Have each group share aloud with the class after they have had the chance to discuss their thoughts. Students may now record notes in the remaining columns as they listen to their peers' findings.

If necessary, you may want to use the following questions to help spur conversation:

- How do the scenes with the aliens interacting with nature compare to the scenes of the humans interacting with nature? (**POSSIBLE RESPONSES**: *Students should notice that when the aliens interact with nature, they seem to do so as conservators—note the "greenhouse" inside the ship as well as how gentle E.T. is when digging up the sapling. The humans, on the other hand, seem to be much more aggressive/destructive toward nature—as evidenced by the tailpipe, for example, or the shot when they all run through the mud puddle.*)

- At one point, we see a long shot of the woods. Giant redwoods dominate the shot. In fact, we almost miss the tiny alien slowly moving through the trees. Why frame the alien this way? (**POSSIBLE RESPONSE**: *Using a long shot makes the alien appear tiny, out of place, and vulnerable. We realize he is not here to conquer. If anything, he appears passive.*)

- How do the aliens use light? How do the humans use light? (**POSSIBLE RESPONSE**: *The aliens have lights on their ship, and they also use light to communicate or connect when their chest cavities begin to glow. Later, we will see E.T.'s finger do the same thing. As for the humans, we see their headlights and flashlights. Additionally, as they chase E.T., they shake those flashlights much more than is necessary, creating a sense of chaos.*)

- When the trucks pull up and stop, the camera focuses on an exhaust pipe. Shortly thereafter, as the humans run through the woods, the camera is focused on a mud puddle. Every one of the humans running down the trail steps into that mud puddle. Couldn't they have just stepped over it? What are these shots supposed to tell us? (***POSSIBLE RE-SPONSE****: These shots show—in contrast to the aliens, who seem to operate in harmony with nature—how humans do not operate in harmony with the natural world. If anything, humans appear destructive.*)

- At one point, we see alien fingers gently digging up a tiny sapling. We cut to a shot of a rabbit, ostensibly looking on. The rabbit does not seem to feel threatened. What is the purpose of this sequence? What do we learn? How are we supposed to feel? (***POSSIBLE RESPONSE****: This scene emphasizes how nonthreatening the aliens are. They appear to have come to earth to learn, not to conquer.*)

- Why does the camera focus several times on the keys on the man's belt? (***POSSIBLE RESPONSE****: Rather than showing us the man's face, which could lead us to begin identifying with him, we are shown the keys. That we come back to the keys more than once implies this is how we will be able to identify the man and that he will be important later.*)

- Why do we see the aliens more clearly than we see the humans? (***POSSIBLE RESPONSE****: When an audience sees a face, they begin to relate to the character. By seeing the aliens, but not the humans, Spielberg seems to be influencing us to relate to the aliens over the humans.*)

- The scene begins looking up at the starry night sky and ends looking down at a brightly lit city grid. Is this use of light intentional, do you think? Are these shots supposed to be related in some way? (***POSSIBLE RESPONSE****: The shots are interesting bookends—the stars in the sky and the grid of streetlights. The shot actually approximates the aliens' arrival on Earth. These shots also help underscore the juxtaposition between the aliens and humans—space versus Earth.*)

- By the end of the scene, we are rooting for the alien to get away. Surely we all realize that the discovery of alien life forms would have an incredible impact on our scientific understanding, and yet, we find ourselves rooting *against* the humans. How has Spielberg led us to root against humanity? (***POSSIBLE ANSWER****: Spielberg, ironically, has "humanized" the aliens more. We see the aliens. We see they seem to have an emotional bond. We see how respectful they are of the environment. We see them as nonthreatening. The humans, on the other hand, are shown in silhouette, which helps to keep them at an emotional distance. We see they are aggressive and are not as respectful of the environment.*)

- How do the techniques we have observed and discussed work together to guide audience expectation? (***POSSIBLE RESPONSE****: By the end of the* scene, the humans remain faceless aggressors whose motives we can only guess. On the other hand, we seem to understand much more about the aliens, whose motives and gentle natures we can see and respect. We see the aliens' faces, which helps us begin to empathize with them. The humans' faces, on the other hand, remain in shadow, thus preventing an emotional connection. We never even hear their voices. On the other hand, we can clearly discern the fear and panic in E.T.'s screams as he tries to escape. In the end, we find ourselves rooting for the aliens and against the humans.)

Remember, the purpose of this activity is to examine in isolation the use of specific film techniques—not just what those techniques are but how they can be used to influence the audience's emotions and perceptions. A good storyteller has at least a basic understanding of psychology; a great storyteller is a fantastic guide.

STEP 5: Write an Original Character Introduction Scene

As a culminating activity, have students write a short scene modeled on the opening scene from *E.T.* Spielberg begins his film with a scene that introduces major characters, establishes the primary relationship between the two sets of characters, and launches the conflict that will drive the action. He does not *solve* the conflict; he merely *introduces* it. Everything else comes later. So, have students write an introductory scene that introduces major characters, establishes the relationship between the characters or groups, and launches the conflict that will drive the story. Students should write the scene in paragraph form, as if they are writing a short story. Feel free to provide a word or page limit.

STEP 6: Storyboard the Scene

Once their story is complete, you may want to have your students extend their learning by trading their writing with another student and then storyboarding their neighbor's scene, including shot list information, using the techniques they observed Spielberg use in this introductory scene.

STEP 7: Reflect on the Process

How has this activity helped you understand how to use the different tools available to filmmakers in tandem to create meaning? Be prepared to share your thoughts with your classmates.

Standards Addressed in This Unit

Conventions of Standard English
CCSS.ELA-LITERACY.CCRA.L.1
CCSS.ELA-LITERACY.CCRA.L.2
Knowledge of Language
CCSS.ELA-LITERACY.CCRA.L.3
Vocabulary Acquisition and Use
CCSS.ELA-LITERACY.CCRA.L.6
Key Ideas and Details
CCSS.ELA-LITERACY.CCRA.R.1
CCSS.ELA-LITERACY.CCRA.R.2
CCSS.ELA-LITERACY.CCRA.R.3
Craft and Structure
CCSS.ELA-LITERACY.CCRA.R.4
CCSS.ELA-LITERACY.CCRA.R.5
Integration of Knowledge and Ideas
CCSS.ELA-LITERACY.CCRA.R.7
Range of Reading and Level of Text Complexity
CCSS.ELA-LITERACY.CCRA.R.10
Comprehension and Collaboration
CCSS.ELA-LITERACY.CCRA.SL.1
CCSS.ELA-LITERACY.CCRA.SL.2
Presentation of Knowledge and Ideas
CCSS.ELA-LITERACY.CCRA.SL.4
Text Types and Purposes
CCSS.ELA-LITERACY.CCRA.W.2
CCSS.ELA-LITERACY.CCRA.W.3
Production and Distribution
CCSS.ELA-LITERACY.CCRA.W.4
Research to Build and Present Knowledge
CCSS.ELA-LITERACY.CCRA.W.9
Range of Writing
CCSS.ELA-LITERACY.CCRA.W.10

10 That Night on the Marge of Lake Lebarge: The Art of the Smooth Transition

◎ Lesson Plan

Essential Question
What is a "seamless transition," and how can the inclusion of such transitions impact the viewing experience?

Objectives
1. Students will be able to identify examples and characteristics of "seamless transitions" and analyze how they impact the viewing experience.
2. Students will be able to plan a film based on Robert Service's "The Cremation of Sam McGee" that will include two "seamless transitions."

Central Text
"The Cremation of Sam McGee" by Robert Service

Agenda
STEP 1: Anticipatory Quickwrite

STEP 2: Read "The Cremation of Sam McGee"

STEP 3: Conduct a Partner Reading of the Poem

STEP 4: Summarize the Poem

STEP 5: Identify an Approach to Filming the Story

STEP 6: Explore Interesting Film Transitions

STEP 7: Develop Transitions into and out of the Story of Sam McGee

STEP 8: Storyboard the Transitions

STEP 9: Connect the Final Scene to Sam McGee

STEP 10: (Optional Extension) Film a "Seamless Transition"

STEP 11: Reflect on the Process

Differentiation

This unit asks students to write, draw, and even, as an extension, film. The overall goal is the development of a seamless transition. If a student would rather draw, feel free to let them draw; if a student would rather write, let them write. Understanding the concept of a good transition is the goal here, not necessarily the drawing or writing about it. Whatever path a student takes to get to that point is not important.

Vocabulary

faithful adaptation (n.)—a transformed text, such as a film made from a print text, that stays close to the original source material

frame story (n.)—a story about someone telling a story

seamless transition (n.)—a transition between scenes that appears to have been done within a single shot

Resources

"28 Creative Cuts from Stranger Things" by Raging Cinema (https://youtu.be/Zs-paBOf2kU)

"6 Creative Video Editing Transitions for You to Try" by Skyler Thomas (https://youtu.be/ADYSsiEQKtc)

"Creative transitions in movies" by Jacob Syrytsia (https://youtu.be/nqt9s4WumDY)

"Cuts & Transitions 101" by RocketJump Film School (https://youtu.be/OAH0MoAv2CI)

"Sherlock - How Creative Transitions Improve Storytelling" by konrad noises (https://youtu.be/1IDBZ5AsUuk)

"The Importance of Scene Transitions" by Film Riot (https://youtu.be/fKgvno6k-og)

"TOP 8 'Smooth' Seamless Transitions" by Parker Walbeck (https://youtu.be/t5k7feqZUD0)

Suggested Timeline
One week

Lesson 10

That Night on the Marge of Lake Lebarge: The Art of the Smooth Transition

Our breath is brief, and being so
Let's make our heaven here below,
And lavish kindness as we go.

—Robert W. Service

STEP 1: Anticipatory Quickwrite

What are transitions? Why are they important? What makes a particularly good transition? Be prepared to share your thoughts with the class.

In my family, Robert W. Service is next to Shakespeare. Not even kidding. From the raucous and entertaining "Shooting of Dan McGrew" to the mystifyingly gorgeous "The Spell of the Yukon," Service was America's first rock-star poet, having made $500,000 on the back of Dan McGrew. "The only society I like is rough and tough," he once said, "and the tougher the better. There's where you get down to bedrock and meet human people." The only other thing that approached that level of devotion from Service was his love of the brutally gorgeous Yukon, immortalized in his collections of poetry *The Spell of the Yukon* and *The Land That God Forgot*.

I have introduced my English students to writing in dialect with his poem "My Prisoner" and had them memorize and present "The Twins." My aunt, a minister, used a portion of "The Song of the Wage-Slave" at my grandfather's funeral. And then there is "The Cremation of Sam McGee." Every member of my family can quote this poem. It is strange, I know, but rather entertaining, too, to be at a family function and begin reciting this poem. Wherever one may stop, someone else is prepared to jump in and keep it going. An odd tradition, perhaps, but then again, I come from a family of storytellers.

This particular unit focuses on Robert W. Service's poem "The Cremation of Sam McGee." More specifically, we are using "The Cremation of Sam McGee" to discuss an often misunderstood or underappreciated part of the storytelling process, both in writing and on film: the art of the smooth transition.

What do your students know about effective transitions? Have their teachers ever told them to include better transitions in their writing? How might this concept apply to filmmaking? What skills or knowledge do students need in order to craft better transitions in their filmmaking?

Hopefully, these questions will inspire your students to consider this critical storytelling element. I recommend using a "think-pair-share" approach here, in which students, having thought about transitions, pair off and share what they have written. And as always, everyone should be prepared to share their thoughts with the class.

Along these lines, Janet Evanovich, author of the Stephanie Plum series, points out that "[t]ransitions are critically important. I want the reader to turn the page without thinking she's turning the page. It must flow seamlessly." One of my teachers once compared transitions to the hitches that connect one railroad car to another, an image that has always stuck with me. Her point was that transitions serve as connections between paragraphs or ideas. They reference the idea that came before, just as they lead the reader to the next idea. From another perspective, they are bridges connecting one cliff face to another. Good connections make for easy travel, but if those connections are weak or missing, well, you have just lost your reader.

Filmmaking is just another method for telling a story, and transitions in film are every bit as important as transitions in print text. Additionally, helping students learn what makes a **seamless transition** in film can go a long way toward helping them understand why transitions are so important in print text as well.

STEP 2: Read "The Cremation of Sam McGee"

To start, your students need to feel the language. Robert W. Service was all about rhythm and rhyme, and feeling that poetic music helps create the spell. Having students read the poem silently first allows them to get a feel for what is being said, which will aid in reading fluency later.

The Cremation of Sam McGee
By Robert W. Service

There are strange things done in the midnight sun
   By the men who moil for gold;
The Arctic trails have their secret tales
   That would make your blood run cold;
The Northern Lights have seen queer sights,   5
   But the queerest they ever did see

Was that night on the marge of Lake Lebarge
  I cremated Sam McGee.

Now Sam McGee was from Tennessee, where the cotton blooms and blows.
Why he left his home in the South to roam 'round the Pole, God only knows. 10
He was always cold, but the land of gold seemed to hold him like a spell;
Though he'd often say in his homely way that "he'd sooner live in hell."

On a Christmas Day we were mushing our way over the Dawson trail.
Talk of your cold! through the parka's fold it stabbed like a driven nail.
If our eyes we'd close, then the lashes froze till sometimes we couldn't see; 15
It wasn't much fun, but the only one to whimper was Sam McGee.

And that very night, as we lay packed tight in our robes beneath the snow,
And the dogs were fed, and the stars o'erhead were dancing heel and toe,
He turned to me, and "Cap," says he, "I'll cash in this trip, I guess;
And if I do, I'm asking that you won't refuse my last request." 20

Well, he seemed so low that I couldn't say no; then he says with a sort of moan:
"It's the cursèd cold, and it's got right hold till I'm chilled clean through to the bone.
Yet 'tain't being dead—it's my awful dread of the icy grave that pains;
So I want you to swear that, foul or fair, you'll cremate my last remains."

A pal's last need is a thing to heed, so I swore I would not fail; 25
And we started on at the streak of dawn; but God! he looked ghastly pale.
He crouched on the sleigh, and he raved all day of his home in Tennessee;
And before nightfall a corpse was all that was left of Sam McGee.

There wasn't a breath in that land of death, and I hurried, horror-driven,
With a corpse half hid that I couldn't get rid, because of a promise given; 30
It was lashed to the sleigh, and it seemed to say: "You may tax your brawn and brains,
But you promised true, and it's up to you to cremate those last remains."

Now a promise made is a debt unpaid, and the trail has its own stern code.
In the days to come, though my lips were dumb, in my heart how I cursed that load.

That Night on the Marge of Lake Lebarge: The Art of the Smooth Transition

In the long, long night, by the lone firelight, while the huskies, round in a ring, 35
Howled out their woes to the homeless snows—O God! how I loathed the thing.

And every day that quiet clay seemed to heavy and heavier grow;
And on I went, though the dogs were spent and the grub was getting low;
The trail was bad, and I felt half mad, but I swore I would not give in;
And I'd often sing to the hateful thing, and it hearkened with a grin. 40

Till I came to the marge of Lake Lebarge, and a derelict there lay;
It was jammed in the ice, but I saw in a trice it was called the "Alice May."
And I looked at it, and I thought a bit, and I looked at my frozen chum;
Then "Here," said I, with a sudden cry, "is my cre-ma-tor-eum."

Some planks I tore from the cabin floor, and I lit the boiler fire; 45
Some coal I found that was lying around, and I heaped the fuel higher;
The flames just soared, and the furnace roared—such a blaze you seldom see;
And I burrowed a hole in the glowing coal, and I stuffed in Sam McGee.

Then I made a hike, for I didn't like to hear him sizzle so;
And the heavens scowled, and the huskies howled, and the wind began to blow. 50
It was icy cold, but the hot sweat rolled down my cheeks, and I don't know why;
And the greasy smoke in an inky cloak went streaking down the sky.

I do not know how long in the snow I wrestled with grisly fear;
But the stars came out and they danced about ere again I ventured near;
I was sick with dread, but I bravely said: "I'll just take a peep inside. 55
I guess he's cooked, and it's time I looked"; ... then the door I opened wide.

And there sat Sam, looking cool and calm, in the heart of the furnace roar;
And he wore a smile you could see a mile, and he said: "Please close that door.
It's fine in here, but I greatly fear you'll let in the cold and storm—
Since I left Plumtree, down in Tennessee, it's the first time I've been warm." 60

There are strange things done in the midnight sun
    By the men who moil for gold;
The Arctic trails have their secret tales

> *That would make your blood run cold;*
> *The Northern Lights have seen queer sights,*   65
>   *But the queerest they ever did see*
> *Was that night on the marge of Lake Lebarge*
>   *I cremated Sam McGee.*

STEP 3: Conduct a Partner Reading of the Poem

Once students have read the poem silently, either pair them off or allow them to select partners with whom to read. Each student reads a portion of the text out loud, and when that student stops, their partner picks up there and continues reading aloud. When the partner stops, the original reader picks back up. Given the structure of this poem, each partner may want to take a stanza at a time.

This poem has always seemed a somewhat scary and silly story that lends itself so perfectly to being told on a camping trip around a campfire. If you feel comfortable allowing students to use their phones, consider cutting the lights and having them use their flashlight feature to create creepy bottom lighting on whoever happens to be reading at the time, to help create the proper mood.

STEP 4: Summarize the Poem

Once students have finished reading the poem, have them reduce each stanza to a single original sentence (not a specific line from the text). What is happening here? Who is doing what? Where are they? What is the problem? And so on.

STEP 5: Identify an Approach to Filming the Story

Earlier, we identified the four elements all stories share (SETTING, CHARACTERS, CONFLICT, and RESOLUTION) and discussed the merits of having students change certain elements in order to make the story their own. In this case, however, we are going for a **faithful adaptation**. We will pull rank on our kids, and in the role of teacher/producer, we will establish restrictions on our students' filmmaking with the goal of getting our students to exercise a bit of creativity.

I mentioned earlier that the story of Sam McGee feels like the perfect campfire story. To that end, we will opt for a **frame story** approach. A frame story is a story about someone telling a story. Structurally, this means our film versions will be divisible into three sections: (1) the situation or context in which one character decides to relate the story (e.g., a camping trip, a bedtime story),

(2) the story of Sam McGee, and (3) the return to the present. *Inception, Titanic, Frankenstein, The Princess Bride, Heart of Darkness*—all of these are frame stories.

This structure inspires certain considerations. For instance, what is going on in the first section? Who are those characters? Why are they inspired to tell stories? How is the story to be told? The answers to these questions will also help inform our understanding of the third section, for obvious reasons.

While those questions are important, what I find most interesting in this case are the transitions from the present into the world of the story and back again. As English teachers, we understand the need for smooth transitions when it comes to writing; we don't want the reader to feel as if they have whiplash as they stagger from idea to idea. The same thing holds true for film. So we need to pay special attention to those transitions here.

STEP 6: *Explore Interesting Film Transitions*

As artists, we should understand there is no need to reinvent the wheel. That said, a quick YouTube search will reveal many fascinating approaches to creating the perfect transitions. For example:

"Cuts & Transitions 101" by RocketJump Film School

"28 Creative Cuts from Stranger Things" by Raging Cinema

"Sherlock – How Creative Transitions Improve Storytelling" by konrad-noises

"TOP 8 'Smooth' Seamless Transitions" by Parker Walbeck

"The Importance of Scene Transitions" by Film Riot

"Creative transitions in movies" by Jacob Syrytsia

"Scott Pilgrim: Make Your Transitions Count" by Nerdwriter1

"Edgar Wright - How to Do Visual Comedy" by Every Frame a Painting

"How to do the "SUPER SMOOTH" Seamless Transition!" by Daniel Schiffer

Some of these videos simply run through a number of interesting transitions while others explore in detail how to pull them off. These are by no means the only videos on transitions out there, so have your students watch a few of them or any other great transition videos you find and then discuss what they saw. What were the most interesting transitions they encountered?

STEP 7: Develop Transitions into and out of the Story of Sam McGee

Now that they have explored a number of creative transitions, students should write two short treatments. In the past, our treatments have covered entire stories; here, they will write treatments only for the "present tense" part of the story—the first and last parts. Pay special attention to the transitions used to shift into and out of Sam McGee's story. You may want to give students a length requirement—three hundred words for each should be enough to get their point across.

STEP 8: Storyboard the Transitions

Once students have written out their transitions, have them storyboard them. Traditionally, we only storyboard one shot at a time (e.g., shot #1, shot #2); however, due to the nature of these transitions, it may be more suitable to storyboard the series of changes within the shot (e.g., shot #1, shot #1.1, shot #1.2, shot #1.3). This will be tricky for your students, no doubt. Your goal, rather than the production of gorgeous artwork, is to have your students think through a challenging element of the storytelling process.

STEP 9: Connect the Final Scene to Sam McGee

There is a moment after a storyteller finishes a campfire story when the audience wonders if the story could possibly be true. Find a way to connect the final scene to the story of Sam McGee—a little detail that leaves the audience thinking, "No way!" Perhaps the storyteller pauses to share a photograph of himself and Sam, we might see something taken from the *Alice May*, or maybe the storyteller contemplates Sam's old pocket watch—anything that ties the story together and gives it some sort of credibility. Storyboard this scene.

STEP 10: (Optional Extension) Film a "Seamless Transition"

As a way to extend students' learning, if they are up for the challenge, have them film a "seamless transition" of their own. This can be done in isolation with two random shots, or students may opt to go back and plug in a "seamless transition" into a film project they have already completed.

STEP 11: Reflect on the Process

What did you learn about transitions? What do "seamless transitions" add to films?

How did adding that final detail in the last scene affect the story's impact? How might you apply the skills you have learned to your future projects? Be prepared to share your thoughts with your classmates.

Standards Addressed in This Unit

Conventions of Standard English
CCSS.ELA-LITERACY.CCRA.L.1
CCSS.ELA-LITERACY.CCRA.L.2
Vocabulary Acquisition and Use
CCSS.ELA-LITERACY.CCRA.L.6
Key Ideas and Details
CCSS.ELA-LITERACY.CCRA.R.1
CCSS.ELA-LITERACY.CCRA.R.2
CCSS.ELA-LITERACY.CCRA.R.3
Craft and Structure
CCSS.ELA-LITERACY.CCRA.R.5
Integration of Knowledge and Ideas
CCSS.ELA-LITERACY.CCRA.R.7
Range of Reading and Level of Text Complexity
CCSS.ELA-LITERACY.CCRA.R.10
Comprehension and Collaboration
CCSS.ELA-LITERACY.CCRA.SL.1
CCSS.ELA-LITERACY.CCRA.SL.2
Presentation of Knowledge and Ideas
CCSS.ELA-LITERACY.CCRA.SL.4
CCSS.ELA-LITERACY.CCRA.SL.5
Text Types and Purposes
CCSS.ELA-LITERACY.CCRA.W.2
CCSS.ELA-LITERACY.CCRA.W.3
Production and Distribution
CCSS.ELA-LITERACY.CCRA.W.4
CCSS.ELA-LITERACY.CCRA.W.5
Research to Build and Present Knowledge
CCSS.ELA-LITERACY.CCRA.W.7
Range of Writing
CCSS.ELA-LITERACY.CCRA.W.10

Documenting the Action: Not Your Everyday Short Story Analysis

Lesson Plan

Essential Question
How might the story change if told as a documentary film?

Objective
Students will analyze the short story "Everyday Use" by Alice Walker and demonstrate their understanding of the text by working collaboratively to transform the short story into a documentary film.

Central Text
"Everyday Use" by Alice Walker

Agenda

STEP 1: Anticipatory Quickwrite

STEP 2: Read "Everyday Use" by Alice Walker and Discuss Plot, Themes, and Characterization

STEP 3: Identify the Elements of Documentaries

STEP 4: In Collaborative Groups, Transform the Text into a Short Documentary Film

STEP 5: Reflect on the Process

Differentiation
This unit provides lots of opportunities for differentiating instruction. In order to successfully complete this unit, some students will act, others will film, others will write, and some will edit. All will have jobs that are important to successfully completing a short documentary film.

Vocabulary

documentary (n.)—a genre of film, usually nonfiction, that includes a number of specific elements such as interviews, cutaways, cinéma vérité, process footage, and archival footage

Resources

"4 Easy Steps to Film a Short Documentary" by Indy Mogul (https://youtu.be/f-K_XbCLtVk)

"7 Fundamental Steps to Film a Short Documentary" by Jesse Cervantes (https://youtu.be/XN8dIQ6vptc)

"8 Tips for your first documentary—International Journalists' Network" by Matthias Sdun (https://youtu.be/W03NUilplRM)

"DOCUMENTARY FILMMAKING TIPS" by Mark Bone (https://youtu.be/c8B0RZ6nEnE)

"How to Craft a DOCUMENTARY" by Mark Bone (https://youtu.be/v62B5DELG5k)

"How to Make a Documentary in One Day" by Indy Mogul (https://youtu.be/-zM2Xl-1kOM)

"How to Shoot a Documentary—Tips & Tricks for Emotional Storytelling" by Kriscoart (https://youtu.be/smE69BTB7Mc)

"Making A Documentary Without Money" by Creative North (https://youtu.be/TYgT6vffWzs)

Suggested Timeline
One week

Lesson 11

Documenting the Action: Not Your Everyday Short Story Analysis

I had the most incredible English and literature teachers in school, and it really influenced my love of storytelling. It's what made me excited to study journalism in college. I love editorials and documentaries. All of that came from being given the opportunity to lose myself in good writing when I was a kid.

—SOPHIA BUSH

STEP 1: *Anticipatory Quickwrite*

The goal of this unit is to analyze a print text, and then transform the story into a short documentary film. What skills and knowledge will you need to successfully accomplish this goal? Be prepared to share your thoughts with your classmates.

STEP 2: *Read "Everyday Use" by Alice Walker and Discuss Plot, Themes, and Characterization*

"Everyday Use" is a short story by Alice Walker published in 1973. The story is told by Mama and follows a specific interaction among Mama, Maggie, Dee/Wangero, and "Asalamalakim"/Hakim-a-barber on a single day. Maggie and Dee/Wangero are sisters with very different perspectives on the place where they grew up. "Asalamalakim"/Hakim-a-barber is Dee/Wangero's male companion (possibly her husband).

The story addresses concepts of cultural identity, assimilation, the complex nature of familial relationships, and the proper way to honor or preserve one's heritage. The conflict comes to a head over a couple of family heirlooms promised to one daughter but which the other daughter very much wants.

STEP 3: *Identify the Elements of Documentaries*

Given the different perspectives present, the story lends itself well to discussion/debate and character analysis. One fun, challenging way to explore this story is to divide students into small groups and have them film the story as a **documentary**. If you take this approach, be sure your students understand how documentaries are constructed. For starters, there are five basic elements to documentaries:

1. **Interviews**: Documentaries tend to include a good deal of interview footage conducted with the principal characters. These individuals tell the story in their own words and from their own unique perspective.
2. **Cutaways**: These are shots of random objects from the world of the story and serve as detail shots providing the flavor of that world.
3. **Cinéma Vérité or Live Footage**: This footage is filmed in real time as the events of the documentary unfold.
4. **Process Footage**: Often, documentaries will include a few shots of the interviewer/film crew, though this element is sometimes omitted.
5. **Archival Footage**: In order to provide a backstory or context for the events unfolding on-screen, documentaries will often include archival footage—footage filmed at earlier points—to fill in the blanks of the story and to help the audience better understand what is going on and why.

Consider showing your students clips from documentaries as well, preferably ones done in several different styles: *I, Tonya*; *Dateline* (television show); ESPN *30 for 30* documentaries; *Supersize Me*; etc. You do not need to show the documentaries in their entirety to successfully demonstrate the relevant components. Have students discuss their responses. Were they able to identify the elements outlined above? Did any of the directors include additional elements or make unusual filming choices? Which storytelling "style" did students prefer? Why?

Once students understand the basic elements of documentaries, go through a few tips with them about planning and implementing their documentaries. Consider the following suggestions:

How to Film Interviews
- Frame your character in either the left or the right third of the screen. However many characters you interview, film roughly half to one side and the other half to the other side for balance.
- Have your character look toward the open two-thirds side of the camera. Typically, the interviewer will sit on that side of the camera to naturally draw the character's eyes in that direction.
- Try to film against a background that reveals information about the character. Audiences will understand that the background will help flesh out

their understanding of the character, so try to use a different background for each character.

- Avoid filming in front of windows. The light from the window will make seeing the interview subject's face more difficult and will generally play havoc with your camera's light sensor.
- If your interview subject wears glasses, be sure they are positioned so that the camera does not catch them reflecting light sources.
- Your interview subject should be between four and fifteen feet in front of a wall in order to provide depth to your shot and prevent your subject's shadow from appearing on the wall.

You do not need to film interview questions. They should, however, be open-ended to encourage the subject to speak more expansively about the topic at hand. One way to encourage the subject to elaborate is simply to repeat the last three words of their previous response. For example . . .

Subject: ". . . which makes me think that bees are important."

Interviewer: "Bees are important?"

Subject: "Well, yes. I mean, think about it. They are responsible for pollinating massive numbers of plants, and without bees, entire ecosystems would collapse."

Interviewer: "Ecosystems would collapse?"

Subject: "Oh, without a doubt. See, it works like this. . . ."

This approach puts the subject at ease and makes them feel they are being heard, which in turn encourages them to speak in greater depth.

How to Film Cutaways

- Take lots of cutaway shots. Then take lots more. Cutaway shots help flesh out the world of the story and provide a bit of "visual poetry." If you shoot lots of cutaway shots, your life will be much easier during the editing process.
- Each cutaway shot should be between eight and twelve seconds long. You can always trim them during the editing phase, but extending them can be problematic.
- Cutaway shots are typically static (i.e., not moving). Treat your cutaway shots like video photographs. Use a tripod.

- A rack focus (a technique in which the camera does not move, but the focal point shifts within the image as framed) can add a sense of poetry or visual interest to your shots, but do not overuse this technique.
- Film cutaways that help the story progress, shots of elements specific to the story: the characters doing things relative to the story, the setting, and any other elements that help to tell the story and make a narrator unnecessary.
- Film cutaways designed to evoke an emotional response—a character's rough hands, a long shot of an isolated character, an old photograph on a mantle, a flickering candle.
- Film lots of cutaways of general details of the world of the story—a rake, old pie tins, a glass on a counter, a butter churn in the corner. These are the details that flesh out the world of the story.
- Film lots of close-ups. Using only medium to long shots creates a distance between the audience and the characters, and you want the opposite effect. You want to pull the viewer into the story. Find interesting details to fill the frame, and shoot more close-ups than you think you will need. You will be glad you did.

How to Film Cinéma Vérité or Live Footage

- This is when you simply follow your subject with a camera to film them doing whatever they typically do. "I'm not here—just pretend I'm not here. You just do your thing."
- Try to get lots of this type of footage, because it may take a while for your subject to relax and be natural.
- This footage allows the audience to see the character in action and therefore encourages the audience members to make up their own minds about who this person really is.
- If you use only interviews and cutaways, your audience can feel manipulated. Live footage of your subject can support the points you make in your film in a more natural way.

How to Film Process Footage

- Process footage refers to footage of the interviewer and the camera crew in action. Sometimes we just hear the interviewer's voice, and at other times, we may get shots of the crew in action, such as when we see over-the-shoulder shots past the subject of the interview being conducted.

- Some documentary filmmakers opt for a more invisible approach, in which they barely appear, if at all. The focus remains entirely on the characters in the story. Other filmmakers almost become characters in their own right, walking and talking with the subject on-screen, doing voice-overs, and appearing in medium close-ups (with the camera very subtly tracking toward them) to explain portions of the story.
- You may consider passing off a camera to a noncrewmember for a while in order to get those "behind the scenes" shots.

How to Film Archival Footage
- The best way to get this footage is to ask your subject for any old photographs or videos they might be willing to share. You will want to make copies, of course.
- Check the archives of the local newspaper for any photographs or videos relative to the story.

STEP 4: In Collaborative Groups, Transform the Text into a Short Documentary Film

As a culminating activity, have your students film a documentary version of the story using the elements of documentary filmmaking you've taught them. Give them a time limit for the completed film (I tend to lean toward ten minutes). I have included a rubric for the documentary project with the other rubrics at the end of this book (see pp. 190–91).

STEP 5: Reflect on the Process

Before this unit, you had likely never filmed a documentary before, especially as a way to study a short story. What have you learned and how has this process contributed to your understanding of the story? Be prepared to share your thoughts with your classmates.

Standards Addressed in This Unit

Knowledge of Language
CCSS.ELA-LITERACY.CCRA.L.3
Vocabulary Acquisition and Use
CCSS.ELA-LITERACY.CCRA.L.5

CCSS.ELA-LITERACY.CCRA.L.6
Key Ideas and Details
CCSS.ELA-LITERACY.CCRA.R.1
CCSS.ELA-LITERACY.CCRA.R.2
CCSS.ELA-LITERACY.CCRA.R.3
Craft and Structure
CCSS.ELA-LITERACY.CCRA.R.4
CCSS.ELA-LITERACY.CCRA.R.5
CCSS.ELA-LITERACY.CCRA.R.6
Integration of Knowledge and Ideas
CCSS.ELA-LITERACY.CCRA.R.7
Range of Reading and Level of Text Complexity
CCSS.ELA-LITERACY.CCRA.R.10
Comprehension and Collaboration
CCSS.ELA-LITERACY.CCRA.SL.1
CCSS.ELA-LITERACY.CCRA.SL.2
Presentation of Knowledge and Ideas
CCSS.ELA-LITERACY.CCRA.SL.4
CCSS.ELA-LITERACY.CCRA.SL.5
CCSS.ELA-LITERACY.CCRA.SL.6
Text Types and Purposes
CCSS.ELA-LITERACY.CCRA.W.2
CCSS.ELA-LITERACY.CCRA.W.3
Production and Distribution
CCSS.ELA-LITERACY.CCRA.W.4
CCSS.ELA-LITERACY.CCRA.W.6
Research to Build and Present Knowledge
CCSS.ELA-LITERACY.CCRA.W.7
Range of Writing
CCSS.ELA-LITERACY.CCRA.W.10

Unbroken: Guiding Audience Response

12

◎ Lesson Plan

Essential Questions

What is the process filmmakers follow when adapting a print text for the big screen?

How do filmmakers decide when to use particular techniques in particular scenes?

Objectives

1. Students will develop a treatment for a scene from the novel *Unbroken* by Laura Hillenbrand in which they use specific film techniques to engender a desired effect on the audience.
2. Students will assess the clarity of their classmates' treatments by using them to craft storyboards.
3. Students will compare the effectiveness of the choices they made through comparison with and evaluation of the scene from the film.

Central Texts

Unbroken (novel excerpt) written by Laura Hillenbrand

Unbroken (film excerpt) directed by Angelina Jolie

Agenda

STEP 1: Anticipatory Quickwrite

STEP 2: Read the Excerpt from *Unbroken* by Laura Hillenbrand

STEP 3: Craft a Treatment for the Scene

STEP 4: Trade Treatments and Construct Storyboards Based on Those Treatments

STEP 5: Compare Students' Versions with the Film

STEP 6: Write a Scene Analysis

STEP 7. Reflect on the Process

Differentiation

You have a few options for differentiating instruction here. For example, you could swap out the text or even give your students the opportunity to select their own text. You might sort your students into two groups, with your writers in one group working on treatments or even scripts, while in the other group your artists create responses to what the writers have written. Generally speaking, I prefer to have my students work on all steps in the process, so when we film actual scenes for our music videos, silent films, ten-minute films, etc., they have a much clearer understanding not only of which aspect of the process they prefer to be responsible for, but also so they better understand the work that goes into the contributions of their peers. That understanding helps my small groups work more smoothly and productively together. Obviously, the choice is yours.

Resources

"Unbroken (2/10) Movie CLIP - Plane Crash at Sea (2014) HD" by Movieclips (https://youtu.be/QU677HiXf6M)

"Unbroken (3/10) Movie CLIP - A Storm and a Prayer (2014) HD" by Movieclips (https://youtu.be/gpgsfivrruk)

"Unbroken (4/10) Movie CLIP - Bullets Above, Sharks Below (2014) HD" by Movieclips (https://youtu.be/xSvW3Gxd-h0)

"Unbroken (5/10) Movie CLIP - Am I Gonna Die? (2014) HD" by Movieclips (https://youtu.be/a2_9fQ0U57w)

Suggested Timeline

One week

Lesson 12

Unbroken: Guiding Audience Response

It takes more discipline than you might imagine to think, even for thirty seconds, in the noisy, confusing, high-pressure atmosphere of a film set. But a few seconds' thought can often prevent a serious mistake being made about something that looks good at first glance.

—STANLEY KUBRICK

STEP 1: Anticipatory Quickwrite

When adapting a print text to film, what are some of the things you must first consider? Be prepared to share your thoughts with your classmates.

In *Understanding by Design,* authors Grant Wiggins and Jay McTighe discuss the importance of beginning the process of planning a lesson by first considering the results one hopes to achieve. The same process is true for filmmaking. In essence, one should begin the process of planning for a film by considering the effect one wishes to engender in the audience. Being a good storyteller means that one must be good at guiding an audience.

Once one identifies the desired response, the next step in the process is to identify the techniques that might achieve that response. Thus far, we have examined dozens of techniques as well as their effects they inspire.

STEP 2: Read the Excerpt from *Unbroken* by Laura Hillenbrand

After students have read the excerpt, they should write an explanation of what they want the audience to feel while watching this particular scene. This step allows them to determine a goal for their scene, which is particularly important, as it helps students determine specific approaches to achieving the desired effects. By this point, students should have a good understanding of which techniques help produce specific feelings or responses in the audience. Even so, encourage them to consider carefully the techniques explained in the back of this book.

Unbroken
Preface

All he could see, in every direction, was water. It was June 23, 1943. Somewhere on the endless expanse of the Pacific Ocean, Army Air Forces bombardier and Olympic runner Louie Zamperini lay across a small raft, drifting westward. Slumped alongside him was a sergeant, one of his plane's gunners. On a separate raft, tethered to the first, lay another crewman, a gash zigzagging across his forehead. Their bodies, burned by the sun and stained yellow from the raft dye, had winnowed down to skeletons. Sharks glided in lazy loops around them, dragging their backs along the rafts, waiting.

The men had been adrift for twenty-seven days. Borne by an equatorial current, they had floated at least one thousand miles, deep into Japanese-controlled waters. The rafts were beginning to deteriorate into jelly, and gave off a sour, burning odor. The men's bodies were pocked with salt sores, and their lips were so swollen that they pressed into their nostrils and chins. They spent their days with their eyes fixed on the sky, singing "White Christmas," muttering about food. No one was even looking for them anymore. They were alone on sixty-four million square miles of ocean.

A month earlier, twenty-six-year-old Zamperini had been one of the greatest runners in the world, expected by many to be the first to break the four-minute mile, one of the most celebrated barriers in sport. Now his Olympian's body had wasted to less than one hundred pounds and his famous legs could no longer lift him. Almost everyone outside of his family had given him up for dead.

On that morning of the twenty-seventh day, the men heard a distant, deep strumming. Every airman knew that sound: pistons. Their eyes caught a glint in the sky—a plane, high overhead. Zamperini fired two flares and shook powdered dye into the water, enveloping the rafts in a circle of vivid orange. The plane kept going, slowly disappearing. The men sagged. Then the sound returned, and the plane came back into view. The crew had seen them.

With arms shrunken to little more than bone and yellowed skin, the castaways waved and shouted, their voices thin from thirst. The plane dropped low and swept alongside the rafts. Zamperini saw the profiles of the crewmen, dark against bright blueness.

There was a terrific roaring sound. The water, and the rafts themselves, seemed to boil. It was machine gun fire. This was not an American rescue plane. It was a Japanese bomber.

The men pitched themselves into the water and hung together under the rafts, cringing as bullets punched through the rubber and sliced effervescent lines in the water around their faces. The firing blazed on, then sputtered out as the bomber overshot them. The men dragged themselves back onto the one raft that was still mostly inflated. The bomber banked sideways, circling toward them again. As it leveled off, Zamperini could see the muzzles of the machine guns, aimed directly at them.

Zamperini looked toward his crewmates. They were too weak to go back in the water. As they lay down on the floor of the raft, hands over their heads, Zamperini splashed overboard alone.

Somewhere beneath him, the sharks were done waiting. They bent their bodies in the water and swam toward the man under the raft.

STEP 3: *Craft a Treatment for the Scene*

Once students have determined the effects they wish to achieve, have them consider how they might use each of the following to achieve their goals: FRAMING, ANGLES, MOVEMENT, LIGHTING, EDITING, and SOUND. By having them focus on each category individually, you will help your students develop a more thorough, more integrated approach to developing their scene. Have your students conduct a think-pair-share by category and then take two minutes to write about how they could use framing techniques effectively, then pair off and share their thoughts, before finally discussing ideas as a class. Then move on to each of the other categories in turn. There are a number of talking points included after the excerpt that you can use to guide the conversation.

STEP 4: *Trade Treatments and Construct Storyboards Based on Those Treatments*

Constructing storyboards from their peers' written treatments encourages students to be more specific in their writing, as no further explanation may be offered beyond what is written on the page. Thus, this activity, though conducted through the lens of film construction, targets one of the common weaknesses of student writing: lack of specificity. If the information is not on the page, it does not matter what the author intended—the information simply is not there.

STEP 5: *Compare Students' Versions with the Film*

Now that students have developed their own plans for filming the scene, have them compare their plans with how the scene was portrayed in the actual film. Remember, this part of the process is about evaluating directors' choices—how and why they made their choices, not who did it "right" or "wrong." Have students pay particular attention to any points where their choices were similar to director Angelina Jolie's version.

Here are some detailed notes you might use to guide students through the process, depending on how much help they need. And if your students are feeling particularly confident, challenge them to film their version!

Things to Consider

As you consider how to film this sequence, there are certain techniques you will want to employ, just as there are some you will wish to avoid, based on how you want your audience to respond to the events unfolding on-screen.

Begin by thinking about how you want your audience to react to what you present to them. In the case of this excerpt from *Unbroken*, your primary goal is to help your audience connect with the three downed airmen. To do that, you will need to use the tools at your disposal regarding FRAMING, ANGLES, MOVEMENT, LIGHTING, EDITING, and SOUND.

- **FRAMING:** You will likely want to begin with one or more establishing shots to let the audience know where the action is taking place. Long shots will be effective in allowing the audience to experience the isolation and vulnerability of the characters. Close-ups of the characters' faces will allow us to better feel their fear and anxiety. Stay away from close-ups of the enemy airman firing at our characters. If the audience sees his face, they will begin to see him as human and begin to relate to him. You want this character to remain distant and disconnected.

- **ANGLES:** Low-angle POV shots will allow us to see the airplane approaching just as the downed airmen see it. These "sea-level" shots will help the audience feel as though they are in the water with the downed airmen. Carefully placed high-angle shots can help the audience see the airmen as vulnerable. While high angles can be effective, avoid using the approaching pilot's POV because we want him to remain a faceless menace to whom the audience does not relate. Ordinarily, high angles are a no-brainer when you want the audience to see a character as weak or vulnerable. In this case, though, you run the risk of slipping into the enemy pilot's POV.

- **MOVEMENT:** Use slow/static shots at first. This will help the audience feel the lethargy that has overcome the downed airmen after so many days adrift at sea. As the enemy airplane makes its strafing runs and the downed airmen attempt to escape, increased camera movement can help build tension. Avoid using too much movement too early. For these downed airmen, afloat for days in a raft on the open ocean, time has lost meaning. Additionally, building tension too early can negate the dramatic increase of tension that should accompany the enemy pilot's attack. Remember, you want the mood of the scene to progress from hopeless complacency to sudden panic in an arc.

- **LIGHTING:** This scene takes place in broad daylight on the open ocean, so high key lighting is the obvious choice. The enemy airplane banking past the sun or approaching while backlit can help build tension and add drama. Given the action in the scene, trying to get creative with bottom lighting, side lighting, etc., would be counterproductive.
- **EDITING:** Initially, the duration of each shot should be a bit longer; however, as the enemy airplane approaches and the downed airmen realize their danger, the pacing of the shots should increase. Quicker shots will help build tension. This scene has an arc; while its mood is initially lethargic and hopeless, the action quickly escalates, and panic ensues. Consequently, the pacing should reflect this idea. Using shots that cut too quickly or dramatically too early can destroy the intended mood.
- **SOUND:** Relying on the diegetic sounds of the water lapping against the sides of the raft and the distant sound of the airplane can help create a feeling of auditory isolation. As the enemy airplane approaches, sparse music in a lower register can help build a sense of tension or foreboding. Using too much nondiegetic sound can make the scene feel staged.

STEP 6: Write a Scene Analysis

Given the lengths to which students have now gone to explore this scene, they should be ready to write a scene analysis. Have students evaluate how well Angelina Jolie tells this scene. Based on everything we now know about filmmaking, could this scene have been shot more effectively? For length, I recommend between 750 and 1,000 words. Feel free to use or adapt the same rubric included in Unit 7.

STEP 7: Reflect on the Process

How has the process of planning the adaptation of a print text for film affected how you read the print text? What has this process taught you? Be prepared to share your thoughts with your classmates.

Standards Addressed in This Unit

Conventions of Standard English
CCSS.ELA-LITERACY.CCRA.L.1
CCSS.ELA-LITERACY.CCRA.L.2
Vocabulary Acquisition and Use
CCSS.ELA-LITERACY.CCRA.L.6
Key Ideas and Details
CCSS.ELA-LITERACY.CCRA.R.1
CCSS.ELA-LITERACY.CCRA.R.2
CCSS.ELA-LITERACY.CCRA.R.3
Craft and Structure
CCSS.ELA-LITERACY.CCRA.R.6
Integration of Knowledge and Ideas
CCSS.ELA-LITERACY.CCRA.R.7
Range of Reading and Level of Text Complexity
CCSS.ELA-LITERACY.CCRA.R.10
Comprehension and Collaboration
CCSS.ELA-LITERACY.CCRA.SL.1
Presentation of Knowledge and Ideas
CCSS.ELA-LITERACY.CCRA.SL.4
CCSS.ELA-LITERACY.CCRA.SL.6
Text Types and Purposes
CCSS.ELA-LITERACY.CCRA.W.2
Production and Distribution
CCSS.ELA-LITERACY.CCRA.W.4
Research to Build and Present Knowledge
CCSS.ELA-LITERACY.CCRA.W.9
Range of Writing
CCSS.ELA-LITERACY.CCRA.W.10

Appendix A
Film Vocabulary

Shots

establishing shot. Often a long shot or a series of shots that sets the scene; used to establish setting and to show transitions between locations

shot. A single piece of film uninterrupted by cuts

Framing

close-up. Generally speaking, the subject is framed such that only the shoulders and head are visible

cowboy shot. A shot framed from mid-thigh up. This technique derived its name from the filming of many Westerns in which this technique was commonly used

extreme close-up. The image being shot is a part of a whole, such as an eye or hand

knee shot. A shot of a person from the knees up

long shot. A shot from some distance. If filming a person, the full body is shown. It may indicate the isolation or vulnerability of the character (also called a **full shot**)

medium close-up. Roughly halfway between a medium shot and a close-up, this shot frames the subject from mid-torso up

medium shot. The most common shot. A medium shot shows the person from the waist up. The intended effect is to ground the story

two shot. A scene between two people shot exclusively from one angle that includes both characters more or less equally. It is used in love scenes, arguments, or scenes in which interaction between the two characters is important

Camera Angles

bird's eye. A steeper angle and shot from some distance. This is a special type of high angle shot

Dutch tilt. A shot composed with the horizon not parallel with the bottom of the frame. Used extensively in *Batman* (1989) and frequently by Orson Welles

eye level. A shot taken from a normal height, i.e., the character's eye level; 90 to 95 percent of shots are eye level because it is the most natural angle

God's eye. The camera is directly overhead. The implication is that the character is being watched by a higher power, whether deity, shadowy government agency, or some other entity

high angle. Camera is above the subject. This usually has the effect of making the subject look smaller than normal, giving them the appearance of being weak, powerless, and/or trapped

low angle. Camera shoots subject from below. This usually has the effect of making the subject look larger than normal and therefore strong, powerful, and threatening

over the shoulder. Shot over one character's shoulder, capturing a second character opposite. This technique is commonly used to show a conversation from the first character's perspective

point of view. Shows what things look like from the perspective of someone or something in the scene. It must be juxtaposed with shots of the actor's face in order to make a connection with the viewer

Camera Movements

arc. The camera itself rotates around the object being filmed, creating a "dizzy" effect

boom/crane. The camera is mounted on a crane over the action. This is used to create overhead shots

crash zoom. A zoom that occurs very quickly. Often used to emphasize a reaction or realization

dolly/tracking. The camera is on a track that allows it to move with the action. It may be used to follow in front, behind, or next to a person as they walk or run

pan. Stationary camera that moves from side to side. Panning is used to create a source of tension or to provide information

rack focus. The camera does not actually move, but the point of focus shifts within the frame so that something that was out of focus comes into focus, and that which was in focus goes out of focus

Steadicam. The camera is attached to a camera operator via a mechanical harness that reduces or eliminates the unsteadiness of the operator's motion

tilt. Pivoting up or down along a vertical axis

trombone shot. The camera moves on a dolly while the zoom is simultaneously manipulated to make the subject appear to be the same distance from the camera. The background, however, will appear to draw closer or fall away. The effect is disorienting. Also referred to as *Vertigo* **effect** after the Hitchcock film that pioneered the technique

whip pan. An extremely fast pan that incorporates a good bit of motion blur. The "whip" in the name refers to the action of the camera operator. Whip pans can be used to build tension or disguise shot transitions

zoom. Stationary camera in which the lens moves to make an object seem to move closer to or farther away from the camera. With this technique, moving into a character is often a personal or revealing movement while moving away distances or separates the audience from the character

Lighting

back lighting. Strong light behind the subject. If the lighting is strong enough, only a silhouette of the subject being filmed will be visible

bottom lighting. Direct lighting from below, often making the subject appear dangerous or evil

front lighting. Soft lighting on the actor's face. It gives the appearance of innocence or goodness or supplies a halo effect

high key. Scene is flooded with light, creating a bright and open-looking scene

low key. Scene is flooded with shadows and darkness, creating suspense or suspicion

side lighting. Direct lighting from one side. This may indicate moral ambiguity or a split personality

Editing Techniques

cross cutting. Cut into action that is happening simultaneously. Also called **parallel editing cut.** The most common editing technique. Two pieces of film are spliced together to "cut" to another image

dissolve. A kind of fade in which one image is slowly replaced by another. It can create a connection between images. Also called a **lap dissolve**

eye-line match. Cut to an object, then to a person. This technique shows what a person seems to be looking at

fade. Can be to or from black or white. A fade begins in darkness and gradually assumes full brightness (fade-in) or the image gradually gets darker (fade-out). A fade often implies that time has passed

flashback. A cut or dissolve to action that has happened in the past

flashforward. A scene that breaks the chronological continuity of the main narrative by depicting events that happen in the future. Contrast with *flashback*

jump cut. An interruption to the continuity of time, in which the image in a shot closely matches the image of the previous shot

lap dissolve. See *dissolve*

montage. A number of images are quickly flashed across the screen to suggest action the director may not have wanted to film directly. Hitchcock used a montage effect when filming the shower scene in *Psycho*, for example, to get the film past the censors

parallel editing. See *cross cutting*

shot-reverse-shot. A shot of one subject, then another, then back to the first. Often used for conversation or reaction shots; shot-reverse-shot is also used with eye-line match

stop motion. A form of animation in which objects are filmed frame by frame and altered slightly between each frame. The original *King Kong* (1933) made extensive use of stop-motion photography

wipe. A new image wipes off the previous image. A wipe is more fluid than a cut and quicker than a dissolve

Sound

diegetic. Sound that would logically be heard by the characters in the film

nondiegetic. Sound that could not be heard by the characters but is designed for audience reaction. An example might be ominous music for foreshadowing

Appendix B
Charts and Rubrics

The following rubrics are included for your use as you teach your students how to read and create film. I have also included notes to help you get the most out of these tools.

This graphic organizer is great for comparing scenes from different directors. One of the goals of this class is to help students understand that given films do not represent the "right" interpretation but merely "an" interpretation. Different storytellers have different voices and different styles. This graphic organizer helps students begin to understand that concept.

Film Comparison Chart

Name:_____Pd._____

Directions: Use the chart below to help you sound smart like a filmmaker as you compare and contrast two related films.

	FILM 1: DIRECTOR:	FILM 2: DIRECTOR:
CINEMATOGRAPHY What do you notice relative to the camera work, including types of shots, movement, framing, color saturation, etc.?		
ACTING How believable are the actors? Do they have good chemistry? (This should be pretty obvious, though the trick can sometimes be in determining the difference between the acting and the writing.)		
SCRIPT How believable is the story line? How compelling? How cliché? Is the action paced well? Are there any obvious plot holes, etc.?		
EDITING Is the action paced well (ties in with script)? Are the transitions smooth?		
DIRECTING Do the director's choices help the story? Is the style consistent? Is the style appropriate?		
OVERALL Do you like the film? Why? Remember, you are a film student, so I expect you to sound like one!		

Film Observation Chart

This graphic organizer is useful when examining a single scene in terms of the basic elements of filmmaking. In essence, students learn to isolate specific contributions to the filmmaking process.

Film Observation Chart

FILM:_____ DIRECTOR:_____

SCRIPT How believable is the story? How compelling? How cliché? Are there obvious plot holes?	
ACTING How believable are the actors? Do the actors have good chemistry?	
DIRECTING Do the director's choices help the story? Is the style consistent?	
CINEMATOGRAPHY How compelling are the images? Are the shots framed well? Do they help tell the story? Would you understand the action without dialogue?	
EDITING Is the action paced well? Are the transitions smooth?	
OVERALL Do you like the film? Why?	

Peer Observation Chart

This graphic organizer is helpful for when students are observing and evaluating their classmates' film projects. Personally, I prefer to have students present their projects twice, the first time with no commentary, so as to get a first reaction. The second time, however, I ask students to teach or explain their work, so that they can be sure we understand what they were trying to do. Only on this second run-through do I and the students in the audience take notes. I encourage audience members to keep their comments as technical and specific as possible.

Peer Observation Chart

Name:_____Pd._____

Directions: One of the major reasons we study film is to determine techniques we might use effectively on our own projects. Use this graphic organizer to keep track of your observations.

FILM TITLE	FILM TYPE	TECHNIQUES I LIKE	TECHNIQUES TO AVOID

Important Takeaways:

Film Rubric/Observation Sheet (Open-Ended, Numeric)

I use these rubrics to record my observations for my students' film projects. I use the same rubric for every project so that my students know what to expect, and because I tend to look for the same elements, regardless. My one caveat here is that I do not assign each category a specific value when determining the grade; rather, I prefer to reward what students have done well. Some students are strong cinematographers; others are great editors. I want to expose my students to all of the skill sets, but I also want to help encourage them as they gravitate toward a specific part of the filmmaking process.

Film Rubric/Observation Sheet

Pd.____

Film Title: _____ **Director:** _____   **Assignment (circle one):**   music video   silent film   animated film   ten-minute film
Camera Work: What does the camera "see"? How well framed are the shots? What angles are used? Do those angles appear to have been chosen for any specific reason?
Editing: How well edited are the shots? Have they been trimmed? Are the proper editing techniques used (cuts, wipes, dissolves, fades)? Are the transitions timed well?
Pacing: Does the story progress too quickly? Too slowly? Do the shots seem to be a comfortable length, or do they go on a bit too long?
Acting: How well do the actors fit their roles? Are they believable?
Lighting: Are the shots well lit? Do they appear too dark? Too bright? Is the lighting consistent throughout the film?
Sound: How well does the sound track match the action? Can the actors' lines be heard clearly?
Special Effects: What special effects, unusual camera work, or interesting editing techniques are used? How do those elements impact the film?
Overall Impression of the Film: Looking at the piece as a whole, what do you think? Does the piece appeal to you? Explain.

Film Rubric/Observation Sheet

Pd._____

Film Title: _____ **Director:** _____

Assignment (circle one):   music video   silent film   animated film   ten-minute film

Camera Work: Are the images well composed? Well framed? Are the angles interesting? Do those angles appear to have been chosen for any specific reason?

1   2   3   4   5   6

Editing: How well edited are the shots? Have they been trimmed? Are the proper editing techniques used (cuts, wipes, dissolves, fades)? Are the transitions timed well?

1   2   3   4   5   6

Pacing: Does the story progress too quickly? Too slowly? Do the shots seem to be a comfortable length, or do they go on a bit too long?

1   2   3   4   5   6

Acting: How well do the actors fit their roles? Are they believable?

1   2   3   4   5   6

Lighting: Are the shots well lit? Do they appear too dark? Too bright? Is the lighting consistent throughout the film? Did the cinematographer white balance?

1   2   3   4   5   6

Sound: How well does the soundtrack match the action? Can the actors' lines be heard clearly?

1   2   3   4   5   6

Special Effects: What special effects, unusual camera work, or interesting editing techniques are used? How do those elements impact the film?

1   2   3   4   5   6

Overall Impression of the Film: Looking at the piece as a whole, what do you think? Does the piece appeal to you? Explain.

1   2   3   4   5   6

TOTAL POINTS:_____

Documentary Rubric/Observation Sheet (Open-Ended, Numeric)

I use these rubrics to record my observations of my students' documentary film projects. The sections are very similar to those from my other film rubrics so that my students know what to expect, and because I tend to look for the same elements, regardless.

Documentary Rubric/Observation Sheet

Pd._____

Film Title: _____ Director: _____
Camera Work: What does the camera "see"? How well framed are the shots? What angles are used? Do those angles appear to have been chosen for any specific reason?
Editing: How well edited are the shots? Have they been trimmed? Are the proper editing techniques used (cuts, wipes, dissolves, fades)? Are the transitions timed well?
Pacing: Does the story progress too quickly? Too slowly? Do the shots seem to be a comfortable length, or do they go on a bit too long?
Acting: How well do the actors fit their roles? Are they believable?
Lighting: Are the shots well lit? Do they appear too dark? Too bright? Is the lighting consistent throughout the film?
Sound: How well does the sound track match the action? Can the actors' lines be heard clearly?
Required Elements: Does the film include interviews, cutaways, live footage, process footage, and archival footage? Are the scenes chosen well? Do they add to our understanding of the story?
Overall Impression of the Film: Looking at the piece as a whole, what do you think? Does the piece appeal to you? Explain.

Documentary Rubric/Observation Sheet

Pd.____

Film Title: _____ Director: _____

Camera Work: Are the images well composed? Well framed? Are the angles interesting? Do those angles appear to have been chosen for any specific reason?

1   2   3   4   5   6

Editing: How well edited are the shots? Have they been trimmed? Are the proper editing techniques used (cuts, wipes, dissolves, fades)? Are the transitions timed well?

1   2   3   4   5   6

Pacing: Does the story progress too quickly? Too slowly? Do the shots seem to be a comfortable length, or do they go on a bit too long?

1   2   3   4   5   6

Acting: How well do the actors fit their roles? Are they believable?

1   2   3   4   5   6

Lighting: Are the shots well lit? Do they appear too dark? Too bright? Is the lighting consistent throughout the film? Did the cinematographer white balance?

1   2   3   4   5   6

Sound: How well does the sound track match the action? Can the actors' lines be heard clearly?

1   2   3   4   5   6

Required Elements: Does the film include interviews, cutaways, live footage, process footage, and archival footage? Are the scenes chosen well? Do they add to our understanding of the story?

1   2   3   4   5   6

Overall Impression of the Film: Looking at the piece as a whole, what do you think? Does the piece appeal to you? Explain.

1   2   3   4   5   6

TOTAL POINTS:_____

Appendix C

Sample Film Technique Assessments

Checking for Understanding: Framing

Directions: *You have decided to film a documentary about this class, because seriously, who would believe what goes on in here? Given the scenarios below, identify the framing technique that would best serve your purpose. Terms may be used more than once or not at all.*

A. establishing shot
B. long shot
C. knee shot
D. cowboy shot
E. medium shot
F. close-up
G. extreme close-up
H. two shot

1. _____ You have an interesting idea for framing your character, Seamus. You have decided to film him standing in front of a mirror. You see Seamus—both of him—in the same frame. The real Seamus is on the right third while his reflection is in the same position on the left. Your shot gives the impression that you are filming two distinct characters. What type of framing are you using?

2. _____ After having studied the films of Kurosawa, you have decided to give your main character, Sally Whatsherface, a facial tic. You feel that such a tic will both serve to humanize little Sally and set her apart from your other characters. You want to showcase this facial tic, so you decide to push in so that only Sally's shoulders and face are visible. Which framing technique have you used?

3. _____ Bobby Vroom-Vroom rides his motorcycle everywhere he goes. Everybody but Bobby, however, realizes the motorcycle in question is really just a figment of Bobby Vroom-Vroom's imagination. To let the audience in on the joke, you will need to show a shot of the school hallway with Bobby weaving in and out of traffic. The camera will show him from head to toe. Which framing technique will you use?

4. _____ You have decided to do a biopic on the mysterious Chuckie Chainsawhands. He doesn't talk much, but that's okay—his chain saw hands make a lot of noise for him. Anyway, you tend to frame your characters from the waist up. In Chuckie's case, you want the audience to be able to see those amazing appendages, so you pull the camera back just a bit. In order to see everything clearly, you decide to frame Chuckie from his knees up. What framing technique have you decided to use?

5. _____ "Given budget constraints," Mr. C addresses the class, "this year's class pet will be Bruce, Bruce the Creek Pebble." He pats down his pockets, looking for Bruce. Suddenly, Mr. C smiles at the class and pulls something from his pocket. "Everybody say hello to Bruce!" The next shot is of Bruce sitting there in Mr. C's hand. Bruce has no legs. Bruce has no arms. Bruce has a lopsided grin, drawn with a black marker, and one of those jiggly stick-on eyes. He had two, but one fell off. Given that you have decided to push in until that one jiggly eye fills the screen, what framing have you used?

6. _____ Sammy the Swashbuckler makes all the ladies swoon. So as to swash all those buckles, Sammy does lots of push-ups. In fact, Sammy's contract stipulates that 75 percent of all shots of him be framed from his waist up. What type of framing must you therefore most often use when filming Sammy?

7. _____ Tammy thinks she is a tiger. When people try to speak to her, she just growls in response. Her favorite t-shirt is orange with black stripes, and she always eats the same cereal for breakfast (the one with the tiger on the front of the box). She even wears a clip-on tail. You decide that you absolutely have to get that clip-on tail in the shot. You therefore decide to film Tammy so that her whole body is visible, head to toe. What framing have you decided to use?

8. _____ Gerald the Garden Gnome just stands in the bushes near Mr. C's front steps all day. It's actually a nice shady spot with a good view of the street. He never says anything to anyone—after all, he *is* a garden gnome. Gerald just stands there clutching his belly and grinning at the world. You decide to push in close enough to frame Gerald from his gold-painted belt buckle up, get a nice shallow focus going, and create a bokeh (out-of-focus) effect in the background. Given that you are filming Gerald from the waist up, what framing have you decided to use?

9. _____ Techno Tracy never goes anywhere without her silver sequined jacket, dark sunglasses, and light-up tennis shoes. She is also a huge fan of neon hair dye, and her super-awesome spiked hair is never the same color twice. To be sure you capture Tracy's sass in all its glory, you'll need to push in close enough to see Tracy from the shoulders up. What framing have you decided to use?

10. _____ Alana, Mother of Iguanas, loves lizards. She is not a real fan of people, but she does love her some lizards. So you decide that when Alana makes her grand entrance with one or two lizards perched on her shoulder in your new film, you want to frame her such that the audience sees her from mid-torso up. What type of framing must you therefore use?

11. _____ When it comes to saving the environment, Alma is all about it. Lately, she has been concerned about how many plastic straws wind up in the ocean, choking sea turtles and other marine life. Ever the entrepreneur, she has had an epiphany and has decided to market short sections of dried, hollowed-out bamboo as Nature's answer to the straw. She decides to start a marketing campaign with a shot of a sea turtle wearing sunglasses drinking from a coconut through a bamboo straw. We see the turtle from his turtle belly button up so as to show off his six-pack. What framing technique has Alma decided to use?

12. _____ Everyone should have a goal, and Jimmy the Fish is no exception. His goal is to be a crime boss on the lower East Side. Sorry—*the* crime boss. He has always heard clothes make the man, so Jimmy likes to wear dark Italian suits with pinstripes. He is never without a flower in his lapel. But his true love is his collection of fine handmade Italian footwear. In order to show off his footwear, Jimmy prefers that when he makes his entrance, the camera is far enough back so as to show him from head to toe. What type of shot is this?

13. _____ Darryl is tall, has crazy eyes, and loves to hug. He is a hugger. Dogs, trees, random shopping carts he finds sitting unattended in parking lots, but mostly he hugs people. Big, bone-crushing hugs. You decide that since one of the first rules of storytelling is the storyteller needs to help the audience relate to the characters, you want to include a shot from a random classmate's POV as Darryl hugs them. The sequence you envision involves the classmate staring at himself in a mirror, wondering which one of himself is real. Then we hear "Darryl hug!" from somewhere off-camera. The classmate spins and is promptly enveloped. The last shot before the blackness of unconsciousness is a giant shirt button taking up almost the entire frame. What framing technique have you chosen if all the audience sees is that button pressing into their vision?

14. _____ Caroline is quite the artist. In fact, she loves art so much, she never goes anywhere without a brush tucked behind her ear or stuck into a pocket of her flower-power overalls. For Caroline, the world is her canvas. In fact, whenever she enters a room, she immediately checks out the wall space, imagining the mural she would like to paint there. You decide to film a scene from Caroline's point of view as she walks into a new room. What type of shot are you using, given that you are showing the area where the next scene will take place?

15. _____ Mr. C likes teaching, but one day, he will achieve his dream of playing in a rock band. That's what he tells himself, anyway. Given his dreams of superstardom, one should not be surprised that he always wears his hot-rod red electric guitar, even while teaching. You want to include a shot in which the bottom of the frame is halfway between Mr. C's knees and his waist in order to include that beautiful guitar. Which framing technique have you decided to use?

ANSWERS: Checking for Understanding: Framing

Directions: Keep in mind as you check these answers that there are many different ways to film the shots described in the quiz. The answers below represent the most likely or obvious way to create the desired effect. If, however, students come up with a different way to film the shot but still manage to convey the desired effect (very important!), you may want to give them the opportunity to explain their reasoning before giving or taking away credit.

#	Letter	Shot	Description
1.	H	two shot	You are, in essence, filming two characters here.
2.	F	close-up	We are close enough to see only Sally's head and shoulders.
3.	B	long shot	We see Bobby head to toe.
4.	C	knee shot	We see Chuckie from his knees up.
5.	G	extreme close-up	Bruce's one eye fills the screen.
6.	E	medium shot	We see Sammy from his waist up.
7.	B	long shot	We see Tammy head to toe.
8.	E	medium shot	We see Gerald from the waist up.
9.	F	close-up	We are close enough to see only Tracy's head and shoulders.
10.	F	close-up	We are close enough to see Alana from mid-torso up.
11.	E	medium shot	We see the turtle from his bellybutton up.
12.	B	long shot	We see Jimmy from head to toe.
13.	G	extreme close-up	We see only that giant shirt button.
14.	A	establishing shot	We are seeing where the next scene will take place.
15.	D	cowboy shot	We see Mr. C from mid-thigh up.

Checking for Understanding: Angles

Directions: *Your documentary is off to a great start, but you have miles to go before you sleep. You have a story to deliver! Given the scenarios below, identify the angles that would best serve your purpose. Terms may be used more than once or not at all.*

A. eye level
B. high angle
C. bird's eye
D. God's eye

E. low angle
F. over the shoulder
G. point of view
H. Dutch tilt

1. _____ You are planning your main character Seamus's entrance shot. You want the audience to understand that your character is in control of the situation—*every* situation. Which angle best conveys your character's total control?

2. _____ Little Sally Whatsherface has had a bad day. At the moment, she is shuffling slowly down a long hallway directly toward the camera. She is drooling, her left eye is twitching noticeably, and she is dragging a broken chair leg behind her. Little Sally is radiating bad intentions. You are filming this shot from the perspective of Vicky Miller, who is standing at the far end of the hallway in question—Vicky, who inadvertently sat in Sally Whatsherface's chair at lunch. Given that we see Sally through Vicky's eyes, which angle are we using?

3. _____ Bobby Vroom-Vroom is in a high-speed chase on his invisible motorcycle through the hallways at school. You decide you could get a really cool shot if you film the chase from the perspective of a terrified passenger on the back of Bobby's invisible bike. (There is no actual passenger on Bobby's bike.) From this angle, you reason, we should be able to see over and past Bobby in order to make out his quarry disappearing around a corner just ahead. Which angle have you chosen?

4. _____ Chuckie Chainsawhands loves going to school. He likes the people, he enjoys his classes, and he especially likes when the cafeteria ladies let him man the meat-carving station at lunch. It's his way of giving back, Chuckie believes. But on this day, in the middle of carving a large hunk of roast beef for Little Sally Whatsherface (who kind of scares Chuckie, to be honest), one of Chuckie's chain saw hands unexpectedly runs out of gas. Chuckie knows Sally won't be happy. What angle could you use to show that things are suddenly not going so well?

5. _____ You'd like to do a dramatic shot of Bruce, the class pet. Bruce the Creek Pebble. You decide normal angles just won't work. You envision Bruce, just sitting there on Mr. C's desk; the camera is directly above Bruce, looking down on Bruce. You think you'd like to imply that old Bruce is being watched…but by whom? That doesn't matter. Given that the camera is directly above Bruce, which angle have you chosen to use?

6. _____ Sammy the Swashbuckler likes to swash buckles and save the day. In fact, he has developed a trademark pose—he stands at a roughly forty-five-degree angle, hands on his hips, head back, chiseled jaw thrust forward, and his eyes twinkling for all they are worth. In fact, his contract stipulates that, when Sammy is in this pose, the camera must film Sammy from close to the ground, looking upward, so as to make Sammy appear large and in charge. Which angle does Sammy's contract stipulate you use?

7. _____ Tammy the Tiger has found the perfect spot to ambush Bobby Vroom-Vroom as he whizzes down the hall to his next class: from on top of the lockers in the main hallway. She figures nobody will ever look up that high. You decide to film the inevitable confrontation through Bobby's eyes as he veers in and out of the pedestrian traffic in the hallway, careening toward a conflict he has no idea is about to go down. Which technique have you chosen to use?

8. _____ Gerald the Garden Gnome is definitely on his game today. He got into a staring contest with a centipede, and guess who didn't blink? This guy! In fact, Gerald has never blinked. Ever. You figure if you place the camera right in front Gerald's grinning face, you can convey Gerald's sunny disposition and rakish charm. You want the audience to see Gerald as the garden gnome equivalent of Jimmy Stewart. Which angle will you use?

9. _____ When it comes to school dances, Techno Tracy has all the moves. First, she scouts the room, identifying the best dancers. Then, she makes her way over to the DJ and baits the hook by requesting "Boom Shaka Laka" — only the best dance song ever. As soon as those first sultry notes cut through the kerosene fog and laser lights, Techno Tracy takes control. You decide you have to include a scene in your film about this giant of the dance floor, and you figure the absolutely coolest shot would be from directly overhead, looking down on Tracy as the crowd forms an admiring circle around her. Which angle did you decide to use?

10. _____ Alana, Mother of Iguanas, loves nothing more than unleashing her iguanas on the unsuspecting public. You decide to get an awesome "carnage shot," in which you film the scene from behind Alana (for your own safety, of course). You notice that, while your focus is on the iguanas getting into *everything* and freaking people out (though you're safe, back there behind Alana), Alana's shoulder, neck, and part of her head still take up part of the left side of the screen as you film past her. Which angle are you using?

11. _____ On a recent trip to the beach, Alma finds several discarded plastic six-pack rings. She is very angry, because she knows the rings are very dangerous for wildlife. She decides to take a picture to post on social media, to which she can then add a fiery message. In order to show just how wrong beach litter is, Alma decides to tilt her camera so the bottom of the frame is not level with the horizon. Which technique does Alma use?

12. _____ Jimmy the Fish has the absolute *best* shoes. Granted, they look straight out of the 1930s, but hey, he's cultivating a look! You decide that a really cool shot would be to tilt the camera down toward the ground and hold it stationary long enough for Jimmy to walk into the frame and stop. Everybody would know who it was because of those cool shoes. Then, you plan to tilt up for the reveal of Jimmy's smirking-but-trying-hard-to-be-nonchalant face. Which angle would you be using as you point the camera down at Jimmy's feet?

13. _____ Darryl is a big dude—big personality, big hands, big ideas. You decide that to drive this point home to your audience, you should film the quad at lunchtime from the corner of the roof of the tallest building on campus as if from Darryl's point of view. That way, the audience can look down at an angle on the entire student body from a good distance away. Which angle have you decided to use?

14. _____ Nothing fazes Caroline. As an artist, she always sees the beauty in the world around her. Plus, she plays rugby. She knows she can handle herself. Given that Caroline is confident and in control, which angle could you use to convey these attributes to your audience?

15. _____ During today's lesson, it becomes obvious to everyone in class that Mr. C is channeling his favorite band, Dude Righteous! As the lesson reaches its exciting climax, Mr. C drops to his knees and plays a few quick

scales far up on the neck of his guitar. His eyes are closed in concentration as he mouths the notes. As he finishes playing, he falls backward onto the floor, his knees tucked awkwardly beneath him. (He realizes he may need help getting back up.) You decide the thing to do instead is to put the audience in the moment by showing Mr. C from the perspective of the students in the classroom. Which technique have you chosen to use?

ANSWERS: Checking for Understanding: Angles

Directions: *Keep in mind as you check these answers that there are many different ways to film the shots described on the quiz. The answers below represent the most likely or obvious way to create the desired effect. If, however, students come up with a different way to film the shot but still manage to convey the desired effect (very important!), you may want to give them the opportunity to explain their reasoning before giving or taking away credit.*

1. E low angle — The camera is low, angled up, and implies control or power.
2. G point of view — We are filming as if through Vicky's eyes.
3. F over the shoulder — We are able to see over and past Bobby.
4. H Dutch tilt — A Dutch tilt is a great way to show that all is not well.
5. D God's eye — The camera is directly overhead and implies surveillance.
6. E low angle — The camera is low, angled up, and implies control or power.
7. G point of view — We are filming as if through Bobby's eyes.
8. A eye level — The camera is right in front of Gerald's smiling face.
9. D God's eye — You're filming from directly overhead.
10. F over the shoulder — You're filming from behind, over her shoulder.
11. H Dutch tilt — The bottom of the frame is not level with the horizon.
12. B high angle — The camera is pointed down at Jimmy's feet.
13. C bird's eye — You're looking down from some distance away.
14. E low angle — A low angle conveys confidence and control.
15. G point of view — You're filming from the students' perspective.

Checking for Understanding: Camera Movement

Directions: *Sure, you're tired, but your film isn't going to make itself. You're making art! Given the scenarios below, identify the camera movement that would best serve your purpose. Terms may be used more than once or not at all.*

A. pan
B. tilt
C. zoom
D. dolly/tracking
E. boom/crane
F. Steadicam
G. arc
H. trombone shot
I. whip pan

1. _____ Our friend Seamus is not very tall. Honestly, he's roughly the size of a hobbit, minus the hairy feet. In any event, having not been paying close attention, Seamus finds himself stuck on an elevator with school basketball team. As Seamus cranes his neck to look up at the player standing in front of him, what camera movement does he approximate with his head?

2. _____ Little Sally Whatsherface is on the prowl, looking for her next victim. You decide you want to film from Little Sally's POV—really "putting the audience in there," so to speak. As Little Sally quickly looks left and right (Little Sally is a bit spastic), searching for that next special someone, which camera movement will you be using?

3. _____ Bobby Vroom-Vroom loves his invisible motorcycle. Just don't make the mistake of telling him it is not real; he rides it everywhere. But Bobby knows his teachers do not want him to ride his bike into their classrooms, so he is always careful to put down his kickstand and park his bike beside the classroom door. One day, though, Bobby walks out of his classroom only to discover that someone has stolen his bike. Which camera movement would help convey to the audience Bobby's moment of horrible realization?

4. _____ Chuckie Chainsawhands, contrary to what one might think, is quite the dancer. The dude has moves; at the school dance, Chuckie decides to show them off. You decide it would be fun to push in close on Chuckie from across the room—besides, it really isn't safe to be close to Chuckie when he is dancing. Given that you are not getting any closer to Chuckie, but Chuckie is increasingly filling your frame, what technique have you used?

5. _____ "Hey, class, it's time for recess," Mr. C announces to the class. "Why don't you take our class pet, Bruce the Creek Pebble, outside and let him play?" Mr. C smiles and sets Bruce on the table. The class begins to slowly gather around him. Bruce's one good eye jiggles just a bit. You envision a shot in which the camera rotates around Bruce as the children close in on him. Given that the camera is rotating around Bruce and that Bruce is always in the shot, which camera movement have you selected?

6. _____ When you think of people who are very conscious of their public image, you think of Sammy Swashbuckler. Sammy studies himself on film to be sure every frame counts. That said, Sammy's contract stipulates that whenever he strikes his signature pose, the camera must slowly move toward him as he stares confidently off-screen. Which type of movement would allow you to dramatically roll the camera in close?

7. _____ Tammy the Tiger is waiting patiently for her archnemesis Bobby Vroom-Vroom to screech into view beneath her perch atop the hallway lockers. She can hear him shifting gears as he careens around a corner in the distance. Next to those stupid laser pointers, Tammy hates Bobby Vroom-Vroom's motorcycle more than anything. Just as Bobby is about to enter the danger zone, he happens to look up and lock eyes with Tammy. Bobby suddenly realizes what is about to go down. Which technique should you use while filming Bobby to convey the idea that he realizes what horrible thing is about to happen?

8. _____ You figure you could get a nice shot of the bird feeder in Mr. C's front yard, then rotate the camera left to right so we see the front yard, then stop rotating as Gerald the Garden Gnome comes into view. Given that the camera does not move but simply rotates, which camera movement have you just used?

9. _____ Yeah, baby! Techno Tracy is working it! Go, Tracy! She's reaching up; she's reaching down! Is there any place Techno Tracy can't reach? Just then, Tracy clasps her hands in front of her and her arms begin to do… the wave! It is as if her arms have become one beautiful sine curve! You decide to rotate around Tracy as she demonstrates this masterpiece of a move, your camera always focused on Tracy like a small moon orbiting a sequin-clad planet on which all the inhabitants rock fuego dance moves! Which camera movement have you just decided to use?

10. _____ You have a fantastic idea. You decide that, at the very moment Alana, Mother of Iguanas, unleashes her iguanas on an unsuspecting public, you will spring up with your camera held low to the ground and just behind a large iguana specimen Alana calls "Walter," and you will follow him as he wanders around and over whatever happens to be on the floor when people freak out and run screaming from the room. Because you cannot predict Walter's movements, you will not be able to lay a track, and the discarded items strewn across the floor mean that anything on wheels will not work. You will have to hold your camera and walk behind Walter. It's all good, though—you have a rig you can attach your camera to with a bit of counterweight to reduce the shakiness. Which movement will you use?

11. _____ Having stumbled upon a clutch of sea turtle eggs on her recent trip to the beach, Alma has a fantastic idea. She can film them emerging and making their way to the open water! Alma decides to add a lightly weighted attachment to the bottom of her camera to reduce the shake when she goes for handheld shots—after all, she figures she will be moving a lot, and a tripod just wouldn't be practical. After days of waiting, the magic moment finally arrives! Unfortunately, Alma forgets to turn the light off on her camera, and the turtles, seeing the light, head in the wrong direction. None of them make it to the water. (Alma doesn't like to talk about that part.) Her camera rig works like a charm, however! Which camera movement does Alma use when filming those doomed turtles?

12. _____ Jimmy the Fish just had his shoes polished, which reminds you of that shot you wanted to capture but have not been able to yet. Well, today is the day! You aim the camera at the ground, and once Jimmy's freshly polished shoes step into the frame, you rotate the camera slowly up from his shoes until you are looking directly at his smug little face. You notice he is chewing a toothpick. Who does that? Anyway, which camera movement did you use?

13. _____ Darryl has decided he wants to be a filmmaker; he feels he has things to say. And when you have something to say, but you don't say it—well, you feel like you might just explode. So, Darryl has begun planning out shots he would like to use. He does not have a story yet, but once he does, he'll be ready. One of his favorite shots involves the camera passing just over the heads of a group of students (who look suspiciously like his classmates) then rising vertically alongside the side of the school building the students are standing next to until the camera reaches the ledge at the

top of the building. That's where Darryl will be standing, dressed in black and wearing a cape and a mask, surveying the action below him. He realizes the shot is complex. Which movement will he use to pull it off?

14. _____ Caroline asked to leave class to get some water, but on the way back, her eye was caught by the invitingly blank walls in the hallway. Caroline decides she must act. You decide you will conceal her work until the end. You're not sure how you'll film the actual act of painting, but you know that at the end, you want the camera to be mounted to a tripod halfway down the hallway, so you can swivel left to right, approximating the perspective of someone seeing the mural for the first time. Given that the camera swivels horizontally but otherwise does not move, which camera movement will you use?

15. _____ Mr. C has enlisted your help in producing a video of the day's lesson, which he can then post online. He feels that, to provide proper emphasis, he will strike an open G chord on his hot-rod red electric guitar every time he makes a particularly good point. In order to drive this effect home, he feels the background should appear to fall away while he continues to be filmed from the knees up. Which technique must you use in order to achieve the effect Mr. C wants?

ANSWERS: Checking for Understanding: Camera Movement

Directions: Keep in mind as you check these answers that there are many different ways to film the shots described on the quiz. The answers below represent the most likely or obvious way to create the desired effect. If, however, students come up with a different way to film the shot but still manage to convey the desired effect (very important!), you may want to give them the opportunity to explain their reasoning before giving or taking away credit.

1. B tilt — Seamus cranes his neck to look up at the tall players.
2. I whip pan — Sally looks left and right, on a horizontal plane, very quickly.
3. H trombone shot — Bobby is having a moment of horrible realization.
4. C zoom — The camera is not getting closer, but Chuckie is getting bigger.
5. G arc — The camera is rotating around Bruce, focused on Bruce.
6. D dolly/tracking — The camera rolls dramatically toward Sammy.
7. H trombone shot — Bobby is having yet another horrible realization.
8. A pan — The camera is rotating left to right.
9. G arc — The camera is rotating around Tracy, always focused on her.
10. F Steadicam — You are holding the camera, and it has a counterweight.
11. F Steadicam — The shot is handheld, and there is a counterweight.
12. B tilt — A vertical rotation—shoes to face—is a tilt.
13. E boom/crane — A complex shot like this one requires a boom/crane.
14. A pan — The camera swivels left to right.
15. H trombone shot — The background falls away, but the framing doesn't change.

Checking for Understanding: Lighting

Directions: *You absolutely cannot believe the things you have seen in this class, and you are not entirely sure your audience will, either. No matter! The show must go on, right? Given the scenarios below, identify the lighting technique that would best serve your purpose. Terms may be used more than once or not at all.*

A. high key
B. low key
C. bottom lighting
D. side lighting
E. front lighting
F. back lighting

1. _____ Seamus is a great kid—everyone says so. But what they don't know is that Seamus is a sociopath. He's like a pumpkin left out too long after Halloween: looks okay on the outside but completely rotten on the inside. Which lighting technique would help your audience understand that Seamus is not all he appears to be?

2. _____ Little Sally Whatsherface has proven to be box office gold, so you decide to add a cool jump scare scene in which a random character puts her books in a locker and then turns to head off to her next class. The pay-off in this particular shot is, as our unsuspecting character turns down the hallway, Little Sally Whatsherface is standing right in front of her. Because of the lighting, we can only see Little Sally's silhouette. We recognize her, though, because of her crazy hair, sprouting from her head in all directions like a cornfield after a tornado. Which lighting technique have you selected for Little Sally?

3. _____ Nothing makes Bobby Vroom-Vroom happier than riding his motorcycle. Bobby knows, though, that riding his bike at night could be very dangerous—especially, as you know, because his motorcycle is really just a figment of his imagination. So, Bobby decides to ride his bike only when the sun is shining brightly to ensure he will be visible to oncoming traffic. As a result, Bobby will typically be filmed in what type of lighting?

4. _____ Of all the nice people in school, everybody agrees that Chuckie Chainsawhands is the nicest. So as to make sure the audience understands how nice Chuckie is, you decide to light him so his face is softly aglow with a bit of a halo effect going on. Which lighting technique have you chosen to use?

5. _____ Bruce is under a leaf with a stick poking him in the back and in a gutter along the roof of the school, where he has been since Mr. C suggested the class take him out at recess to play. He cannot see anything because the moisture has caused his one stick-on eye to fall off. Plus, Bruce is a creek pebble. Given that Bruce is under a leaf in the dark, how would you describe the lighting?

6. _____ When it comes to making dramatic entrances, Sammy Swashbuckler is a pro. Sammy is a huge fan of proper lighting, mostly because he knows how to use it to his advantage. His favorite entrance involves ensuring that all anyone can see of him is a dramatic silhouette. Sammy likes to imagine his foes writhing in fear and consternation when they behold his shadowy self. Which lighting technique allows Sammy to make his signature entrance?

7. _____ Tammy the Tiger is working on a report on tigers, and she just came across some interesting information: tigers, it would seem, are ambush predators. Tammy decides ambushing some prey seems like a great idea. She just needs to choose her prey. Chuckie is out, given he has chainsaws for hands, and nobody has seen Bruce since a week ago last Tuesday. Bobby is in the infirmary getting nasty scratches tended to. Might as well try little Sally Whatsherface. Tammy decides her best bet is to find the darkest corner she can, so she will be practically invisible. Which lighting technique has Tammy decided will give her the best chance of remaining invisible until the last possible moment?

8. _____ Gerald the Garden Gnome is just doing his thing, standing there, not blinking, staring at the house across the street. As it happens, Gerald happens to be positioned just over one of those little spotlights Mr. C set up in the flowerbed to illuminate the front of his house. Now that the sun has gone down and the spotlights have come on, Gerald's happy-go-lucky blue-eyed grin takes on a much more sinister air. Which lighting technique has caused this dramatic transformation?

9. _____ Tracy is sitting quietly in class, doing her assignment. To the casual observer, Tracy looks like the model student. But Tracy is so much more. When the lights go down and the kerosene fog comes creeping across the floor, Tracy turns into Techno Tracy, queen of the dance floor. Which lighting technique helps the audience understand that Tracy is so much more than what she first appears?

10. _____ Alana, Mother of Iguanas, likes to hide in the shadows. That way, she can sneak up on people more easily and release her iguanas to wreak havoc. If there is a shadow in a room, that is where you will find Alana. Plus, hiding in the darkness will help make her entrance all the more dramatic once she decides to emerge. Which lighting technique does Alana prefer while she waits to make her move on an unsuspecting public?

11. _____ After the recent sea turtle debacle, Alma decides to hire a public relations firm to clean up her image. The firm decides to do an infomercial, most of which includes shots of baby animals in order to appeal to viewers' emotions. The final shot is a push in to a close-up on Alma, smiling, and lit so she appears to have a halo. Which lighting technique does the PR firm decide to use for this epic final shot?

12. _____ Jimmy the Fish made a big mistake, and it is going to cost him. Jimmy wants to be a crime boss—the crime boss on the lower East Side. So Jimmy has hired a lighting technician to follow him around and ensure he is lit so as to command the proper level of respect. Unfortunately, the lighting technician misunderstood Jimmy's intent and thought Jimmy wanted the world to know that he had a heart of gold. The lighting technician chose an angle for his lights that would create a halo effect, thereby showing the world Jimmy the Fish's sweet and innocent side. Which lighting technique did the now-out-of-work lighting technician choose?

13. _____ Darryl is a storyteller. He loves the way he can tell a story and make people laugh, or feel angry, or experience acute anxiety. Daryl figures that's about as close as anybody can come to having actual superpowers. And sometimes, when Darryl wants to get an especially noteworthy reaction, he cuts the lights and whips out a flashlight he carries for just this purpose. Once he's switched on the light and placed it under his chin so that the shadows splay ominously upward across his face, his audience can't help but be terrified. Which lighting technique does Darryl use to achieve this effect?

14. _____ Caroline loves art. During the day, she always has a sketchbook under one arm and a pen or a paintbrush tucked behind one ear. But at night, Caroline dons a Guy Fawkes mask, sneaks into old people's windows, and steals their dentures. Then once the sun comes up, she's back to her artsy self, and she uses the dentures to create cool jewelry. Which light-

ing technique could you use for Caroline to indicate to the audience her dual nature?

15. _____ For today's lesson, Mr. C has decided to pep things up by bringing in a laser light rig and a smoke machine. Oh, yeah! Unfortunately, Mr. C did not realize the laser light rig uses real lasers, resulting in some painful burns on his backside, an obliterated classroom wall, and an unscheduled visit from the local fire department. Before things completely unraveled, though, the effect was quite cool. Given that the light source is behind Mr. C and creates a silhouette effect so the students see only his shadowy rock-star outline, which lighting technique has been created by the super-cool lasers?

ANSWERS: Checking for Understanding: Lighting

Directions: Keep in mind as you check these answers that there are many different ways to film the shots described in the quiz. The answers below represent the most likely or obvious way to create the desired effect. If, however, students come up with a different way to film the shot but still manage to convey the desired effect (very important!), you may want to give them the opportunity to explain their reasoning before giving or taking away credit.

1. D side lighting   There is more to Seamus than meets the eye.
2. F back lighting   We only see Little Sally's silhouette.
3. A high key   The sun is shining brightly, so Bobby is clearly visible.
4. E front lighting   His face is softly aglow, and there is a halo effect.
5. B low key   Everything is dark.
6. F back lighting   All we see is Sammy's shadowy self.
7. B low key   Tammy is in the darkest corner she can find.
8. C bottom lighting   Gerald is standing over a spotlight.
9. D side lighting   Tracy is more than she appears to be.
10. B low key   Alana hides in the shadows.
11. E front lighting   Alma has a halo effect, which makes her look innocent.
12. E front lighting   Jimmy has a halo, and appears sweet and innocent.
13. C bottom lighting   Darryl has a flashlight under his chin.
14. D side lighting   You are trying to imply Caroline's dual nature.
15. F back lighting   The light source is behind the subject, creating a silhouette.

Checking for Understanding: Editing

Directions: If Scorsese could see you now, he'd call you "Butter," because you're on a roll! You have a ton of fantastic footage, but you have to figure out how best to put it all together. Given the scenarios below, identify the framing technique that would best serve your purpose. Terms may be used more than once or not at all.

A. cut
B. dissolve
C. wipe
D. flashback
E. flashforward
F. shot-reverse-shot
G. cross cutting
H. eye-line match
I. fade
J. jump cut
K. montage
L. stop motion

1. _____ You decide to get symbolic (or maybe metaphorical, you're not sure which) with your editing: you plan a close-up shot of our good buddy, Seamus, which will slowly become a close-up of an old Halloween pumpkin. The transition is gradual rather than instantaneous. Which transition have you chosen to use?

2. _____ Uh-oh! Little Sally's on a rampage again! Maybe it is because she has lost her shoe, or maybe it has something to do with the stick protruding from her ear. In any event, Little Sally has decided someone must pay. You want to do a shot of little Sally staring off screen, absently ripping the wings off a grasshopper, then a shot of Vicky Miller on the far end of Little Sally's glare, and the obvious focus of Little Sally's growing ire. Which editing technique have you just used?

3. _____ Bobby is sitting in his math class, thinking how nobody ever uses math in real life. Motorcycles, on the other hand…well, people use those all the time. This leads Bobby to think back to when he first got his bike. As Bobby considers that glorious day—which the audience is able to see along with Bobby—we see a clean, instantaneous break between the image of Bobby in class, reminiscing, and Bobby discovering the bike so long ago, though this shot is in sepia, because, yeah. Which editing technique describes that instantaneous break?

4. _____ Nobody knows where Chuckie Chainsawhands came from, and Chuckie doesn't talk about it much. But one day, his emotions brimming, Chuckie begins to tell his assembled friends his life story. You decide that Chuckie's story is pretty boring, so you switch over to an altercation brew-

ing in the hallway between Little Sally Whatsherface and a malfunctioning water fountain. She is using a broken chair leg to beat the bejonky out of that fountain, but the fountain just does not seem to want to cooperate. As you are redirecting your audience to events transpiring at the same time but in another place, which editing technique have you just used?

5. _____ Bruce the Creek Pebble is still in the gutter. The leaf is gone, thanks to a recent rain, but so is Bruce's one good eye, washed away down the drain spout. It's okay, though, because Bruce is a creek pebble, and creek pebbles don't need jiggly stick-on arts-and-crafts eyeballs. There was a time, you know, when Bruce was part of something bigger. A bigger rock, in fact. And that rock was once part of an even bigger rock, and so on back to the time when Bruce was formed in a volcano. You have decided you wish to include this sequence in your hard-hitting exposé about the school where Bruce is still, remember, sitting in a gutter. Which editing technique allows you to explore Bruce's backstory?

6. _____ Sammy Swashbuckler has a favorite editing technique, and it isn't what you might think. Sammy loves when he swings his sword across the screen (It's not a real sword; it's actually just a stick wrapped in tinfoil, which he affectionately named Cattywampus), and as he does so, a new image takes the place of the old. It is more fluid than a cut, which Sammy, ironically, finds dull and boring. To which editing technique is Sammy partial?

7. _____ Tammy the Tiger has found the perfect dark corner from which to ambush little Sally Whatsherface. Tammy begins to think about how the encounter will go down. In her mind, she sees little Sally Whatsherface approaching from the far end of the hallway. Sally's left eye is twitching, and she is dragging a broken chair leg behind her. Sally gets closer, Tammy pounces, blah, blah, blah…but then Tammy sees in her mind Little Sally continuing on her way, her left eye twitching, now holding a tattered tiger tail in her free hand. Which editing technique has helped Tammy come to the conclusion that today is not the day to ambush little Sally Whatsherface?

8. _____ Gerald the Garden Gnome is just standing there, not blinking, as Mr. C heads out the door to go to work. What Gerald doesn't know is that Mr. C has been torn up over the loss of Bruce the Creek Pebble, an erstwhile class pet. As Mr. C shuts the front door and turns to head down the walk, he makes eye contact with Gerald. Gerald stares back. Mr. C, still staring at

Gerald, stops in his tracks, an idea forming behind his tired eyes. Given that your camera shows Mr. C, then Gerald, then Mr. C, which editing technique have you just used?

9. _____ Sometimes the DJ really knows how to catch lightning in a bottle, whatever that means; Tracy isn't really sure. All she knows is that the music is incredible tonight! Suddenly, as someone singing "everybody was kung fu fighting…" drifts across the dance floor, the strobe light malfunctions. AND THEN A REAL KUNG FU FIGHT ERUPTS! It is like some sort of audio fractal. Tracy is enraptured. As she looks around, she catches only the quickest glimpses of what can best be described as dancing ninjas in mid-fight. It is as if their movements are jerky and machine-like, something would see in a flip-book: A FLIP-BOOK ABOUT DANCING FIGHTING NINJAS! Which editing technique most closely approximates what Tracy is seeing around her?

10. _____ Alana, Mother of Iguanas, really likes to imagine the chaos and confusion her army of iguanas, led by a particularly large specimen named Walter, will cause. You would like to show this chaos before it happens, as if the camera were actually in Alana's head. As this action has not yet happened, which editing technique have you chosen to use?

11. _____ Alma wants to make a difference by becoming class president, which will give her the platform she needs to make real and lasting change. She figures her chances are decent, given that only Bobby Vroom-Vroom, Chuckie Chainsawhands, and Bruce the Creek Pebble have been nominated. Bobby has already said he doesn't want to do it because "the open road is calling." Nobody has seen Bruce in a couple of weeks—plus, he's a rock. That just leaves Chuckie. Alma gets her PR team to make a commercial for her. They decide to use a series of quick shots of Alma doing lots of (really) good things, like taking that six-pack ring off that seagull's neck, giving the Heimlich to a dolphin that had ingested a wad of Styrofoam, and— Wait, what is she doing with those baby sea turtles? How did that shot get in there? Given that Alma's PR team has opted to go with a series of quick shots of Alma doing lots of (mostly) good things, which technique have they opted to use?

12. _____ Jimmy the Fish is sad. Ever since that unfortunate incident with the lighting technician, everyone thinks Jimmy is a great guy. Now he is

being invited to sleepovers and birthday parties, and his dreams of running a crime syndicate on the lower East Side are going up in flames. Ah, the good old days! You decide to insert a story about Jimmy's first big score—the first great caper that put him on the charts as the next bad guy to reckon with. Since you are showing something that occurred long ago, which technique will you use?

13. _____ Every superhero needs a costume, so Darryl has decided to make one for himself. He gathers up his supplies: four yards of black velvet, a pair of sunglasses with glow-in-the-dark frames, a pair of bright yellow rain boots, three rolls of black electrical tape, a scarf with an image of an eagle in mid-flight on it, a navy beanie (the closest he could find to black), and a custom utility belt he salvaged from his little brother's costume last Halloween. Once he's down in his basement, he gets to work fashioning his new look. This is going to take a while, so you decide to include a quick shot every couple of minutes or so. In the end, the process takes Darryl three hours; on-screen, however, the process will appear to take thirty seconds (all the time you could spare). Which technique have you decided to use?

14. _____ Caroline has just walked into a new room, and she is blown away by the untapped potential of the massive blank wall space she sees in front of her. Seriously—she could practically hear the walls screaming out to be painted. You decide to include a close-up of Caroline, face squenched (you're pretty sure that's a word) as she considers which colors will work best. She taps her paintbrush against her chin as she considers. Then you want to cut to a shot of the wall that Caroline is considering. Then you want to cut back to Caroline as her expression reveals she has just made up her mind. Given that you are planning a three-shot sequence here, which technique are you considering?

15. _____ Mr. C is in the middle of his lesson, and things are going well. Things are going so well, in fact, that Mr. C begins to daydream about what his life will be like when his rock-star dreams come true. The screen slowly goes black—so black. It's like, how much more black could this be? And the answer is none. None more black. Then, it explodes in a dizzying display of laser lights and kerosene fog. He is up there under the bright lights, shredding some gnarly solo action, and maybe he'll even have dyed his hair! Given that Mr. C's daydream started with the screen slowly going completely black, which technique are we using here?

ANSWERS: Checking for Understanding: Editing

Directions: *Keep in mind as you check these answers that there are many different ways to film the shots described in the quiz. The answers below represent the most likely or obvious way to create the desired effect. If, however, students come up with a different way to film the shot but still manage to convey the desired effect (very important!), you may want to give them the opportunity to explain their reasoning before giving or taking away credit.*

#	Ans	Term	Description
1.	B	dissolve	One image gradually becomes another.
2.	H	eye-line match	We see Sally looking off screen, then we see what she sees.
3.	A	cut	We see a clean, instantaneous break between images.
4.	G	cross cutting	We are jumping to other events transpiring at the same time.
5.	D	flashback	We are exploring Bruce's backstory.
6.	C	wipe	As Sammy's sword crosses the screen, we see a new image.
7.	E	flashforward	Tammy is thinking through what has not yet happened.
8.	F	shot-reverse-shot	We see Mr. C, then Gerald, then back to Mr. C.
9.	L	stop motion	We see action that is jerky and machine-like, like a flip-book.
10.	E	flashforward	This action has not yet happened.
11.	K	montage	We are showing lots of quick shots to tell a story.
12.	D	flashback	We are showing events from long ago.
13.	J	jump cut	The action is long and tedious, but you are only showing clips.
14.	F	shot-reverse-shot	We are shooting a three-shot back-and-forth sequence.
15.	I	fade	Mr. C's daydream begins with the screen slowly going black.

Checking for Understanding: Sound

Directions: You're in post now, baby! Your footage has been shot and edited, and now you are working with your techs on the sound design. Given the scenarios below, identify the type of sound that would best serve your purpose. Terms may be used more than once or not at all.

A. Diegetic B. Nondiegetic

1. _____ The climax of your film is going to be amazing. It will culminate with this kid Seamus pushing a walrus off the roof of the school cafeteria. It isn't nice, of course, but then again, Seamus has always been a bit off. Which type of sound describes the sound of the walrus landing, as gently as a walrus can, on the patio below?

2. _____ Little Sally has a habit of mumbling incoherently, sometimes even growling randomly, as she goes about her business. Which type of sound (aside from "disconcerting") should we consider Little Sally's… vocalizations?

3. _____ The best motorcycles make the coolest sounds; just ask Bobby Vroom-Vroom. And as Bobby rides his motorcycle down the hallway from English to history class, Bobby supplies all of those cool noises himself—from the sound of kick-starting his ride to the rapid acceleration as he takes off down the hallway to echo of screeching tires as he rounds a turn. Given that Bobby is making all of these noises, which type of sound are we experiencing?

4. _____ Chuckie Chainsawhands is everybody's best buddy, but don't try to play Red Rover with him! After all, those chain saw hands are actual functioning gas-powered chain saws. So, which type of sound do those chain saw hands make?

5. _____ Something is tapping, tapping, tapping. The sound is coming from the gutter lining the roof of the school. As the camera rises slowly toward the sound, we see it is a seagull trying to eat Bruce, Bruce the Creek Pebble. The seagull's eyes jiggle weirdly as the bird shakes its head, then it abruptly bends and tries once more to eat Bruce. You find the scene oddly fascinating, perhaps even metaphorical. Regardless, which type of sound describes the noise the bird's beak makes as it slams, yet again, into Bruce?

6. _____ Sammy Swashbuckler is a huge fan of drama. He likes dramatic poses, dramatic lighting, dramatic entrances. He even went so far as to save up his allowance for an entire year to pay a sound tech to "edit in a whooshing sound" every time Sammy swings his mighty sword, Cattywampus. Unfortunately, the sound tech did not have that sound available. He did, however, have a perfectly good sound file of a goat bleating. Sammy will never know, not unless he watches the final edit; no one on the set can hear the sound since it was added in post. But boy the audience sure can, and they think it's awesome! Which kind of sound is this awesome sound?

7. _____ Whenever Tammy the Tiger comes into the frame, you decide to include faint jungle sounds. Her classmates cannot hear these sounds, but the viewers at home most definitely can. Which type of sound have you decided to use?

8. _____ Gerald the Garden Gnome's senses are being assaulted. His life until this moment had been a veritable Garden of Eden (or at least a Flowerbed of Eden). Now he finds himself surrounded by a kid who thinks he's a pirate, another who keeps beating things with a broken chair leg, and another who thinks he is riding a nonexistent motorcycle. Then there is the kid with the chainsaws for hands. And why does Gerald have green paint smeared on his beautiful blue jacket? And seriously, who glued a tongue depressor and giant pink feather to his back? Turns out, you're not in Kansas anymore, Gerald! Which type of sound describes the cacophony assaulting poor Gerald's porcelain ears?

9. _____ Techno Tracy always hears the music. The problem is that no one else can. Given that Tracy's music does not really exist except in her own imagination, which term best describes the sound?

10. _____ In your film, whenever Alana, Mother of Iguanas, leaps out from the shadows with two or three of her favorite iguanas, "War Pigs" by Black Sabbath begins playing loudly from somewhere. As only the audience hears the music, which type of sound have you used?

11. _____ Alma is happy with how well her PR team did on that commercial for the morning announcements at school, the one in which she announced she is running for class president. Her favorite shot is the

close-up they used of that mama sea turtle, the one in which that single tear trickles down the sea turtle's cheek. Alma wanted to use the sound of a mama sea turtle weeping, but she realized that they do not actually make any sound. So, she decided to use sad and patriotic background music instead. Which type of sound has Alma used?

12. _____ You want to show your audience the story of how Jimmy the Fish got his name. It all goes back to a time when Sammy the Squealer—an admittedly unfortunate name—gave the coppers the goods on Jimmy and his crew. Jimmy, realizing he'd been double-crossed, began slapping Sammy repeatedly with a flounder. FWAP! FWAP! FWAP! FWAP! Which type of sound describes the meaty noise of the flounder smacking Sammy across his two-timing face?

13. _____ Superheroes need theme music. It's a rule. Everybody knows that. So, Darryl rigs a couple of small wireless speakers into his costume to play music whenever he fights crime. Which type sound has Darryl opted to use?

14. _____ Whenever Caroline paints, she goes into what she refers to as her "creative space." While she is in this space, Caroline cannot hear anything around her, no matter what else is going on. Instead, she hears the dulcet tones of Tchaikovsky's "1812 Overture." She really likes the cannons. Given that the music is only in Caroline's head, so none of the other characters can actually hear it, which type of sound would this be considered?

15. _____ Sometimes we all need a little theme music. Mr. C is feeling it today, so he limbers up his fingers and, with the invigorating tones of one of his favorite *Dude Righteous!* songs plowing through his mind like a summer storm on the prairie, begins ripping a solo as he enters the classroom to deliver the day's lesson. Unfortunately, none of the kids can hear what Mr. C is playing because Mr. C forgot to plug his air guitar into his air amp. As the music is only in Mr. C's mind, which technique have we just used?

ANSWERS: Checking for Understanding: Sound

Directions: When it comes to sound, diegetic and nondiegetic are definitional terms, which does not leave a great deal of room for interpretation. As a rule of thumb, if the characters in the shot can hear the sound, it is diegetic. If they cannot hear the sound, it is nondiegetic.

1. A diegetic — The characters would hear that sound.
2. A diegetic — The other characters would hear Sally's vocalizations.
3. A diegetic — Bobby's making the noises, so the other characters would hear.
4. A diegetic — Everyone can hear those functioning gas-powered hands.
5. A diegetic — Anyone nearby would be able to hear this sound.
6. B nondiegetic — No one on set can hear this particular sound effect.
7. B nondiegetic — Tammy's classmates cannot hear these sounds.
8. A diegetic — All of these sounds are produced in Gerald's presence.
9. B nondiegetic — No one else can hear Tracy's music.
10. B nondiegetic — Only the audience can hear this music.
11. B nondiegetic — We are hearing music that was added after the fact.
12. A diegetic — That meaty *thunk* could be heard by all who were present.
13. A diegetic — The speakers are in his costume, so people can hear the music.
14. B nondiegetic — The music is only in Caroline's head.
15. B nondiegetic — Mr. C didn't plug in his amp, so the music is only in his head.

Appendix D

Storyboard Templates

Template 1

Story:_____ Author:_____
Director:_____

Shot #_____

Shot #_____

Shot #_____

Shot #_____

Shot #_____

Shot #_____

Template 2

Story:_____Name:_____
Author:_____Date:_____Pd.:_____

SCENE:_____

STORYBOARDS	SHOT LIST	CAMERA SCHEMATICS

Appendix E

Common Core State Standards

Your state may or may not subscribe to the Common Core State Standards. In the event your state does not, odds are the language and focus of your standards are at least similar. In either case, these standards are included for reference purposes.

College and Career Readiness Anchor Standards for Language

Conventions of Standard English

CCSS.ELA-LITERACY.CCRA.L.1

Demonstrate command of the conventions of standard English grammar and usage when writing or speaking.

CCSS.ELA-LITERACY.CCRA.L.2

Demonstrate command of the conventions of standard English capitalization, punctuation, and spelling when writing.

Knowledge of Language

CCSS.ELA-LITERACY.CCRA.L.3

Apply knowledge of language to understand how language functions in different contexts, to make effective choices for meaning or style, and to comprehend more fully when reading or listening.

Vocabulary Acquisition and Use

CCSS.ELA-LITERACY.CCRA.L.4

Determine or clarify the meaning of unknown and multiple-meaning words and phrases by using context clues, analyzing meaningful word parts, and consulting general and specialized reference materials, as appropriate.

CCSS.ELA-LITERACY.CCRA.L.5

Demonstrate understanding of figurative language, word relationships, and nuances in word meanings.

CCSS.ELA-LITERACY.CCRA.L.6

Acquire and use accurately a range of general academic and domain-specific words and phrases sufficient for reading, writing, speaking, and listening at the college and career readiness level; demonstrate independence in gathering vocabulary knowledge when encountering an unknown term important to comprehension or expression.

College and Career Readiness Anchor Standards for Reading

Key Ideas and Details

CCSS.ELA-LITERACY.CCRA.R.1
Read closely to determine what the text says explicitly and to make logical inferences from it; cite specific textual evidence when writing or speaking to support conclusions drawn from the text.

CCSS.ELA-LITERACY.CCRA.R.2
Determine central ideas or themes of a text and analyze their development; summarize the key supporting details and ideas.

CCSS.ELA-LITERACY.CCRA.R.3
Analyze how and why individuals, events, and ideas develop and interact over the course of a text.

Craft and Structure

CCSS.ELA-LITERACY.CCRA.R.4
Interpret words and phrases (lighting, framing, editing, and other techniques) as they are used in a text, including determining technical, connotative, and figurative meanings, and analyze how specific word choices (film techniques) shape meaning or tone.

CCSS.ELA-LITERACY.CCRA.R.5
Analyze the structure of texts, including how specific sentences, paragraphs, and larger portions of the text (e.g., a section, chapter, scene, or stanza) relate to each other and the whole.

CCSS.ELA-LITERACY.CCRA.R.6
Assess how point of view or purpose shapes the content and style of a text.

Integration of Knowledge and Ideas

CCSS.ELA-LITERACY.CCRA.R.7
Integrate and evaluate content presented in diverse formats and media, including visually and quantitatively, as well as in words.

CCSS.ELA-LITERACY.CCRA.R.8
Delineate and evaluate the argument and specific claims in a text, including the validity of the reasoning as well as the relevance and sufficiency of the evidence.

CCSS.ELA-LITERACY.CCRA.R.9
Analyze how two or more texts address similar themes or topics in order to build knowledge or compare the approaches the authors/directors take.

Range of Reading and Level of Text Complexity
CCSS.ELA-LITERACY.CCRA.R.10
Read and comprehend complex texts independently and proficiently.

College and Career Readiness Anchor Standards for Speaking and Listening

Comprehension and Collaboration
CCSS.ELA-LITERACY.CCRA.SL.1
Prepare for and participate effectively in a range of conversations and collaborations with diverse partners, building on others' ideas and expressing their own clearly and persuasively.

CCSS.ELA-LITERACY.CCRA.SL.2
Integrate and evaluate information presented in diverse media and formats, including visually, quantitatively, and orally.

CCSS.ELA-LITERACY.CCRA.SL.3
Evaluate a speaker's point of view, reasoning, and use of evidence and rhetoric.

Presentation of Knowledge and Ideas
CCSS.ELA-LITERACY.CCRA.SL.4
Present information, findings, and supporting evidence such that listeners can follow the line of reasoning and the organization, development, and style are appropriate to task, purpose, and audience.

CCSS.ELA-LITERACY.CCRA.SL.5
Make strategic use of digital media and visual displays of data to express information and enhance understanding of presentations.

CCSS.ELA-LITERACY.CCRA.SL.6
Adapt speech to a variety of contexts and communicative tasks, demonstrating command of formal English when indicated or appropriate.

College and Career Readiness Anchor Standards for Writing

Text Types and Purposes

CCSS.ELA-LITERACY.CCRA.W.1

Write arguments to support claims in an analysis of substantive topics or texts using valid reasoning and relevant and sufficient evidence.

CCSS.ELA-LITERACY.CCRA.W.2

Write informative/explanatory texts to examine and convey complex ideas and information clearly and accurately through the effective selection, organization, and analysis of content.

CCSS.ELA-LITERACY.CCRA.W.3

Write narratives to develop real or imagined experiences or events using effective technique, well-chosen details, and well-structured event sequences.

Production and Distribution

CCSS.ELA-LITERACY.CCRA.W.4

Produce clear and coherent texts in which the development, organization, and style are appropriate to task, purpose, and audience.

CCSS.ELA-LITERACY.CCRA.W.5

Develop and strengthen texts as needed by planning, revising, editing, rewriting, or trying a new approach.

CCSS.ELA-LITERACY.CCRA.W.6

Use technology to produce and publish texts and to interact and collaborate with others.

Research to Build and Present Knowledge

CCSS.ELA-LITERACY.CCRA.W.7

Conduct short as well as more sustained research projects based on focused questions, demonstrating understanding of the subject under investigation.

CCSS.ELA-LITERACY.CCRA.W.8

Gather relevant information from multiple print and digital sources, assess the credibility and accuracy of each source, and integrate the information while avoiding plagiarism.

CCSS.ELA-LITERACY.CCRA.W.9
Draw evidence from literary or informational texts to support analysis, reflection, and research.

Range of Writing
CCSS.ELA-LITERACY.CCRA.W.10
Write routinely over extended time frames (time for research, reflection, and revision) and shorter time frames (a single sitting or a day or two) for a range of tasks, purposes, and audiences.

Works Cited

Clerehan, R. "How Does Dialogic Learning Work? What Do We Learn from Teaching One-to-One That Informs Our Work with Larger Numbers?" *Proceedings of the Language and Academic Skills Conference*, La Trobe U, 1996.

"55 Fiction: How to Enter." *New Times* of San Luis Obispo, www.newtimesslo.com/sanluisobispo/55FictionHowtoEnter/Page.

"Foley (Filmmaking)." *Wikipedia*, Wikimedia Foundation, 27 May 2019, en.wikipedia.org/wiki/Foley_(filmmaking).

Gottlieb, Carl, and Peter Benchley. *Jaws*. Film script. 1975.

Helgeland, Brian. *42*. Film script. 2012.

Karasek, Hellmuth. "Lokomotive Der Gefühle." *Der Spiegel* (in German). 26 December 1994. Ein Kurzfilm wirkte besonders nachhaltig, ja er erzeugte Furcht, Schrecken, sogar Panik.

Lang, Kevin. "Is *Jaws* a True Story? Learn the Real Inspiration for *Jaws*." HistoryvsHollywood.com, History vs. Hollywood, 9 May 2018, www.historyvshollywood.com/reelfaces/jaws/.

LeMind, Anna. "Geometric Shapes: Simple and Unusual Personality Test." *Learning Mind*, 5 Sept. 2018, www.learning-mind.com/geometric-shapes-simple-and-unusual-personality-test/.

Loiperdinger, Martin. "Lumiere's Arrival of the Train: Cinema's Founding Myth." *The Moving Image*: Volume 4, Number 1, Spring 2004, pp. 89–118.

Mabillard, Amanda. "Sources for Othello." *Shakespeare Online*, 20 Aug. 2000, www.shakespeare-online.com/sources/othellosources.html.

Mamet, David. *On Directing Film*. Penguin, 1992.

Mathison, Melissa. *E.T. The Extra-Terrestrial*. Film script. 1982.

McGrail, Lauren, et al. "What Is a Film Treatment, and When Do You Need One?" Lights Film School, 7 Aug. 2018, www.lightsfilmschool.com/blog/what-is-a-film-treatment-afx.

Moreton, Cole. "'The Plays Weren't Written to Be Read, They Were Written to Be Spoken out Loud and Acted': Sir Ian McKellen on Why It's a Waste of Time Reading Shakespeare." *Daily Mail Online*, Associated Newspapers, 16 Apr. 2016, www.dailymail

.co.uk/home/event/article-3539598/The-plays-weren-t-written-readwritten-spoken-loud-acted-Sir-Ian-McKellen-s-waste-time-reading-Shakespeare.html.

Raiders of the Lost Ark. IMDb, IMDb.com, www.imdb.com/title/tt0082971/trivia?ref_=tt_trv_trv.

"Rules for the 55 Fiction Short Story Contest." *New Times* of San Luis Obispo, 15 June 2019, www.newtimesslo.com/sanluisobispo/rules-for-the-55-fiction-short-story-contest/Content?oid=2950668.

"Skills Employees Need to Succeed in the Workplace." FCC, Florida Career College, 1 Mar. 2017, www.floridacareercollege.edu/blog/skills-employees-need-to-succeed-in-the-workplace.

Springer, Mike. "Hitchcock on the Filmmaker's Essential Tool: The Kuleshov Effect." *Open Culture*, 2 May 2012, www.openculture.com/2012/05/alfred_hitchcock_on_the_essential_filmmakers_tool_the_great_kuleshov_effect.html.

Tarantino, Quentin. *Inglorious Basterds*. Film script. 2009.

Thayer, Ernest Lawrence. "Casey at the Bat." Poetry Foundation, 1888, www.poetryfoundation.org/poems/45398/casey-at-the-bat.

Thompson, Caroline. *Edward Scissorhands*. Film script. 1990.

Wachowski, Larry, and Andy Wachowski. *V for Vendetta*. The Internet Movie Script Database, www.imsdb.com/scripts/V-for-Vendetta.html.

Wiggins, Grant, and Jay McTighe. *Understanding by Design*. Association for Supervision and Curriculum Development, 1998, educationaltechnology.net/wp-content/uploads/2016/01/backward-design.pdf.

Wujec, Tom. "Build a Tower, Build a Team." TED, Feb. 2010, www.ted.com/talks/tom_wujec_build_a_tower.

Index

The letter *d* following a page number denotes a definition and an *f* denotes a figure.

action element of a spec script, 44
actors, responsibilities of the, 9
adaptations. *See also* directorial freedom, adapting a film from a published print text; texts, adapting in different ways
    faithful, 102, 115, 117
    research for, 130
    text to film, 131–34
    textual elements, changing in, 99–100
allusion in *Edward Scissorhands* (Burton), 82
angle
    analyzing, 63, 145, 147
    checking for understanding of, 197–201
    considering when filming, 176
    vocabulary, 180–81*d*
arc, 181*d*
archetypes, 83
archival footage, 168–69
assessment
    angles, 197–201
    camera movement, 202–6
    collaboration, 14–16
    editing, 212–16
    framing, 192–96
    of group projects, 14–16
    lighting, 207–11
    sound, 217–20
audience expectations, techniques for influencing, 136–38
audiences, judging by, 89

background elements
    anticipatory quickwrite, 75
    five-minute film clips, analyzing, 84–85
    overview, 72–74
    reflecting on, 85
background elements in *Edward Scissorhands* (Burton), analyzing
    opening credits, 76
    opening scene, 81–84
    the score, 76
    the script, 76–80
    think-pair-share activity, 76
back lighting, 181*d*
back space, 53
Barthes, Roland, 21
Bay, Michael, 104
bird's eye, 180*d*
boom/crane, 181*d*
bottom lighting, 181*d*
Boyd, William, 30
Bush, Sophia, 165

camera
    Rule of Thirds, selecting the, 90–92
    using the phone for a, 89
camera angles, vocabulary, 180–81*d*
camera movement
    checking for understanding of, 202–6
    motivated, 82
    vocabulary, 181*d*
"Casey at the Bat" (Thayer), 99–102, 104–7
character element in stories, 63, 98–99
character name element of a spec script, 44

Christ figure archetype, 83
cinematographer, responsibilities of the, 8
cinéma vérité, 168
circle shape, 35–36
classroom learning, connecting to the real world, 9–14
close-up, 180*d*
collaboration, 5–6, 14–16
color palette, 76
color symbolism in *Edward Scissorhands* (Burton), 82
Common Core State Standards, 224–29. *See also* individual units/lesson plans
composition, analyzing, 62
conflict element in stories, 63, 98–99
course objectives, developing effective, 4–5
cowboy shot, 180*d*
crash zoom, 181*d*
"The Cremation of Sam McGee" (Service), seamless transition in
　connecting the final scene to Sam McGee, 161
　filming a, 159–61
　partner reading of, 159
　reflecting on, 161–62
　silent reading, 156–59
　storyboarding the transitions, 161
　summarize, 159
　transitions into and out of, writing, 161
cross cutting, 182*d*
cutaways, 167–68

Designing a Studio Logo activity, 37–38
dialogue element of a spec script, 44
diegetic sound, 182*d*
differentiation, 5–6
director
　modeling thinking like a, 127–30
　responsibilities of the, 7
directorial freedom
　anticipatory quickwrite, 96–97
　in "based on a true story" films, 111–12
　ethics of storytelling, discuss the, 118
　faithful adaptations, using research for, 115, 117
　historical accuracy, evaluating for, 112–15, 118–19
　overview, 94–96
　reflecting on, 118
　storyboards, 110, 115, 117
　truth, researching the, 115
directorial freedom, adapting a film from a published print text
　"Casey at the Bat" (Thayer), 99–102, 104–7
　faithful adaptations, 102, 115, 117
　42 (film), 112–15, 118–19
　graphic organizer, using a, 103
　historical accuracy, evaluating for, 118–19
　reflecting on, 110
　scripts into storyboards, 110
　scripts into treatments, 109–10
　textual elements, changing, 99–100
　treatment, writing the, 104–9
　treatments into scripts, 109–10
director of photography (DP) responsibilities of the, 8
director's form, using the, 126
dissolve, 182*d*
documentaries
　definition, 165–66
　elements of, 165–66
　"Everyday Use" (Walker), transforming to a, 169
　reflecting on, 169
　short stories into, 163–65
documentaries, filming
　archival footage, 169
　cinéma vérité, 168
　cutaways, 167–68
　interviews, 166–67
　live footage, 168
　process footage, 168–69
Documentary Rubric/Observation Sheet, 189–90
dolly/tracking, 181*d*
Dutch tilt, 180*d*

editing
　checking for understanding of, 212–16
　considering when filming, 177

vocabulary, 182d
editor, responsibilities of the, 8–9
Edward Scissorhands (Burton)
    allusion in, 82
    camera movement, motivated, 81–82
    Christ figure, use of the, 83
    color palette, 76
    color symbolism, 82
    magical realism, 81
    snow globe imagery, 81–82
    soundstage, using a, 83
    visual rhyming, 82, 84
Edward Scissorhands (Burton) background elements, analyzing the
    opening credits, 76
    opening scene, 81–84
    the score, 76
    the script, 76–80
    think-pair-share activity, 76
Eisenstein, Sergei, 23
Elfman, Danny, 76
establishing shot, 180d
ethics of storytelling, 118
E.T. The Extraterrestrial (Spielberg), technical analysis, opening scene
    overview, 136–37
    reflecting on, 150
    script excerpt, reading for format/structure, 138–43
    sketch three shots to include in the film, 138, 144f
    storyboarding, 150
    writing an original scene, 150
"Everyday Use" (Walker)
    read and discuss plot, themes, characterization, 165
    transforming to a documentary film, 169
extreme close-up, 180d
eye level, 180d
eye-line match, 182d

fade, 182d
faithful adaptation, 159
film, responses to early, 21
Film Comparison Chart, 184
film from text, 131–34

film language, 145
filmmakers, goals of, 2–3
Film Observation Chart, 185
Film Rubric/Observation Sheet, 187–88
film set hierarchy, roles in the
    actors, 9
    cinematographer, 8
    director, 7
    director of photography, 8
    editor, 8–9
    producer, 7
    scriptwriter/supervisor, 7–8
film set hierarchy, specific responsibilities in the, 6–7
film study
    as an effective teaching tool, 2
    introduction to, group dynamics, 28–39
film techniques, 64–66
    anticipatory quickwrite, 52
    camera movement, 56f
    commonly used, exploring the, 52–54
    four elements all stories share, 63–64
    overview, 50–51
film techniques, storyboard activities
    co-construction, 54–60
    evaluate the samples, 54, 62–63
    "If My Life Were a Movie" poster and one-minute trailer, 69–70
    revision, 67
    shots, determine the required number of, 66–67
    shot sequence, written analysis of a, 68
    storyboard a new story, 68
film techniques, storyboards
    short stories, 64–66
film texts, difficulty of reading, 1–2
Fincher, David, 104
Fish, Stanley, 21
five-minute film clips, analyzing, 84–85
The Five Shapes activity, 34–36
flashback, 182d
flashforward, 182d
foley sound assignment, 12–13
Follows, Stephen, 66
Forming Small Groups activity, 36–37

42 (film)
    evaluating for historical accuracy, 115, 118–19
    examining a scene from, 112–15
frame story, 159
framing
    analyzing, 62, 145, 146–47
    checking for understanding of, 192–96
    considering when filming, 176
    vocabulary, 180*d*
Franta, Connor, 4
front lighting, 181*d*

genre-bender movie trailer assignment, 11
God's eye, 180*d*
Gow, Kailin, 5
Gracey, Michael, 111
graphic organizers
    Film Comparison Chart, 184
    Film Observation Chart, 185
    Peer Observation Chart, 186
group dynamics
    anticipatory quickwrite, 30–31
    overview of, 28–29
group dynamics activities
    Designing a Studio Logo, 38
    Forming Small Groups, 37
    Marshmallows and Spaghetti, 31–32
    Movie Poster Tableau, 38
    One-Word Stories, 32–33
    Personality Test: Myers-Briggs Type Indicator, 36
    Personality Test: The Five Shapes, 34–36
group projects, assessment of, 14–16
guiding audience response in *Unbroken* (Hillenbrand)
    explain what the audience should feel, 173
    filming, considerations for, 176–77
    preface, 174–75
    reflecting on, 177
    scene analysis, writing a, 177
    student version, compare with the film version, 175–76
    treatment, crafting a, 175

Hansberry, Lorraine, 42
headroom, 53
Hepworth, Cecil, 21
high angle, 180*d*
high key lighting, 181*d*
historical accuracy, evaluating for, 115–18
Hitchcock, Alfred, 23–24
Holland, Norman N., 21
Howe, Katherine, 9

"If My Life Were a Movie" poster and one-minute trailer, 69–70
interviews element of documentary, 166–67
Iser, Wolfgang, 21

Jauss, Hans Robert, 21
jump cut, 182*d*
juxtaposition, making meaning through, 19–27

Karasek, Hellmuth, 21
knee shot, 180*d*
Kubrick, Stanley, 94, 172
Kuleshov, Lev, 21
Kuleshov Effect: making meaning through juxtaposition, 19–27

lap dissolve, 182*d*
lesson plans. *See also* specifics under individual units
    background elements, 72–86
    directorial freedom, 94–120
    film techniques, 50–71
    group dynamics, 28–39
    guiding audience response, 171–78
    introduction, 18
    Kuleshov Effect: making meaning through juxtaposition, 19–27
    seamless transition, 152–62
    shot composition, 87–93
    spec scripts, 40–49
    technical analysis, opening scene of *E.T. The Extra-Terrestrial* (Spielberg), 136–50
    texts, adapting in different ways, 121–35

lighting
  analyzing, 63, 145, 147
  checking for understanding of, 207–11
  considering when filming, 177
  vocabulary, 181–82d
literature, goals of teaching, 2
live footage element of documentary, 168
Loiperdinger, Martin, 21
long shot, 180d
low angle, 180d
low key lighting, 182d
Lucas, George, 75
Lumière brothers, 21

magical realism, 81
Mamet, David, 21
Mapp, Craig, 52
Marshmallows and Spaghetti activity, 31–32
mashed-up movie trailer assignment, 10–11
McKellen, Ian, 124
medium close-up, 180d
medium shot, 180d
Méliès, Georges, 21
mise en scène. *See* background elements
montage, 182d
movement, considering when filming, 176–77
Movie Poster Tableau activity, 38
music video assignment, 10
Myers-Briggs Type Indicator activity, 36

Naskar, Abhijit, 6, 124
Nolan, Christopher, 104
nondiegetic sound, 182d

One-Word Stories activity, 32–34
opening credits, view and analyze in *Edward Scissorhands* (Burton), 76
opening scene, view and analyze in *Edward Scissorhands* (Burton), 81–84
Othello (Shakespeare), adapting in different ways
  director's form, using the, 126
  film versions, evaluating, 131–34
  Moors clothing, researching, 130
  provide stage directions, 131
  read an excerpt for, 125, 127–30
  reflecting on, 132–34
  set design for, 131
  thinking like a director for, 127–30
  translate the script into modern English, 125–26
over the shoulder, 180d

pacing, analyzing, 145, 147
pan, 181d
parallel editing, 182d
parallel editing cut, 182d
parentheticals element of a spec script, 44
partner reading in seamless transitions, 159
Paul, Robert W., 21
Peer Observation Chart, 186
Personality Tests
  The Five Shapes activity, 34–36
  Myers-Briggs Type Indicator activity, 36
phone, using for a camera, 89
photographs, Rule of Thirds, 90–92
point of view, 181d
posters, 69–70
print texts, film texts and, 1–4
process footage element of documentary, 168–69
producer, responsibilities of the, 7

rack focus, 181d
A Raisin in the Sun (Hansberry), 42–43, 45–47
reader-response criticism, 21
real world, connecting to the, 9–14
rectangle shape, 35
resolution element in stories, 63, 98–99
rubrics
  Documentary Rubric/Observation Sheet, 189–90
  Film Rubric/Observation Sheet, 187–88
Rule of Thirds, 90–92

scene heading element of a spec script, 44
Schrader, Paul, 1, 42

score, analyzing, 76, 145, 147–48
screenplay
   defined, 42
   the five basic elements, 44
screenplay activities
   compose a spec script for a scene not in the play, 47–48
   identify the five elements, 47
   rewrite an excerpt in spec script format, 44–47
scripts
   examine and make predictions, for *Edward Scissorhands* (Burton), 76–80
   into storyboards in film adaptations, 110
   into treatments in film adaptations, 109–10
scriptwriter/supervisor, responsibilities of the, 7–8
seamless transitions
   anticipatory quickwrite, 155–56
   "The Cremation of Sam McGee" (Service), 156–61
   exploring in film, 159–60
   filming a, 161
   overview, 152–54
   reflecting on, 161–62
Service, Robert W., 155
set design, 131
setting element in stories, 63, 98–99
Shakespeare, experiencing, 124–25. *See also Othello* (Shakespeare), adapting in different ways
Shapes Personality Test, 34–36
shooting script, 43, 76
short documentary assignment, 13
short stories
   into documentaries, 163–65
   four elements, identify the, 63–64
   group storyboarding, 64–66
shot composition
   alternative approaches to, 92
   anticipatory quickwrite, 89–90
   overview, 87–88
   reflecting on, 93
   Rule of Thirds in, 90–92
   using the phone for a camera, 89
shot list, 54

shot-reverse-shot, 182*d*
shots
   analyzing single, 62
   determine the required number of, 66–67
   vocabulary, 180*d*
shot sequence, written analysis of a, 68
side lighting, 182*d*
silent film assignment, 11
silent reading in seamless transitions, 156–59
slugline element of a spec script, 44
Small Groups, Forming activity, 36–37
Smith, George Albert, 21
sound
   checking for understanding of, 217–20
   considering when filming, 177
   vocabulary, 182*d*
soundstage in *Edward Scissorhands* (Burton), 83
spec script
   anticipatory quickwrite, 42–43
   overview, 40–41
   shooting script vs., 43
spec script activities
   compose for a scene not in the play, 47–48
   five elements, identify the, 47
   rewrite an excerpt in spec script format, 44–47
square shape, 34–35
stage directions, 131
Steadicam, 181*d*
stop motion, 182*d*
stories, four elements shared in all, 63–64, 98–99. *See also* short stories
storyboard
   based on treatments, constructing, 175
   elements of, 110
   faithful adaptations, using research for, 115, 117
   goal of, 54
   model for creating, 55*f*
   scripts, translating into, 110
   shot list, 57
   templates, 221–23
   transitions, 161

storyboard activities
    co-construct a, 54–56
    evaluate the samples, 54, 57–63
    "If My Life Were a Movie" poster and one-minute trailer, 69–70
    revision, 67
    shots, determine the required number of, 66–67
    shot sequence, written analysis of a, 68
    storyboard a new story, 68
    storyboard the short story, 64–66
    technical analysis, opening scene of *E.T. The Extra-Terrestrial* (Spielberg), 150
storytellers, goals of, 2–3
storytelling, ethics of, 118
students, role in assessment, 14–16

tableau, 38
A Talk with Hitchcock (documentary), 23
technical analysis, opening scene of *E.T. The Extra-Terrestrial* (Spielberg)
    analyzing, 145–50
    overview, 136–37
    reflecting on, 150
    script excerpt, read for format/structure, 138–43
    sketch three shots to include in the film, 138, 144f
    storyboards, 150
    writing an original scene, 150
ten-minute film assignment, 13–14
ten-minute film proposal/preproduction notebook assignment, 12
texts, adapting in different ways. *See also* directorial freedom, adapting a film from a published print text
    anticipatory quickwrite, 124–25
    Othello (Shakespeare), 125–34
    overview, 121–23
textual elements, changing in film adaptations, 99–100
Thayer, Ernest Lawrence, 99–102
think-pair-share for *Edward Scissorhands* (Burton), 76
tilt, 181d

trailer assignments, 11, 69–70
treatments
    constructing storyboards based on, 175
    in film adaptations, 104–10
    guiding audience response, 175
    into scripts, 109–10
    storyboards based on, constructing, 175
    Unbroken (Hillenbrand), 175
triangle shape, 35
trombone shot, 181d
truth, researching the, 115
two shot, 180d

Unbroken (Hillenbrand), guiding audience response in
    explain what the audience should feel, 173
    filming, considerations when, 176–77
    film version, compare with student versions, 175–76
    preface, 174–75
    reflecting on, 177
    scene analysis, writing a, 177
    treatment, constructing storyboards based on, 175
    treatment, crafting a, 175
units. *See* lesson plans

visual rhyming, 82, 84
vocabulary
    camera angles, 180–81
    camera movement, 181
    editing techniques, 182
    framing, 180
    lighting, 181–82
    shots, 180
    sound, 182

Wexler, Haskell, 89
whip pan, 181d
wipe, 182d

zigzag shape, 36
zoom, 181d

Author

Robert B. Crisp is a magna cum laude graduate of North Carolina State University. He has taught at Myers Park High School in Charlotte, North Carolina, since 1997, where he serves as a National Board Certified English and film teacher. During his more than two decades at Myers Park, he has coauthored five nationally adopted ELA textbooks (Pacesetter/SpringBoard) for the College Board, for which he served as a national trainer and curriculum writer for more than fifteen years. While at Myers Park, he has helped develop a popular Literature and Film program, where he conveys his undying love for and devotion to his family, Alfred Hitchcock, Guillermo del Toro, Kubrick-inspired conspiracy theories, and Black Keys Fridays. To schedule speaking engagements or workshops on the use of film in the classroom to positively impact student literacy, contact the author at RobertBCrisp@gmail.com.

This book was typeset in TheMix and Palatino by Barbara Frazier.

The typeface used on the cover is Kiln Sans.

The book was printed on 50-lb. White Offset paper by Seaway Printing Company, Inc.

www.ingramcontent.com/pod-product-compliance
Lightning Source LLC
Chambersburg PA
CBHW060247240426
43673CB00047B/1888